Mortgage-FREE!

The Real Goods Solar Living Books

Wind Power for Home & Business: Renewable Energy for the 1990s and Beyond
by Paul Gipe

The Independent Home: Living Well with Power from the Sun, Wind, and Water
by Michael Potts

*Real Goods Solar Living Sourcebook: The Complete Guide to Renewable
Energy Technologies and Sustainable Living,*
Ninth Edition, edited by John Schaeffer

The Straw Bale House by Athena Swentzell Steen,
Bill Steen, and David Bainbridge, with David Eisenberg

The Rammed Earth House by David Easton

*The Real Goods Independent Builder:
Designing & Building a House Your Own Way* by Sam Clark

The Passive Solar House: Using Solar Design to Heat and Cool Your Home
by James Kachadorian

A Place in the Sun: The Evolution of the Real Goods Solar Living Center
by John Schaeffer and the Collaborative Design/Construction Team

Hemp Horizons: The Comeback of the World's Most Promising Plant
by John W. Roulac

Mortgage-Free! Radical Strategies for Home Ownership by Rob Roy

Real Goods Trading Company in Ukiah, California, was founded in 1978 to make available new tools to help people live self-sufficiently and sustainably. Through seasonal catalogs, a periodical (*The Real Goods News*), a bi-annual *Solar Living Sourcebook*, as well as retail outlets, Real Goods provides a broad range of tools for independent living.

"Knowledge is our most important product" is the Real Goods motto. To further its mission, Real Goods has joined with Chelsea Green Publishing Company to co-create and co-publish the Real Goods Independent Living Book series. The titles in this series are written by pioneering individuals who have firsthand experience in using innovative technology to live lightly on the planet. Chelsea Green books are both practical and inspirational, and they enlarge our view of what is possible as we enter the next millennium.

Ian Baldwin, Jr.
President, Chelsea Green

John Schaeffer
President, Real Goods

Mortgage-FREE!

RADICAL STRATEGIES
FOR HOME OWNERSHIP

Rob Roy

CHELSEA GREEN PUBLISHING COMPANY
White River Junction, Vermont
Totnes, England

To Don and Mary Ann Osby, Ted Holdt and Sara Mapelli,
Ki and Judith Light, Rob and Bonnie Watt, Gregg and Janet Butz,
Jim Schley and Rebecca Bailey and friends at Blue Moon,
and all the other heroes who have generously shared of their
experiences so that the way might be made a little smoother for
those that follow. And to you, the reader. Good luck . . . and,
when luck comes, take advantage of it!

Designed by Andrea Gray.

Printed in the United States.
First printing, March 1998.
01 00 99 98   2 3 4 5

Library of Congress Cataloging-in-Publication Data

Roy, Robert L.
    Mortgage free! : radical strategies for home ownership / Rob Roy.
      P. cm. — (Real goods solar living book)
    Includes bibliographical references and index.
    ISBN 0-930031-98-9 (alk. paper)
    1. House construction—Amateur's manuals. 2. Dwellings—Energy
conservation. 3. Housing—finance. 4. Home ownership. I. Roy,
Robert L. Money-saving strategies for the owner/builder © 1981.
II. Title. III. Series.
643' . 12—do21
                                    98-10080

Chelsea Green Publishing Company
Post Office Box 428
White River Junction, VT 05001
(800) 639-4099
www.chelseagreen.com

Contents

Acknowledgments

Many of the strategies listed in *Mortgage-Free!* have been recycled, polished, and updated from my earlier book, *Money-Saving Strategies for the Owner/Builder* (Sterling, 1981). Readers who have read several of my books have told me that *Strategies* was the one that helped them the most to reach financial security. I hope this total remake, which contains whole new chapters, strategies, and a variety of new present-day case studies from all over North America, will be even more useful. I wish to thank Charles Nurnberg, Executive Vice President of Sterling Publishing Company, for his kind permission to reprint much of the earlier material in this new work.

Thanks also to the gang at Chelsea Green for providing encouragement, research materials, and the occasional gentle kick in the pants. Thanks to assistant editor Rachael Cohen for valuable suggestions and to manuscript reader and critic extraordinaire Michael Potts for straightening me out when I needed it. Thanks to Publisher Stephen Morris for his humorous but true story of how he and his wife became mortgage-free early in their marriage. Special thanks to Editor-in-Chief Jim Schley, not only for his own contribution to chapter 7, but for his personal attention in supervising the editing of the entire manuscript. And extra special thanks to project editor Alan Berolzheimer, who read my manuscript and wrestled with it so many times that it started to make sense, and then suggested how it could be improved so that other readers could make sense of it in a single reading. Last, but not least, the Gold Pen award goes to fellow undergrounder Malcolm Wells for all the great drawings throughout the book. They help to lighten the poor reader's load when the author starts taking himself too seriously. *Muchas gracias*, Mac.

Introduction

When people tell me this book is radical or outrageous, I thank them, for then I know that it has found its place among good company. When they tell me the book is simplistic or that the strategies are unworkable, I smile, because I know they're wrong. They're wrong because I've proven to myself and to others that the strategies for mortgage freedom work. And they're wrong because thousands of others—not fat cats—have lived in their own homes without ever signing a mortgage agreement. The several case studies detailed in this book are but a tiny tip of a gigantic iceberg.

For many North Americans, the words *mortgage-free home* take on a dreamy quality, and suggest the completion of a twenty-five- or thirty-year economic trial, or, perhaps, winning the state lottery. Among the very rich, and, paradoxically, many of the rural poor (as we will see in chapter 1), the mortgage-free home is the *status quo*. Only the vast middle class seems to suffer from the mortgage manacle.

Housing costs, whether by way of rent or mortgage, are the single largest after-tax expenditure for most Americans. It needn't be that way. Housing costs can be drastically reduced. Rental housing should only be considered as a short-term necessity in situations, for example, where an individual, couple, or family has just moved to a new area, and has not yet found ownership possibilities. Long-term, even a mortgage is better than rent, which returns no equity. Renting a house or apartment is like hiring a car. When the ride is over, the car (or rental unit) is returned to its true owner.

A mortgage is like hiring money, particularly in the first years when most of the payments go toward interest. In the early years, little equity is built up. If you get no further in this book than this, the fourth paragraph, take one investment strategy away with you, and you will be better

off. It is this: Whenever you have extra money to invest—from tax re-
fund, hard work, gift, windfall, whatever—make a principal payment on
your mortgage. Many economists will tell you that acceleration of mortgage principal payments is one of the best investments you can make.
Even a $50 prepayment early in the mortgage might save you a couple of
$400 payments at the end. Steve Carlson, author of *The Best Home For
Less* (Avon, 1989), asks, "Where else can you get a return of $800 on a
$50 investment?"

THE VAGARIES OF AMORTIZATION SCHEDULES

The chart below is part of an actual amortization schedule used in a
property transaction with which I was acquainted. I have abbrevi-
ated the long schedule to make certain points. The amount of the
mortgage is $36,500, the rate is 10 percent, and the number of
monthly payments is 300 (25 years). Each payment is $331.68, but
the breakdown of that payment between principal and interest
changes dramatically as the years proceed. Note how almost all of
the early payments go toward interest.

Payment	Principal	Interest	Balance Due
1	27.51	304.17	36,472.49
2	27.74	303.94	36,444.75
3	27.97	303.71	36,416.78
217	166.56	165.11	19,647.19
227	179.48	152.20	18,084.27
300	328.94	2.74	.23

Look at the first three payments. Combined, they have reduced
the balance by a whopping $83.22!

Now check out payment number 217. This is the first payment
where more than half goes toward principal, eighteen years into the
schedule!

At payment 227, the loan is half paid after nineteen years of payments, six years to go.

Payment 300 leaves a balance of 23¢ due. Maybe they'll tell you
to keep the change. Maybe not.

The loan is $36,500. The total amount paid over twenty-five years
is $99,504. I hope you can readily see why prepayment of mortgage
principal is a very sensible investment.

Knock Nine Years Off Your Mortgage

Maybe you decide that building a house is not for you. Well, here's a tip, suggested by Bob Duquette of Adirondack Funding Services of Plattsburgh, New York, that can save you nine years of payments (and $41,500 in the example given) on a thirty-year mortgage, or two and one-half years on a fifteen-year loan. It's something you can do right now, and it is practically painless. At least, you won't notice the pain. This mathemagical strategy involves making biweekly mortgage payments instead of monthly payments. And the biweekly payments are exactly half of what you would pay by the month. There, isn't that easy? "But how can that save me time and money?" you ask. The trick is that you are making twenty-six *half* payments in a year instead of twelve *full* payments. This is like making an *extra* full payment a year. As we've already seen, prepayment of your mortgage is the best investment you can make. In 1995, the typical conversion cost of refinancing your mortgage along these lines was about $295. In an article by Joe Lo'templio (*Plattsburgh Press-Republican*, May 21, 1995), Duquette says that about three-quarters of the people who learn about the biweekly payment scheme go for it. He says, "The nice thing about it is that it doesn't interrupt your cash flow and you don't have to come up with that large amount once a month."

Original Mortgage: $70,000 at 8.5%, 30 years, monthly payments of $688.24
     (payments include $150 per month escrow for property taxes and insurance)
Loan Curtailment Strategy: convert to biweekly payments of $344.12
Interest on the original loan: $122,774
Interest if biweekly schedule is used: $81,268 ($41,506 saved!)

Year End	Principal, Original	Principal, Biweekly	Year End	Principal, Original	Principal, Biweekly
1998	$69,697	$69,353	2013	$53,578	$31,974
1999	69,141	68,081	2014	51,597	27,401
2000	68,536	66,699	2015	49,441	22,423
2001	67,877	65,195	2016	47,095	17,006
2002	67,160	63,558	2017	44,541	11,109
2003	66,380	61,776	2018	41,761	4,692
2004	65,531	59,837	2019	38,736	DEBT FREE!
2005	64,607	57,727	2020	35,443	
2006	63,601	55,430	2021	31,860	
2007	62,506	52,586	2022	27,959	
2008	61,314	49,837	2023	23,714	
2009	60,018	46,843	2024	19,093	
2010	58,606	43,584	2025	14,065	
2011	57,070	40,037	2026	8,591	
2012	55,398	36,176	2027	2,634	

Be Mortgage-Free

If prepaying a mortgage is such a great financial investment, it follows that an even better strategy is to avoid the mortgage altogether. This is the real purpose of this book, but there are no one-paragraph shortcuts. You'll have to read the whole thing.

Historically, the burden of shelter costs has only grown worse. Once, human shelter was *found*, in the form of caves. Later it was built of indigenous materials on land owned by no one. One's right to live in a shelter had nothing to do with money, which was nonexistent, and everything to do with cunning, strength, and a variety of negotiating strategies.

Let's jump ahead many thousands of years to the European Middle Ages, when civilization had aggregated family units into larger blocks, and defense became a tribal or clannish concern. In the Middle Ages, tenant farmers worked three months of the year for the lord of the estate. In return, they got land, house, and the advantages of the communal defense system. *Three months.* And we call these people serfs. In grade school, we thought of serfdom as only slightly removed from slavery. Yet in my home state of New York, "Tax Freedom Day" is in late May. We work the first 140-odd days of the year just to pay local, state, and federal taxes . . . and we still haven't done anything about the shelter itself. With roughly a third of the average after-tax middle-class income going toward housing, we can conservatively add another 90 days to reach "Shelter Freedom Day" sometime in late August. So now we're committed to eight months labor to achieve what the peasants of the Middle Ages accomplished by their three-month contract with their lords. If those poor wretches were *serfs*, what word can we find to describe ourselves?

The saddest part of this unsavory scenario is that modern humankind accepts our fate as normal; truly "quiet desperation" if I ever saw it. Keep this in mind: a $75,000 mortgage at a fixed rate of 9 percent over thirty years costs $217,249 to pay off, almost three times the original loan.

We're talking about more than shelter costs here. To pay a high monthly mortgage, it is necessary to earn higher salaries, which also means paying higher taxes. More of our earnings are garnisheed and Tax and Shelter Freedom Day gets pushed even later into the year. Labor Day takes on new meaning. Speaking from thirty years' experience, mortgage-free living means savings at every turn. It is possible to live well on a relatively low self-employment income, and still have the freedom to pursue personal interests, travel, and work; work not just for a paycheck, but for job satisfaction. I once asked the owner of a café in Corfu about the Greek words on a sign above the table. With a smile, he translated, "First you must be happy at your work." An unholy percentage of American men and women are working largely for their houses, at jobs they would not choose were pay not the overriding consideration. I spent nearly five years at that game, surrounded by co-workers caught in the mortgage trap. My escape was made possible largely by our mortgage-free home.

In chapter 6, I will relate our complete personal story of mortgage freedom, including how my wife and I utilized strategies described in the first five chapters. Here is a brief overview of how we have managed to own five mortgage-free homes in the past twenty-five years. This will introduce you to my family, help you to make sense of some of the references in the first five chapters, and, I hope, establish my credibility as the author of a book called *Mortgage-Free!*

Using grubstake strategies described in chapter 2 and land search ideas enumerated in chapter 3, I moved from the United States to Scotland to buy a dilapidated Highland cottage. There, twenty-five years ago, I met the lovely Jacqueline Bates, hereinafter known as Jaki.

In 1974, in search of a more self-reliant lifestyle, Jaki and I embarked for the United States. We moved to northern New York in 1975, where we bought land on Murtagh Hill and built Log End Cottage, a cordwood masonry home. We made use of the Temporary Shelter strategy detailed in chapter 4, our grubstake coming from the sale of our cottage in Scotland. The home had a wonderful rustic atmosphere, a romantic cottage for a freshly married couple. From a practical standpoint, though, the place was not energy-efficient. And the romance part led to the birth of our first son, Rohan, who made it clear right away that the place was too small for our growing family. Rather than add on to a house with flaws, we built a truly practical house, the warm and cozy earth-shelter called Log End Cave. There were no do-it-yourself books about either cordwood masonry or underground housing in those days, so I wrote a book about each house, hoping to share with other potential owner-builders what we did right, and what we did wrong.

Log End Cave was cute and cozy, but the building bug had bit, and I wanted to experiment with ideas about incorporating whole living systems (not just shelter) into a home. Influenced by Henry David Thoreau, Helen and Scott Nearing (*Living the Good Life*), and the homesteading movement of the 1970s, I was beginning to see the importance of integrating Food and Fuel with Shelter at the design stage of construction, as well as other modern necessities such as Recreation and Home Industry. Chapter 1 speaks of what I call Thoreauvian economics, distilling life down to the basic "necessaries of life." Chapter 5 lists design ideas for building a low-cost home, strategies that we made great use of at

Earthwood, the round, two-story, earth-sheltered, cordwood masonry home where we have lived since 1982. And chapter 6 describes how we made use of integrated living principles at Earthwood.

Our family grew to four with the addition of our second son Darin in 1985, and now varies between three and four as Rohan comes and goes. (He has inherited a predilection for travelling from his parents.) Earthwood the house has become the physical core of Earthwood Building School, where we make our living sharing what we have learned about cordwood masonry, earth-sheltered housing, and related subjects.

Our fifth mortgage-free home is Mushwood, a little summer cottage on a nearby lake, a place we built on a pay-as-we-could-afford basis. It took several years to complete, but we never borrowed a penny. Laughably, Mushwood now carries a higher valuation than Earthwood, so our sweat and dollar equity over the years has translated into the best darned investment we could have made. If we ever get in a bind financially, we could, reluctantly, sell Mushwood, another advantage of mortgage freedom.

Our work has introduced us to hundreds of owner-builders and would-be owner-builders, most of whom would like to include in their dream the words Mortgage-Free! The six case studies in chapter 7 show how people from a variety of backgrounds, living in rural areas all over North America, have made use of the strategies described in this book to achieve mortgage freedom, adding to and improving on them as inspiration, imagination, opportunity, and good fortune allowed. (Good fortune, it will be seen, is all around us. All we need do is recognize it.)

I have been asked who the audience is for this book. While it seems obvious that everyone would like a mortgage-free home, if handed to them on a plate, not everyone has what it takes to bypass the thirty-year road toward owning one's home. The audience, I like to think, are those among you, mostly middle-class North Americans, with imagination, flexibility, and courage. You have the imagination to visualize yourself as mortgage-free; if you can't visualize a goal, you can't achieve it. You have the flexibility to free yourself from preconceived notions about some heady life and lifestyle issues: the real reasons you work at a particular job, the differences between necessity and desire, whether you are living in the area that best suits your personality. How much are you willing to change to get what you really want? Are you willing to earn less? To relocate? Imagine what it would mean to work to save money instead of to earn money to pay others to do things for you. This book poses some tough values questions. And courage? To be mortgage-free takes the courage to march to a different drummer, the courage to doggedly pursue your dream in spite of every obstacle, the courage to recognize that maybe it's you that's right and the rest of the world that's crazy.

Despite all the high-falootin' rhetoric of the previous paragraph, some down-to-earth generalizations might be helpful here:

First, the book and its philosophies will no doubt feel more comfortable to those who have a dream of pursuing a self-reliant lifestyle, which could run the gamut from homesteaders to survivalists, with other types of rugged individualists in between. Many of the strategies require a very physical personal involvement. Good health, not great strength, will be of benefit, although I am convinced that a change from the consumer to a conserver lifestyle (one of the strategies described in detail in chapter 2) will improve health as an added bonus. Owner-builders or even owner-builder wannabes will derive more benefit from these pages than those who do not take as personal an involvement in creating their own shelter. Still, it is possible to be mortgage-free without heavy physical involvement, for example, by setting oneself up as a contractor for the home-building project, while others actually pound the nails and run the electrical and plumbing lines.

Second, I acknowledge from the start that the strategies described in this book work best in rural areas, although you may figure out ways to adapt them to an urban environment. If you are a city person and plan to remain that way, it's not too late to put the book back on the shelf now . . . unless you're just looking for a scintillatingly good read. How many lives change by circumstances stemming from old-fashioned curiosity?

With regard to owner-building and even rural living, we must first take into account some paper realities, particularly building and zoning regulations, which are becoming ever more stringent in both the United States and Canada. I recognize the need for health and building codes to protect ourselves, our neighbors, and the environment from pathogens and other types of pollution. Indeed, as standards have risen in the past couple of decades, it has become easier to promote and implement some ecological practices, such as energy efficiency. Those of us who are owner-builders are especially responsible for holding ourselves accountable to the best intentions of these regulations.

At the same time, contemporary building and zoning regulations can impose many restrictions that hinder the prospective mortgage-free homeowner. In Britain, zoning (called *planning* there) has made it difficult (but not impossible) to build a home on an individual lot. Building codes there have stifled the development of innovative housing techniques, although some brave individuals have persevered, even in Britain, despite restraints by the paper people.

In certain parts of North America, such as Massachusetts, California, Ontario, and the Adirondack Park of New York, the permitting process is almost as difficult as it is in the United Kingdom. In Britain, population pressures on a relatively small land area are readily apparent, and the tough regulations are understandable if not always common-sensible. The planning boards have preserved the charming character of the English towns, villages, and countryside. The typically North American suburban nightmare of strip malls, gas stations, and fast food shacks is virtually nonexistent in the United Kingdom. Sometimes these codes and rules can be expensive to the owner-builder, and sometimes they seem to lack common sense in individual cases, but we benefit from the protection they afford.

With regard to building in rural areas, I am most keenly aware of the fact that nature is under attack by the human species. While I believe in the right of people to provide their own shelter, every prospective builder must realize that he or she has a responsibility to the land and to the future of the planet. Legality and individual rights are no longer primary ; the primary issue now is the survival of the diverse species that live on the planet, including ourselves. That we are only stewards of the land—not truly owners—has been said many times before, but a sheep farmer friend in Scotland made the point most clear to me many years ago: "You can't own the land, Rob. The land owns you."

Developers taken as a whole seem to have little concern for the land. Yes, some, to their credit, go to considerable effort to minimize environmental impact, but all too often the American pattern of development prevalent since World War II has held sway: bulldoze the land to lifeless moonscape, build the houses (or malls), landscape with lawns and young trees. Owner-builders generally do better than this, but we must do a *lot* better. In this book, at every opportunity, I will advocate green strategies and green solutions. I make no apology for this. The governments and citizenry of Western Europe, by necessity, have taken this approach. Because of a more favorable resources-to-population ratio and a lesser population density, the majority of Americans, at least in rural areas, have not felt the coming crunch, but coming it is. There's no point in achieving personal economic freedom at the cost of the environment, our larger nest. Fortunately, the two do not have to be mutually exclusive.

1

The Mortgaged Home

On applying to the assessors, I am surprised to learn that they cannot at once name a dozen in the town who own their own farms free and clear. If you would know the history of these homesteads, inquire at the bank where they are mortgaged.

—HENRY DAVID THOREAU, WALDEN

It is late January, 1997. I am nearing the completion of a three-week visit to Chile. A few days ago, my oldest son and I conducted a cordwood masonry workshop here, our way paid for by a visionary who wants to see a fairly large tract of land made into a "park-village" of homes that harmonize with nature in many ways, not the least of which is in the use of indigenous materials. It is an idea worth pursuing no matter where you build.

In this part of Chile, the indigenous people are the Mapuche Indians. Historically, these people have maintained a fierce independence. The Spanish, who had a relatively easy time conquering the rest of what is now Latin America, were repelled by the Mapuche for centuries. In the valleys of this beautiful lake district of Chile, the native people still live in their hand-made houses, mortgage-free of course. Though "poor" by the definition and standards of most Americans, they are free of debt. Whole Earth founder Stewart Brand's outlook, however, is more to the point: "Living below your means is a cheap way to be rich. It's the only way to be rich" (*The Next Whole Earth Catalog*. Random House, 1980, p. 292). By this standard, the Mapuche might be considered to be rich, as is anyone who is free of debt and has two pesos to rub together.

MOST PEOPLES ARE FREE OF MORTGAGE!

For over four years, in my recent past, I worked as a "housing rehabilitation specialist" for a not-for-profit company. My job was to administer federal HUD (Department of Housing and Urban Development) home improvement grants for "income eligible" people. Eligibility required that the household income not exceed a certain level for the family size, and that the home possessed certain "substandard" elements (foundation, roofing, plumbing, electric, etc.). And, if there was a mortgagor, that person or institution would need to give approval, in writing, for the grant to be made. My "target areas" were in townships in the two most northeasterly counties of New York State. Amazingly, out of roughly a hundred income-eligible clients that I worked with, only two or three had any kind of mortgage on their homes. The lower the income, the less was the likelihood that a mortgage existed on the property.

At the other end of the scale, the very rich are also mortgage-free, or could be. Some actually find tax advantages to having a mortgage, I hear, but this is not a strategy that has any meaning in the context of this book. Further, I note (with no facetious intent) that birds, bees, beavers, and other building species besides humankind, also build without "benefit" of mortgage. Indigenous people I have visited, like the Mapuche, the Mayans in Belize and Mexico, the Zulus in Southern Africa, and others, also find the idea of a mortgage to be a strange one.

But north of the Rio Grande, most people in the great middle class have mortgages on their homes (or, worse, pay rent to live in someone else's home). This is troubling. How is it that the rich and the poor are mortgage-free and a large part of the other 80 percent (or so) of the rest of North Americans are not? How is it that indigenous peoples and other building species are mortgage-free while the middle class that you—I am guessing here—and I and most of our friends belong to, is not?

Without hard proof, I can only speculate, and my speculation runs like this:

Poor people cannot afford mortgages. As soon as they can, they are no longer poor, at least by the standard connotation of poverty. But they will remain less poor in the true empiric sense if they stay away from mortgage. Banks will not deal with "unqualified" borrowers. Thankfully, the rural poor often live on mortgage-free land, passed down through the family, in homes that were built by the people (or the forebears of the people) who live in them. One of the prerequisites of mortgage freedom is ownership of the land. Country people— Mapuche or McCoy—start with this prerequisite in many cases. The situation among the urban poor is entirely different. They are living on "land"—or, at least, "space," for is there truly any land in the city?— which is incapable of supporting the people who live on it. It will take a more difficult book by a smarter writer to address the kind of desperation found in our inner cities. One of the parameters of this current work, by necessity, is that the strategies described to achieve mortgage freedom, are, for the most part, applicable mainly in rural areas. Readers preferring an urban lifestyle might still find this book of interest, in a dreamy, romantic kind of way, and some of the economic philosophies and strategies may be of genuine and positive value. The reality, however, is that it is much more difficult, though not impossible, to obtain early mortgage freedom with a purchased house in the city. And owner-building in built-up areas is all but precluded by expensive and restrictive bureaucratic regulations.

I have said that poor people cannot afford mortgages, but this rather simplistic and perhaps obvious statement is not intended to imply that if they could get one, they should. (They might entertain the idea with a view, perhaps, to improving the home where state and federal grant monies are not at work.) The North American population has come to accept the mortgage as an unfortunate but necessary part of living in their dream home. Even the rich, very often, wish to live beyond their means, and the mortgage, by its very definition, is a mechanism that allows them to do this.

> mortgage—n. (from the Old French, *morgage*, *mort gage*, literally death pledge; *mort*, death, and *gage*, a pledge.) 1. the pledging of property to a creditor as security for the payment of debt.

And what's so wrong with that? Maybe the mortgage makes a kind of sense. On the surface, it would appear that mortgages are the only means for many people to "own" their own home, or so we have been coerced to believe. (The reader, I hope, will excuse the use of conditional quotation marks around the word *own*. Make no mistake, it is the lending institution that has the greatest equity in the house over the longest part of the mortgage contract, not the person or persons actually living in the home. We can deduce this fact from the fragments of the typical amortization schedule appearing in the Introduction.) The indoctrination runs deep, but it can be overcome.

QUIET DESPERATION

About 1847, Henry David Thoreau wrote, "The mass of men lead lives of quiet desperation." I submit that today, 150 years later, his famous observation is more true than ever. Some residents of Concord, Massachusetts in the mid-nineteenth century had mortgages, but televisions, credit cards, and automobiles, the other major contributors to quiet—or not so quiet—desperation, did not yet exist.

For more than half of my fifty years on this planet, I have been haunted by the image of a young couple backing submissively out of a lender's office, sophomoric grins on their faces, forever grateful to the loan officer for condescending to enslave them economically for the best part of their remaining natural lives. The young couple will pay the "points" (a point is one percent of the amount of the mortgage loan), perhaps the valuation costs, most closing costs, and, for the first few years at least, mostly interest payments and very little principal. The home, we will see, starts out at a higher price than necessary because it contains elements required not by the occupants, but by the

ON SELF-DISCIPLINE

I knew a couple that used going into debt as a means of saving money. Really. They did not have the self-discipline required to save money to buy a car, for example. Yet they could make car payments, because they knew that if they didn't, the car would be repossessed. The discipline was imposed on them, always an easier kind than that which one imposes upon oneself. Going into debt to have something is actually the common method today, the American way. People buy "on time," using plastic as their magic card to ownership. But things cost a lot more this way, you're a slave to the payments, and the thing you've bought has worn out before it is fully paid for.

Similarly, it's easy to show up at work every morning at 8 a.m. If (without good reason) you don't, you lose your job. It's much harder to show up at your own word processor every morning to write. I can assure you of this. But being mortgage-free is going to require self-discipline. If you haven't got it, get it. Besides land, it's the one absolute requirement. I'll try to help.

One of the most valuable keys to unlocking self-discipline is to be methodical. Break the desired goal down into chewable bites. A common thread in chapter 7 is that the heroes and heroines tell of making plans, lists, goals, priorities, and then going through them, one by one. What satisfaction comes from crossing something off a list! Once in a while, my wife Jaki and I devote ourselves to a "day in town." There is shopping to do, lots of places to go, business items to look into, a million things it seems. We make a list, ordering the places to go, with lists within lists telling what we must get or do at each stop. The hard work is done before leaving home. If we didn't make a list, the day in town would take twice as long and we'd forget half the stuff. We've done it that way, too.

bank, elements that do not necessarily grace the lives of the buyers, but just add further economic burden. Sometimes, in my vision, I see the young couple backing out of the office in bowed positions, boot-black on their lips. This may sound like a surrealistic nightmare, but events like this happen hundreds of times each business day.

Some might call my views extreme, even nutsy-cuckoo. Let us examine the facts in detail.

LOW MORTGAGE RATES STILL COST YOU A LOT

As I attempt to put this manuscript to bed (December 1997), we are in a period of relatively low interest rates, about 7.75 percent on fixed thirty-year mortgages in northern New York State. If the reader really wants to be economically indentured, now would be a great time to do it. The graph in figure 1-1 shows the average fixed-rate interest rate for mortgages from 1965 through 1997.

Interest rates have a tremendous impact on the amount of money paid back to the bank over the lifetime of the mortgage. Let's compare a twenty-five-year mortgage of $60,000 at various fixed rates:

$60,000 MORTGAGE FOR 25 YEARS, FIXED RATE

Rate	Monthly Payment	Total (300) payments	Total Interest
7%	$424.07	$127,221	$67,221
8%	$463.09	$138,927	$78,927
9%	$503.52	$151,056	$91,056
10%	$545.23	$163,569	$103,569
11%	$588.07	$176,421	$116,421
12%	$631.94	$189,582	$129,582
13%	$676.71	$203,013	$143,013

It is difficult for anyone to predict which way interest rates will go, but it seems clear, by the graph on the next page, that they are unlikely to fall below current levels. While I do not claim any clairvoyant abilities in these matters, ordinary statistics and probability theory would suggest that mortgage rates are more likely to go up than down. If rates are still low by the time you read this, and you absolutely must take out a mortgage (whatever your reason), then a fixed (rather than a variable) rate would probably be the best choice. But I hope that by

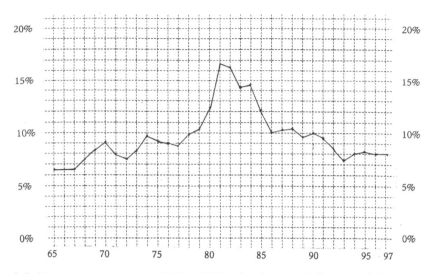

1-1. *Mortgage interest rates, 1965 to 1997, after* Statistical Abstract of the United States, *1992 and 1996 (U.S. Dept. of Commerce, Washington, D.C.) and* Economic Indicators Handbook *(Gale Research, 1992). Rates for 1996 and 1997 are based on averages found in current periodicals.*

the time you finish reading this book, you will be armed with enough strategies and courage to avoid the mortgage ("death pledge") route altogether. Or nearly so.

CLOSING COSTS

At closing, there are costs borne by the seller and costs borne by the buyer. Commonly, the breakdown will resemble that shown in the sidebar on page 9.

As bad as the chart in the sidebar looks, from the mortgagee's perspective, it doesn't tell the whole story on closing costs. The realtor's commission, for example, is really a buyer's cost because it is built into the price of the home. It is "passed on" to the buyer. And, in many parts of the country, including northern New York where I live, a home that qualifies for a mortgage is generally quite a bit more expensive than one that does not. A drilled well is required in our area, for example, even though a perfectly adequate, tested spring or shallow well exists on-site. Add between $5,000 and $6,000 to the mortgage amount, which translates to $10,000 to $20,000 over a twenty-five-year lifetime depending on the interest rate. The bank may require that the home have a recognized "central heating" system, such as oil, gas, or electric baseboard. Add another $2,000 to $4,000 to the mortgage, or $6,000 to $12,000 over twenty-five years. See the sidebar on page 11, "On Central Heating."

LIVING COSTS

For the average American family, typically 32 percent of after-tax income goes toward shelter, either in the form of rent or mortgage payments, plus costs associated with maintaining the home, including utilities. This figure varies from state to state; in California, for example, it's closer to 50 percent. (For interest's sake, the next two biggest living cost items are the automobile at 18 percent and food at about 14 percent, according to 1994 figures from *Statistical Abstract of the United States*.)

For people with mortgages, the cost of shelter is a very much higher percentage of after-tax income than for those without mortgages or for renters. In 1995 the average monthly mortgage payment was $1,062,

---

CLOSING COST BREAKDOWN

Costs borne by the buyer	*Costs borne by the seller*
1. All points (each point is 1% of mortgage)*	1. The balance due on any existing mortgage
2. Mortgage recording fees	2. Title research fees
3. Title insurance	3. State and local transfer taxes
4. Appraisal fee	4. Seller's attorney fees
5. Buyer's attorney fees	5. Realtor's commission
6. Survey fees, if necessary	
7. Credit report fee	

In addition, private mortgage insurance fees might be added to the mortgage payment schedule, as well as escrow funds for property tax and homeowner's insurance (required).

* Points can be paid upfront, if you can afford them. The interest rate will be reduced by a certain amount, a quarter percent or thereabouts, for example, per point paid.

which represented 32.6 percent of income for this group. When utilities and maintenance are added in, shelter cost is right around 50 percent of income. In 1976, incidentally, mortgage payments represented 24 percent of income, so things aren't getting any better.

The median monthly rent was $487 in 1993, the latest year for which I have figures. So rental is generally less expensive than the mortgage route. And so it should be. While it will be obvious by now that I am no great fan of mortgages, I am even less enthralled with the idea of renting my shelter, a condition that builds no equity whatsoever.

Now, eliminating a third of after-tax expenditure (by achieving shelter cost freedom) can actually save you a whole lot more than just the shelter (mortgage) cost. If the home was designed sensibly, fuel costs can also be greatly reduced, as at Earthwood. If the home accommodates home industry, car and clothing costs connected with holding an outside job can be eliminated. Perhaps food costs can be reduced by growing and storing food in a shelter designed to promote these activities. An often overlooked savings comes from potential income reductions. While it is true that mortgage interest payments are income tax deductible, even greater tax savings can be realized in another, superior way: by moving to a lower tax bracket.

Some of what I'm saying here might sound just a little bit radical, but really, it is not. Perhaps some important groundwork will help, groundwork that requires a journey back in time and space, 150 years, to be precise, to the gentle shores of a small pond near Concord, Massachusetts.

THOREAUVIAN ECONOMICS

Writer and philosopher Henry David Thoreau is best known for his American classic, *Walden*, which tells of his famous two-year "experiment in living" at Walden Pond near Concord, Massachusetts, from July 4, 1845 through September 6, 1847. Thoreau might truly be called the father of the owner-builder movement in America, although he was not a strong defender of ownership. The first and longest chapter of *Walden*, called "Economy," influenced a long line of empiric economists, who could be categorized as those who tear down economy to its barest essence, and who believe in the paramount value of practical

ON CENTRAL HEATING

Writer Steve Carlson, in his excellent book *The Best Home For Less* (Avon, 1989, p. 119), says, "There was a time when central systems were necessary to ensure comfort. That has changed. Houses have become tighter, better insulated, and more open in design. Meanwhile, individual heating units have become both safer and more efficient. Comfort and convenience are no longer dependent upon central systems. A central system is one of the most expensive components of a house. It adds substantially to the mortgage bill. Tax assessors recognize how much it costs, so the more expensive a system you have, the more it will add to your tax bill."

In addition, the central system will be more expensive to operate than either individual heating units or woodstoves. In our cold climate, people are happy if they can get away with an annual heating oil bill of $1,800 or less. At Earthwood, our 2,000-square-foot home described in chapter 6, we buy almost all of our firewood (most of which is burned cleanly and efficiently in a masonry stove) and our annual heating bill is about $200 per year, about 10 percent of heating costs acceptable to other North Country folks living in similarly sized homes. But our 23-ton masonry stove does not qualify as a central heating system for purposes of securing a mortgage; however, neither do we have nor desire a mortgage. Once a slave has tasted freedom, it's really hard to get him to put on the fetters again, even gold and silver ones. He'd sooner die. And our masonry stove is more efficient and more reliable than any system subject to mechanical or electrical failure, or which requires a constant fuel supply. In short, your money is better spent on double-pane south-facing glass and extra insulation than on a central heating system. Incorporate plenty of thermal mass, which is cheap, and the house will carry itself through long periods of winter inoccupancy, such as when you go to Chile for three weeks in January, which you can more likely afford to do if you're mortgage-free.

experience. Along with Hermann Hesse's short novel, *Siddhartha*, the seventy-odd pages of "Economy" had a profound and lasting effect on my own sense of fiscal responsibility, most particularly as it relates to the problem of shelter. To create his snug little house in the woods, Thoreau adapted many strategies (though he did not use the word) that are still in use by owner-builders in the creation of their mortgage-free homes today. He used a small grubstake to finance his experiment. He made use of recycled materials, as well as indigenous ones found near the house site. For land, he adapted "squatter's rights," which, in this case, meant building his house (with permission) on land belonging to his friend and mentor, the essayist Ralph Waldo Emerson. And Emerson, incidentally, after Thoreau's early death in 1862 at the age of forty-five, said of his friend, "No truer American existed."

Thoreau was the village handyman, amateur naturalist, sometime surveyor and pencil maker, and "unsuccessful" writer—at least in his own lifetime—in the way that Van Gogh was an unsuccessful painter. When he couldn't find a willing publisher for his book, Thoreau paid one to print it. Only 214 copies were sold in the first four years and the publisher returned the remainder of the thousand-copy print run to the author, which precipitated this wry comment: "I now have a library of nearly nine hundred volumes, over seven hundred of which I wrote myself."

How did such a man, even considered a "ne'er do well" by some of his neighbors, manage to exercise such a profound influence on intellectual giants like Tolstoy, Gandhi and (by way of Gandhi) Martin Luther King? The answer, I think, is that Thoreau had the uncanny ability to strip important philosophies down to their bare bones, subjects such as empiric economy, opposition to slavery, or even "on the duty of civil disobedience," his famous essay of the same name that helped change the history of the Indian subcontinent.

In the interests of space, I must necessarily reduce Thoreau's basic economic tenets, insofar as they are applicable to this current work, to an even barer essence. There is a danger in this. Important links might be lost by this approach. But if the reader's interest is tweaked by the next few paragraphs, then he or she would be well advised to travel to any library or bookstore and procure a copy of the original work in the philosopher's own inimitable words.

Henry David Thoreau and friends.

The Necessaries of Life

Animal life, says Thoreau, is nearly synonymous with animal heat. Today, we think of human body heat in terms of numbers like 37° Celsius or 98.6° Fahrenheit. If the body is at the optimum temperature, there is a very strong likelihood that the body is healthy. If it is healthy, it ought to be happy, for what is more important than health? Many a "rich" man wishes he could buy it. And how do we maintain our body heat? Thoreau speaks of the four necessaries of life, which "for man in this climate may, accurately enough, be distributed under the several heads of Food, Shelter, Clothing, and Fuel; for not till we have secured these are we prepared to entertain the true problems of life with freedom and a prospect of success."

Food, Shelter, Clothing, and Fuel are the basic means by which we keep our bodies at a healthy temperature. Food is "the fuel which keeps up the internal combustion in the lungs." Shelter creates a microclimate in which we can move about with some comfort. Clothing is close body insulation which slows immediate heat loss. And Fuel changes the ambient temperature of our Shelter to something more conducive to our idea of comfort. In actuality, we could probably survive on Food and proper Clothing alone, and, in the right climate, even reduce the Clothing requirement to nothing or nearly so.

Clothing. Thoreau takes us through many wonderful commentaries on reducing the four necessaries of life to their basics, including a delightful treatise on Clothing which runs for several pages, but which can be reduced to eighteen famous words: "I say beware of all enterprises which require new clothes, and not rather a new wearer of clothes." If it is possible to reduce life's costs enough that enterprises requiring new clothes can be eliminated, then further savings can be realized. Jaki and I are less concerned with fashion than with clothes of practicality. As a registered nurse at a pediatric office, Jaki must maintain a "uniform" conducive to instilling confidence in her patients (and her patients' parents). For my part, I must look at least presentable at building workshops, but a suit and tie might detract from my credibility. Our Clothing budget, if we had such

A dollar saved is worth a whole lot more than a dollar earned, because we have to earn so darned many of them to save so precious few.

a thing, would be very low indeed. Today, as I write these words, Jaki is mending some old clothes, instead of earning money to buy new ones. There is true economy in this sort of enterprise. Roy's First Law of Empiric Economics can be stated thus: "A dollar saved is worth a whole lot more than a dollar earned, because we have to earn so darned many of them to save so precious few."

Suffice it to say that Clothing is the least part of Thoreau's necessaries of life. The average American consumer unit (this space-age term has replaced "family" or "household" among statisticians) spends 5.2 percent of after-tax income on clothing and related expenditures annually, or $1,644. The present Roy consumer unit of 3.5, I'm sure, comes in at less than half of this figure. We are warm and, for the most part, presentable.

Fuel. Thoreau warmed his little house with a wood fire, but he speaks less of Fuel than of the other three necessaries. His small 10-by-15-foot house would have been easy to heat to a bachelor's satisfaction, and he had no worry about pipes freezing, as there was no indoor plumbing. His best-known observation about heat involves another famous nineteenth-century author and student of nature: "Darwin, the naturalist, says of the inhabitants of Tierra del Fuego, that while his own party, who were well clothed and sitting close to a fire, were far from warm, these naked savages, who were farther off, were observed, to his great surprise, 'to be streaming with perspiration at undergoing such a roasting.' So, we are told, the New Hollander goes naked with impunity, while the European shivers in his clothes."

A few sentences later, Thoreau comments that "Fuel serves only to prepare that Food or to increase the warmth of our bodies by addition from without."

This book is about designing and building a house that you own, instead of the bank owning it for you. Let's compound the savings by designing a house that is easy (and cheap) to heat or cool. Let's design it so that cooking and water heating are accomplished by sensible and fuel-efficient means, rather than by the wasteful systems so common in American homes today. For example, using electricity to heat resistance coils either for range-top cooking or immersion water heating is wasteful in terms of both money and fuel. Even propane and natural gas are more efficient, and some enterprising homesteaders, particularly in areas of high insolation (exposure to sunlight), are using solar energy for these purposes, as well as for space heating.

Food. Although Henry David was not averse to eating out with friends and relatives in town, he did take most of his meals at his cabin in the woods, and he grew and gathered a good part of what he consumed. In fact, he tended a small market garden, earning a profit of $8.71½ the first year, mostly in beans and potatoes. When he took into account the amount of food that he grew and consumed himself, and "considering the importance of a man's soul" and "the short time occupied by my experiment," he concluded that he'd done "better than any farmer in Concord did that year." Bravado notwithstanding, Thoreau ate simply and does not report that he suffered from more mealtimes than meals. Today, we have made advances in Food production with intensive growing methods, better seeds, and devices for extending the growing season. Although the modern homesteader is probably not as skilled or practiced as the nineteenth-century farmer at storing food, such knowledge is available to all who want it, and we have no excuse for not incorporating methods of Food production and preservation into our home design. From the start of the mort-gage-free endeavor, we should be considering the potential savings in all of the other "necessaries of life."

Shelter. The largest of the after-tax expenditures for most middle-class Americans is Shelter, the subject of this book. In the ensuing chapters, we will examine strategies and methods for designing and building a home that is so affordable that involvement with lending institutions will be non-existent or, at the least, limited to short-term seed money loans. Jaki and I have renovated a house in Scotland, and built four houses in New York, and we have never borrowed a cent on any of them. No, we're not rich fat cats. We simply employed sensible strategies that precluded bank "assistance" (read: indentured servitude). Our complete story is related in chapter 6. Thoreau's Shelter story is one of the main themes of the first chapter of Walden, and is best read in its original form in order to derive the full inspirational experience. And, in chapter 7, others will relate the personal odysseys that led them to the same result, freedom from the death pledge.

There are other life-cycle costs, such as low maintenance and lower property taxes that we can attend to at the design stage. More on this later.

Modern Needs

Now, on the verge of the twenty-first century, we must acknowledge other items that most people would consider necessities today, that were not for a cerebral bachelor philosopher of 1850. Transportation (car), Home Industry, and Recreation are three that come to mind, three potentially expensive items.

Transportation. Home design has only a minimal impact on the costs of owning and maintaining a car. Garage size and design, per-haps even the elimination of a garage (at least in the early days), are the main opportunities for reducing costs here. In the city, a car might be more of a burden than a benefit, but in rural areas, where most of the mortgage-free homes are, I am personally aware of only one young couple who make use of bicycles for all local transportation. They also happen to be top competitive bikers and triathletes, the fittest couple I've ever known. And, of course, many of the Amish and Mennonite people live high-quality lives untroubled by either cars or mortgages. They do not need this book. They could write their own.

Home industry. Home industry can easily be incorporated into the design strategies of home-building, and should be. Include in this category such considerations as a home workshop, sewing, crafts, and various computer-related activities. Some home industries might earn an income. Others, such as beer-making, might simply save money. In either case, great life-cycle cost savings can be derived, further reducing reliance on a fat and steady paycheck. Remember Roy's First Law?

Recreation. In its broad sense, recreation has taken on the status of a necessity. For Thoreau, recreation may have been a walk in the woods or an hour's reading by lamplight. This much I have learned in my five decades of sojourning in this life: *Everybody's different.* But I suspect that even the most addicted workaholic needs a break once in a while.

TO WHAT END?

I ask the reader to take a quantum leap with me. For purposes that will become clear, I ask you to accept, for a moment, that, yes, you can achieve mortgage freedom. (You really can. Believe it.) The next question, logically, would be: Having achieved freedom from the single largest cost of living, how can you best make use of this fortuitous situation? Put another way: To what meager purpose do we concern ourselves with retaining the body heat? Thoreau answers this in an eloquent passage:

> When a man is warmed by the several modes which I have described, what does he want next? Surely not more warmth of the same kind, as more and richer food, larger and more splendid houses, finer and more abundant clothing, more numerous, incessant, and hotter fires, and the like. When he has obtained these things which are necessary to life, there is another alternative than to obtain the superfluities; and that is, to adventure on life now, his vacation from humbler toil having commenced.

To adventure on life now, whatever it is that you might perceive that to be. We hear people saying, I wish I had the time to do this, that, or the other thing. Take care of the necessaries by an economy of effort and money—build a mortgage-free home—and the time will present itself.

The answers to these kinds of questions cut to the essence of our being. What is it that we want out of life? How, truly, do we escape

Our Lost Leisure

In 1991, Harvard economist Juliet Schor wrote a fascinating treatise on our entrapment in a voluntary (or involuntary) work ethic that turned us into a nation of workaholics, *The Overworked American: the Unexpected Decline in Leisure* (Basic Books, 1991). Some of her observations are startling:

> Since 1948, the level of productivity of the U.S. worker has more than doubled. In other words, we could now produce our 1948 standard of living in less than half the time. Every time productivity increases, we are presented with the possibility of either more free time or more money. We could have chosen the four-hour day. Or a working year of six months. Or every worker in the United States could now be taking every other year off from work—with pay (p. 2).
>
> Half of this country's population now say they have little time for their families (p. 11).
>
> "Nearly two-thirds of adult women are now employed" (p. 20).

At regular paying jobs. And weigh the previous fact against this:

> For women, gaining a husband adds about five hours of domestic work per week (p. 38).
>
> Before capitalism, most people did not work very long hours at all. The tempo of life was slow, even leisurely; the pace of work relaxed (p. 44).
>
> A Harris poll finds that since 1973 free time has fallen nearly 40 percent—from a median figure of 26 hours a week to slightly under 17 (p. 22).

All this is very interesting, but what does it have to do with a mortgage-free home? Simply this: Released from the need of having to come up with the monthly mortgage payment, less money needs to be earned. Less taxes need to be paid. This can translate into more leisure time. Or not. It's up to you.

from "lives of quiet desperation?" Which way is really up, and which way is the illusion? The answer, my friends, is not blowing in the wind. The answer, like truth, is personal and transient. That is to say, "Everybody's different. Everybody changes."

I read or heard this recently, I don't remember where: "A dying man's final words are unlikely to be 'I wish I'd watched more TV.'" No, there has got to be something more than that. For me, I've got enough interests to last a lifetime, ten lifetimes. I do not understand boredom, don't have the time for it. Life is exciting at fifty, because I have so many interests, so much to do. And I couldn't do it, or, at least, my style would be severely cramped, if I were not mortgage-free.

I have found a way of life that works for me. I enjoy my work. I could tell you all about it, but it wouldn't do any good. Thoreau says, and I agree, "I would not have any one adopt my mode of living on any account; for . . . before he has fairly learned it I may have found out another for myself . . ." No, the best I can hope for is to show workable strategies toward mortgage freedom, not necessarily all the strategies, the only strategies, even the best strategies, for this field is as long as it is wide. And what you do with the freedom is entirely up to you.

Mortgage freedom can come in three different ways. First, you can slog through the twenty or thirty years of the death pledge, tied to your salary and your monthly payments, until the long-awaited day of the mortgage-burning party. Second, you can live frugally until you can afford to buy a home without a mortgage. While difficult, this is not impossible, and it will require either a sudden windfall or adaptation of what writer Charles Long calls a conserver (as opposed to consumer) lifestyle. (Long's very practical economic philosophies, as explained in his book *How to Survive Without a Salary,* are examined more closely in chapter 2.) Or, third, you can build your own house, using strategies described throughout the remainder of this book.

ADVANTAGES OF OWNER-BUILDING

The very act of building your own shelter will virtually guarantee you a substantial dollar savings because of the elimination of labor costs, profit, and a proportional amount of bank interest, but even if this were not so, owner-building still would have many positive attractions, both practical and spiritual.

Quality

One of the most common fears of potential owner-builders is that they do not have the skills or knowledge to build a house with the same standards of the contractor-built home. This fear stems from the myth that building a home is a very complicated procedure. A great deal of experience is deemed mandatory, ergo, only a professional builder should be entrusted with the task. This line of uninformed reasoning can lead to ignorant conclusions, such as, "Owner-builders construct shacks."

The truth is that the quality of a home does not depend on whether or not it is owner-built or contractor-built. Quality depends, first and foremost, on conscientious attention to detail. Thus, in many cases, the owner-built home is of higher quality because the owner's long-term interests are the prime motivating force rather than merely a profit or a wage reward for punching the clock. Now, this is not to say that professional builders are not craftsmen; many most certainly are. But craftsmanship can be present in the owner-built home, too.

While only 20 percent of houses in America today are owner-built, a majority of the rest of the world's population lives in "homemade" houses, many of which have harmonized with the landscape for hundreds of years and more. Contractors are unknown in the animal world, where some excellent examples of craftsmanship can be found. The truth is that building a home is not all that complicated. The late writer and owner-builder advocate Ken Kern said, "Not everyone has the attitude and physical ability necessary to begin a house and proceed to a successful conclusion. But most people, once they have made the initial decision to proceed, do find these qualities in themselves. Success is more a matter of determination than of previous experience" (Kern, Kogon, and Thallon, *The Owner Builder and the Code*. Scribner's, 1976, p. 78).

Years ago, I was working with a construction crew on a house for an out-of-state customer. One morning, the contractor told us, "Look, the loan officer is coming to inspect the foundation at one o'clock. We're backfilling this afternoon. We've got to have the Thoroseal™ on the wall before we can backfill. Now, let's go!" (Thoroseal™ is a waterproofing material used to keep water out of basements and foundations.)

So we applied a single coat of Thoroseal™ to the foundation, although a double coat is called for by the manufacturer with a twenty-four-hour wait between coats. The bank loan officer was on time and saw that the Thoroseal™—still damp—was on the basement wall. He was satisfied. That afternoon, the foundation was backfilled. The bank was happy. The contractor saved a day. But, what did the customer get? A few days later, after another incident involving the structural integrity of a different house, I quit my job.

Previous to these events, Jaki and I built our first home, Log End Cottage, and applied the Thoroseal™ correctly to the block wall. We were inexperienced, but all we had to do was to follow the directions on the bag.

There are many excellent contractors, of course, who endeavor to put out a quality product, but they can't always be present to supervise every detail. From my experience on construction crews, I've learned that the workers do not always do things quite as carefully as they would on a job for themselves. Personal involvement on a project can provide that all-important difference.

You will make mistakes, to be sure, and certain skills—stone masonry, for example—take years to achieve aesthetic mastery. But a strong, long-lasting house can be built by most people, even of stone, although it may not have quite the polished appearance found in the work of master masons.

Ease of Repair and Maintenance

If something goes wrong in your contractor-built home, you would, in all likelihood, call in a contractor or tradesman to repair it, especially if it's within the period of time (usually one or two years) during which the contractor is legally responsible. An owner-builder, on the other hand, would find it counterproductive to call in a tradesman for normal maintenance or repairs. For a start, the tradesman does not know the house at all, while the owner-builder is familiar with each nail and board. Having built their own homes, owner-builders are rarely inclined to pay twenty or twenty-five dollars per hour to have someone else do the repairs. Therefore, the life-cycle cost of the owner-built home is less.

Comfort

Your home should not only be built by you, its future occupant, but designed by you as well. Can your architect know you better than you know yourself? As often as not, architects design homes at least partially to satisfy some personal, structural, or aesthetic whim, and the client's requirements are molded to that whim, instead of vice versa. Again, to quote Ken Kern:

> [Owner-builders] imagine being able to have a house of any shape they want, designed by themselves to meet their most practical needs and their most whimsical fancies. They wonder what it would be like if no one else made these decisions for them. What would it be like to be an artist house-builder in the only true sense, in a way that architects, who interpret clients' visions, and builders, who are allowed no visions at all, cannot? What would it be like to touch all the materials, to learn about placing them one against the other? What would it be like if the mistakes were made by their own hands instead of by the mechanisms of technology? What would it be like to have stories to tell about the creations of their houses? (Ibid., p. 60).

An owner-built home fits the designer-occupant like an old shoe. A special comfort, as well as economic advantage, can be derived from using indigenous and recycled materials in the construction. A house of stone on a stony site will be in harmony with its surroundings, as will be a log or cordwood masonry house built in a wooded area. Some of the quality and detailing in recycled materials is difficult, impossible, or extremely expensive to match today with modern materials. Finally, but not least, the use of recycled and indigenous materials makes infinitely more environmental sense than buying new energy-wasteful building materials, and hauling them across country to your site.

Owner-built homes are often constructed on a pay-as-you-go basis. This is a sound and time-proven strategy, as we will see. One of the byproducts of this building strategy, however, is that the original plans tend to change as time goes on. But change should be seen as a positive development when it's based on your newest requirements instead of your distantly anticipated requirements. In this way, the house molds naturally to the "contours" of its inhabitants. A change of plans in a contractor-built home normally carries a heavy penalty, and rightly so; it adversely affects how a contractor budgets time for his other

An owner-built home fits the designer-occupant like an old shoe.

work. Changes in code-approved plans involve unacceptable delays within the bureaucratic machine.

Special design features found in owner-built homes are often spontaneous ideas: the use of a burled branch as a handrail, for example, or bottles included in cordwood masonry as a purely aesthetic effect. It is a rare carpenter or mason who will take it upon himself to improvise. And, even if he did, and his improvisation was successful visually or functionally, it would still have been his idea. To the occupant, the meaning and feeling derived from the improvisation is of a different kind than that felt by the owner-builder, which leads us to:

Satisfaction and Pride

An intangible part of comfort comes, not so much from what has been built, but rather from who built it. Now this quality may only be manifest to the builders themselves, and perhaps to their family and close friends, and would be largely lost if the house were sold to a stranger, but it is present as long as the builders occupy their own home.

Renowned owner-builder Cliff Shockey, of Saskatchewan, says, "The satisfaction of designing and building your own home cannot be measured. It is truly one of the most rewarding things I have done."

Sam Felts says of his experience building a round cordwood house in Georgia, "This has been the most rewarding experience in my life. I feel that I have created a fun place in which to live."

Bonny Pond of New Brunswick says, "Our house is more than a beautiful, ecologically sound, economically attuned domicile. It is a statement of what we feel about ourselves, each other, and the world in which we live."

A dramatic exaggeration? Not at all. If owner-builders seem just a wee bit sinful in their pride, they are forgiven. They deserve it.

Economics

A third of after-tax income is commonly spent on shelter, whether the shelter is rented or mortgaged. If an individual works from the age of 20 to the age of 65, it can be argued that 15 years of his 45-year working life have been devoted to keeping a roof over his head. By the mortgage route, the individual has at least built up an equity in his home—albeit very slowly, thanks to the nature of amortization schedules in the early years of a mortgage—and, in most cases, the retirement years are relatively free of shelter costs, property taxes and normal maintenance excluded. The rental route is an economic disaster in all but the most unusual individual circumstances, as no equity is built up at all. The mortgage road seems the better of the more common approaches to paying for shelter. But, to obtain a mortgage commonly requires a substantial down payment which may even exceed the total land and materials cost of the owner-built home.

Obviously, the magic key is the addition of the owner's labor. In some cases, people take six months off from regular employment to build; in others the construction is done after work and on weekends. People say to me, "That's okay for golf pros, writers, and other layabouts, but I can't afford to take six months off work to build my house." I argue that to save the equivalent of fourteen and one-half years of their working life, they can't afford *not* to.

2

The Grubstake

consumer

conserver

With respect to luxuries and comforts, the wisest have ever lived a more simple and meagre life than the poor.

—Henry David Thoreau, *Walden*

Leaving our share of the national debt aside—after all, I've never heard of an individual actually called on to repay his or her portion—it can be safely asserted that most of us enter this world with a clean ledger, a nice tidy zero balance sheet. And, for most of us, what happens to our fiscal balance sheet over the next eighteen years is probably more of a function of parental influences and contributions than personal initiative, although cases exist of successful entrepreneurs doing quite well for themselves by the time they reach voting age. Certainly, our habits of spending and saving, as well as the value we place on money (determined by the amount of time and work we're willing to exchange for the stuff) are established early in life. If your habits lean toward the saving side, this chapter will be easier to take than if your spending habits lean more toward the buy-now-pay-later outlook. But I heartily believe that almost anyone can develop the kinds of habits necessary for laying up a grubstake, because I've seen successful examples time and again.

The word "grubstake" originally referred to money or provisions advanced to a prospector in return for a share of his findings. "Grub"—yes, it often meant food as well as prospecting supplies—was advanced for a "stake" in the claim. Nowadays, the term commonly refers to monies laid aside for the purchase of homesteading land or to start a business.

Basically, there are two grubstake strategies that you can pursue toward owning your own home. I call them the "full grubstake" and the "land grubstake," and I'll look at their relative applicability to people in various circumstances. I'll discuss considerations for determining what size of a grubstake is needed. And I'll introduce a way of living called the Conserver Lifestyle that will enable you to procure the grubstake. Finally, I'll share some specific money-saving tips that will shorten your grubstake savings time. First, I'd like to share my thoughts about a different kind of investment: the college tuition grubstake.

THE COLLEGE TUITION GRUBSTAKE

College tuition money is probably the most common form of grubstake today, whether it was set aside by your parents, yourself, or both. The parents' "stake" in this case is the natural instinct to see their children do as well or better than the parents have done themselves. The

27

stake is nothing less than the perceived improvement of the family situation and the betterment of the human race. The wisdom of a college education is not questioned by the overwhelming majority of Americans, and yet how many have examined this "standard wisdom" analytically and considered the alternative? The thoroughly American Thoreau says, "No way of thinking or doing, however ancient, can be trusted without proof."

College is great for those who know exactly what career they desire, and which degree they require to get there. Unfortunately, for many, college becomes an expensive extension of high school for at least the first couple of years. To be sure, there is a social life that has a value— even if its main component is "party time"—but the worth of the entire package must be weighed against the alternatives. In her book *Possum Living* (Universe Books, 1978), Dolly Freed compares college costs with one such alternative, the one that is the subject of the book in your hand:

> Owning your own home free and clear—that's the key to all the rest. Once you have your snug harbor, your safe base, all else comes easy. You can tell the rest of the world to go to hell if you want, once you own the roof over your head. I believe that some parents who are willing to give kids a college education would be doing the kid a better turn by giving him that money to buy a house instead. Once he realizes he doesn't have to worry about his future—once he has security and leisure to think about it, instead of having his future rammed down his throat— he'll make his own future.

Anne Herbert, writing in *The Next Whole Earth Catalog,* observes, "I've noticed that when I meet people my own age who seem to have had a truly incredible number of adventures, they turn out to have not gone to college, so instead of doing one thing for four years, they started doing two or three things as soon as they left high school" (p. 545).

I resemble that remark. Upon leaving high school, I continued to operate a small summer business, earning enough for extensive world travel in the winter. I soon realized that input (another word for education) was entering my life several times faster than the rate at high school. Eventually, monies laid aside for college by my parents became the grubstake for my first mortgage-free home. I'm sure that my parents were somewhat disappointed that I didn't attend college, but they knew I received an education, and they saw me achieve a comfortable financial freedom by my early twenties, thanks mostly to mortgage freedom.

Thoreau, who had been to college, asks, "Who would have advanced the most at the end of a month—the boy who had made his own jackknife from the ore which he had dug and smelted, reading as much as would be necessary for this—or the boy who had attended the lectures on metallurgy at the Institute in the meanwhile, and had received a Roger's penknife from his father? Which would be most likely to cut his fingers?"

Jaki and I believe in Mark Twain's adage: "Never let schooling get in the way of your children's education," and we have home-schooled each of our sons at different times during their primary school days. We have never hesitated to pull them out of school for travel abroad, with no doubt whatsoever about which course returned the better education. Academically, home schooling and travel didn't seem to hurt the boys: they each stayed at or near the top of their class. Upon completion of high school, our oldest son Rohan, despite excellent scholarships to some good colleges, realized that he was not yet ready for college. He did not know what qualifications he would need for an as-yet-unknown career. Following in his father's footsteps, he has traveled close to the wind on four continents, and has been involved in innovative building in France, Chile, British Columbia, and throughout the United States. To paraphrase Thoreau's question, "Would he be better prepared to build a house had he attended the Institute? Would he know as much about economy?"

I admit that, as a parent, it was tough to swallow Rohan's decision to turn down scholarship opportunities that, in all likelihood, would not recur. "Standard wisdom" (wise or not) is hard to cast aside. But Rohan has learned a wisdom that many of my middle-aged paycheck-hunting contemporaries have still not realized, and he didn't need to have anyone translate it for him: "First you must be happy at your work."

I *do not* encourage anyone to stay away from college who knows exactly what they want or need out of it. I *do* suggest that for those who don't have fixed goals, consider, at least, some of the educational and financial benefits that come from *not* going. People who go back to formal education as adults generally do extremely well, because they are going back for some specific purpose. My sister returned to academia in her mid-forties, gained a law degree, and became a successful lawyer. Someone else might go back to school to learn art, computer literacy, a new language, any number of disciplines.

THE FULL GRUBSTAKE

This strategy requires that you lay by all the money needed to buy a piece of land and build a house upon it. This is nice if you can do it. Its primary advantage is that you can "strike while the iron is hot." Enthusiasm carries over from the purchase of the land to the construction of the house, as there is no saving and waiting period. In addition, a complete break can be made from your current mode of existence, a boon when your current mode isn't really what you want out of life anyway.

If the land is close to your place of employment, money for land purchase and building materials is sufficient. If a move is anticipated and outside employment cannot be counted upon right away, additional money for ordinary living expenses during construction will be necessary. And you'd better know where your living is to come from after the house is finished. Even though the cost of living diminishes greatly when shelter costs are eliminated, and even further if food and fuel expenses are attended to simultaneously, it is still necessary to come up with a certain amount of money to live. The whole exercise has been a waste of time if you cannot earn the "paper costs" of living, such as mandatory insurance, land and school taxes, registrations and licenses, and the like. Also, a certain number of luxuries seem almost to have become necessities in today's society: recreation, entertainment, labor-saving devices.

Perhaps you've already built up enough equity in your currently mortgaged home to sell out and clear enough cash to build a new, more economically attuned home, thus releasing you from the death pledge. Or, you may already own your home free and clear, but want to make use of the economic benefits of owner-building in some other way, downsizing to a smaller home for retirement, for example, while releasing more money for the enjoyment of that retirement.

Here's a typical scenario: a couple in their late forties live in a large, fashionable, but energy-inefficient home which they own or almost own. The value of the house has appreciated. Family income is steady. But the place is too big for them now that the children have left. And the new reality of energy costs looms heavy on the landscape. They're interested in energy-efficient homes, such as passive solar designs and earth shelters. Still young enough to tackle a building project, they see it as both a personal challenge and an adventure. So, they clear $120,000 on the sale of their home, buy a piece of land, and build a sensible and customized home at a combined cost of $80,000, putting the extra toward investment for retirement. Nice.

If you are starting from "scratch," the problems connected with laying up the full grubstake may outweigh the benefits. Inflation can be an enemy. Land and building material prices often rise even faster than the general inflation rate.

Say a young couple calculates that they need $10,000 for land and $15,000 for materials to build their own home: $25,000 in all. They figure that by tightening the belt—they've already read the rest of this chapter—they can save $5,000 per year. In five years, it seems, they'll have their grubstake. Sadly, this is not the case. If they invest their savings at 6 percent interest, but the cost of land and building materials escalates at 10 percent, it actually takes nine years to put aside the full grubstake.

The exact figures cited above are not as important as understanding the relationship between savings and prices. Both inflation and interest rates have been low during the 1990s. Only the stock market seems to be growing at a hyper rate, which I don't pretend to understand. If inflation returns to the high levels of the 1980s, savings will take a tremendous dive in terms of spending power. Our young couple will stand still, at best.

The only way that this hypothetical couple could manage to save the necessary grubstake in five years would be to increase the amount that they are laying aside each month or each year. If they are paying shelter costs already, this may be extremely difficult. Even if their salaries rise, occasional but major expenses such as a replacement vehicle or medical care may cause a setback in the savings strategy.

Roy's Second Law of Empiric Economics might be stated: Savings accounts have a certain optimum size, neither too thin nor too fat. A fat savings account is one of the poorest hedges against inflation. After a healthy savings account is established, a better strategy to further dollar accumulation is to invest the monthly savings immediately in the very things required for the house: land payments, tools, building materials. A "healthy" bank account, in this case, is one that allows you to take advantage of genuine bargains when they come up. I feel that five to ten thousand dollars is the ballpark at this writing. This is usually enough to place a down payment on a piece of property, for example, when "just the right piece" becomes available.

A nine-year or even a five-year strategy has another built-in problem which negates its value for all but the most patient and methodical visionaries: the strong initial enthusiasm for the project wanes over time. It's easy to do things when we have to; self-discipline is very much harder. We are creatures of habit and our economic servitude begins to take on the guise of security. Another danger: one of the partners in a marriage gets impatient with far-in-the-future schemes, that castle in the air under which no foundation seems to be forthcoming. The relationship is severely strained.

Savings accounts have a certain optimum size, neither too thin nor too fat.

But there is a good chance you will not be "starting from scratch" in an economic sense. By the time most people have reached the prime age of the first-time home buyer, say 25 to 34, a certain amount of equity has been accumulated. This equity may be in stocks or bonds, a bank account, cars, appliances, or some other investment. Perhaps there is a modest inheritance. Many people reaching the age of thirty may be surprised to find that their estate has grown to a value of $10,000 to $20,000, or more. Sadly, others attain this age only to find that they have accumulated little of liquid value. If *you* resemble *this* remark, don't despair! Read on. And take comfort that tomorrow really is the first day of the rest of your life.

Anyone who can afford to buy a contractor-built home with a down payment and the assumption of a very expensive mortgage, can certainly afford to build his or her own home at a great savings.

Jaki and I were fortunate in being able to start our homesteading venture in northern New York with the full grubstake. Our grubstake came mostly from the sale of an old stone cottage in the Scottish Highlands, which I'd bought in 1969 for $2,400, renovated (sweat equity), and sold in 1974 for $26,000. This enabled us to move to the United

States, buy the land and a small pick-up truck, build Log End Cottage, and cover our living costs while building. Chapter 6 tells the whole story.

To summarize on the full grubstake strategy: If you've got it, use it. If not, that's fine, too. The land grubstake, the temporary shelter, the pay-as-you-go house, and other strategies are all open to you.

THE LAND GRUBSTAKE

This land grubstake strategy is one of the most common routes toward mortgage freedom. Most of the case histories in chapter 7 illustrate this strategy. In brief, the plan is to save the money for the land (or at least a substantial down payment), to move onto the land by one of the various temporary shelter strategies discussed in chapter 4 (saving interim housing costs), and then to build the permanent house on a pay-as-you-go basis. The total cycle from starting with zero savings to owning your own land and home can range from three to six years, depending on your tenacity and the degree of lavishness reflected in your house plans.

One couple living near us started with an irregular income and a grubstake of about $1,000. They were living in their own home on a 20-acre woodlot within a year! The home was not completely finished in that time, but it was comfortable even in the North Country winter. Within five years, the land was paid off and the home was completed.

Because of the favorable price obtained through collective purchase, and the fact that the seller did not wish to take in too much money the first year for tax reasons, many of the people who originally joined in with us on Murtagh Hill in 1975 were able to buy their land for a down payment of $600. The value of these two strategies—collective buying and securing owner-financing—cannot be overemphasized. Each individual family obtained a warranty deed (the best kind; see appendix 4) for its parcel. Acreages varied from 15 to 23, selling prices from $2,800 to $3,600. The owner carried the mortgage for five years. Land payments were made once a year, one-fifth of the principal each year plus interest at 6 percent on the unpaid balance. This meant that each year's land payment was a little less than the previous year's. Combined with the decreasing value of money through inflation, this is a very favorable situation for the buyer.

All of the parties who joined together in 1975 to buy land on The Hill, and at least three families who have moved to riparian land since, own their own homes and land now, free of debt. There have been some divorces in our community over the past twenty years, at about the same rate as the national average, and I won't deny that some of the break-ups were related in part to the pressures of owner-building. In fact, this is an important consideration which I will return to now and again throughout this book. At least one member of each of the original families still lives on or makes use of the land on The Hill, a remarkable record after twenty-two years for a community drawn together as haphazardly as ours.

Buying land on a mortgage may seem almost the same as buying a house on a mortgage. While there are similarities in kind, there is a vast difference in degree. The average home in the United States today costs $85,000. Let's say that $20,000 was put down on the purchase (a reasonable grubstake, by the way, for building a mortgage-free home). The $65,000 mortgage over 30 years at 8 percent (the current fixed rate as I write) would require monthly payments of $502, or $6,024 per year. The total cost of the $85,000 house is $20,000 for the down payment plus $180,720 for 360 payments of $502, or $200,720 altogether, not counting closing costs. By comparison, a piece of land costing $10,000, with terms of $2,000 down and four annual payments of $2,000 plus 8 percent of the unpaid balance costs $11,600 over the four years: $2,000 d.p. + $2,640 + $2,480 + $2,320 + $2,160 = $11,600. The relatively small land purchase winds up costing 11.6 percent more than the original price, whereas the home on the long-term mortgage costs 236 percent more.

Unless you're Henry Thoreau or have a beneficent Aunt Minnie or just a great mother like Sara Mapelli does—you'll hear Sara's story in chapter 7—the cost of land is an unavoidable part of the cost of a home. If you want to build something, you have to build it somewhere. And, for the many members of the buy-now-pay-later generation who are only able to lay money aside to meet payments, the self-imposed kind of discipline needed to accumulate savings is extremely difficult. For these people, making land payments and building equity is certainly preferable to blowing the money away, the inevitable alternative.

Okay, but we've still got to start with something, even if it's only $600 for a down payment on the land, $300 for a temporary shelter, and another $300 or $400 for living expenses until income starts to flow again. Ki Light's mother and father started thus 22 years ago. You'll meet Ki, too, in chapter 7, and learn about his wonderful straw bale house. Ki and his wife Judith are the first of the second generation on The Hill to build their own mortgage-free home.

HOW MUCH IS ENOUGH?

You will need to answer this question, or at least make a fair stab at it, whether you employ the Full Grubstake or the Land Grubstake strategy. Plenty of courageous people all over this country have started out with a $2,000 full grubstake or less, but this is not so common and not so easy. A proper balance between time and money should be the goal in determining the amount of the grubstake. Low-budget living can be a spiritual experience, but just as often, money worries can be a disturbing cause of friction within the family.

How is this paradox resolved? And how much is the right amount for the grubstake? There are no hard and fast answers to these questions, as the answers will vary from individual to individual, couple to couple. There are people who think of themselves as "hard up," but would consider themselves destitute if forced to live the way of the Roy family during our first three years on The Hill: hand pumping every drop of water used in the home, flushing the toilet with a bucket, lighting with kerosene lamps and a few 12-volt lights. (Conversely, many Third World citizens would be ecstatic with the sudden wealth.) Never mind that for the first eight months we made use of an outhouse (sometimes in sub-zero temperatures), had no electricity at all, and used buckets to haul water from a distant pump. All of the folk in our community started under similar circumstances, yet I doubt that any one of them thought of himself or herself as poor. On the contrary, I suspect that, upon reflection, most of us would say we have always enjoyed true wealth: fresh air, peace and quiet, good neighbors, clean water, untainted vegetables, and lack of debt; in short, real, not paper, security. Any one of us could trade in our sweat equities for a profit in the dollar sense and readopt the ways of the "masses of men." I, for one, am not so inclined. A person who has once known freedom makes a poor slave compared with the one who has never known an alternative.

The resolution to the paradox might be that there is a tremendous psychological difference between voluntary poverty and involuntary poverty. Eliminating the "gold and silver fetters" should not be thought of as a regression, but, rather, as a giant step toward freedom.

Even though Jaki and I started our homestead with the full grub-stake, we were each well acquainted with dollar poverty before we began our partnership, and, as a kind of refresher course, we returned to that vantage point after the completion of Log End Cave, our second home. We were broke. Nickle-and-diming it isn't much fun. Like Hesse's Siddhartha after his years in the materialistic world, we'd forgotten how to be at peace with dollar poverty. We buckled down again to make the switch from enforced poverty, in which piddling dollar concerns overwhelmed us, to voluntary poverty, in which we'd have enough to meet our needs. We were fortunate that our relationship was strong enough to take us through a trying period.

If the move to the land can be accomplished via the Temporary Shelter strategy (chapter 4), and regular income from employment continues without interruption, you only need to grubstake the materials cost of the temporary shelter before making the move to the land. Monies formerly delegated toward shelter costs, usually rent, can be put directly into building materials, so the accumulation of the house portion of the grubstake can now proceed at a greatly accelerated pace. The problem here is often one of insufficient funds to maintain the momentum of building. Time spent waiting for enough money for the next stage of construction is frustrating. Preferably, you should have enough additional money so that you can make a substantial start on the permanent dwelling, keeping the time you have to spend in the temporary shelter to a minimum. A year in cramped quarters is quite enough for anyone, and especially for a family. With the full grub-stake, the period spent in your temporary shelter can be reduced to the six or eight warmest months (time enough to build the house), when being outside provides pleasant escape from the cramped conditions.

If your regular income terminates with the move to the temporary shelter, you'd better have enough to build the permanent home and for at least six months' worth of life's normal expenses during con-

ON HOMESTEADING

A visit with *Webster's Unabridged* helps avoid the kind of confusion that can "crop up" with a word like *homestead*. The first definition is pretty good for our purposes: "A home; the seat of a family, including the land, house and outbuildings; especially, a dwelling retained as a home by successive generations." The second definition is also interesting: "In law, such a place occupied by the owner and his family and exempted from seizure or forced sale to meet general debts." Bankruptcy, although it protects people from getting kicked out of their houses, is not a strategy that I can endorse. Others are hurt by bankruptcy, not just the one going bankrupt. And even a staunch believer in "if you can't afford it, don't buy it" like myself can imagine situations where a good credit rating might be useful, such as when renting a car.

The third definition of *homestead* adds spice: "A 160-acre tract of public land granted by the United States government to a settler to be developed as a farm." This, of course, refers to the famous—or infamous if you happen to be a Native American—Homestead Act of 1862, which granted "land not to exceed 160 acres to any citizen or alien intending to become a citizen, to be developed as a farm." And where did this "public" land come from? Well, we can speak of Thomas Jefferson's canny "Louisiana Purchase" of nearly 800,000 square miles of land for $15,000,000—just 3¢ an acre—but where did France get title to it in the first place? The plight of the indigenous people, not even afforded the status of aliens, brings a new appreciation of the expression "falling through the cracks." Many plots of land in the Midwest and West still derive from the Homestead Act, and stolen land was still being given away until the 1950s. But no more.

You don't have to homestead—yes, there is a verb—to have your home protected under the law. A home that you own—*not a mortgaged home*—affords the same protection. And you don't have to homestead to use the strategies described in this book. The grubstake, the temporary shelter, designing a low-cost home, and all the rest are just as useful to wage-earners as to homesteaders, and those two categories don't have to be mutually exclusive either. When I think of homesteading, I think of the additional economic, environmental, and health advantages of providing one's own Fuel (energy) and Food, as well as Shelter. *But you don't have to!*

struction. Combine the estimates for these items and add 20 percent as a safety margin. For example, you may estimate that your house will require $10,000 and take six months to build. Figure to spend $150 a week over and above building costs, or $3,900 for six months. Building and living totals $13,900. The 20 percent safety margin of $2,780 brings the grand total to $16,680. If land payments are due during construction or shortly thereafter, they must be added.

Are you shocked at these figures, finding them unreasonably low? "What kind of house can be built for $10,000?" you may ask. The answer is: a comfortable, debt-free home, with a minimum of frills. Others might ask, "How do you expect us to live on $150 a week?" Well, three of the biggest costs of living are income taxes, shelter costs, and fuel costs. Living on the land in a temporary shelter eliminates the first two of these, and substantially reduces the third. This new economic reality bears little resemblance to the system you've been used to. Still others might despair at the thought of saving $16,000 or more. Don't! Remember, it can be done for less, as illustrated by some of the case histories in chapter 7. The point is that $16,000—or $8,000 or $25,000—is better invested in building your own home than in a down payment on a bought home or in spending the equivalent on two or three or four years' rent. Or buying a new car. Or smoking two packs of cigarettes a day for eight years.

A charming little $10,000 cottage.

The problems in determining how large a grubstake you will need stem from four variables, and the first one won't surprise you: (1) Everybody's different. Their abilities are different. Their fiscal responsibility and earning potential varies. Their house and land requirements are different. (2) Land prices vary tremendously around the country. (3) Earnings and cost of living also vary around the country. (4) Building and planning codes range from restrictive to nonexistent. (The chart in appendix 1 shows what strategies are possible with different combinations of grubstakes and earning power.)

Even if the Temporary Shelter strategy isn't employed, the land grubstake is still a viable strategy. Your savings are better invested in land, which tends to rise in value at least as fast as inflation. And you can enjoy the land and get to know it, even if you're not yet actually living there. Some people camp on the land for several years before they finally build, but, by then, they know the land intimately, and it is friendly to them.

The "roughing it" implied with the temporary shelter may not appeal to you or your partner, and is not imperative as long as you buy the land outright or on a mortgage, and live fairly close to the property. If you convert further savings directly into building materials, which can be stored on the land providing that they are safe from theft and deterioration, the problem of escalating building costs is also kept under control. Converting indigenous raw material on the land—standing trees into logs and log-ends, for example—and recycling building materials such as are found in old barns in the area, can bring the building reality in sight, perhaps within a year or two. A well can be dug and capped, a septic system installed, a driveway built, all at current prices and not at some future inflated price. The grubstake does not have to be measured in cash. Tools, building materials, and improvements to the property can all be thought of as part of the grubstake.

You can take lots of other valuable and inexpensive steps in the interim period between purchasing the land and constructing the house. One neighbor, a single lady, found all sorts of helpful things to do while awaiting her move to the land: "I started a notebook on gardening and homesteading ideas, and in it I also made lists—of equipment, tools, books to read, clothing I'd need, goals, crops to grow, and so on. I began gathering hand tools, kerosene lamps, ropes, buckets, mosquito netting, water cans, work gloves, compass, tarps, first aid supplies, and my closets bulged. I experimented with raising earthworms in my apartment, making yogurt, baking bread and candlemaking. I took a class in gardening and got hands-on practice by spending a week on a friend's homestead and helping another friend prune grapes." Your list may be different and might include learning about your chosen building method by reading or through a course of study, planning the house, getting to know the land, constructing useful outbuildings, and pursuing other related activities. The point is that there are lots of other gainful activities that you can pursue at the same time you're grubstaking.

THE CONSERVER LIFESTYLE

Barring an unexpected inheritance or lottery prize, you will have to lay up your own grubstake. The rate at which this money can be saved is proportional to the degree of austerity that you can accept. In other words, exactly how much are you willing to do without in order to reach your goal in the shortest possible time?

Most North Americans are caught up in what is universally known as the consumer economy. We are called consumers. Say that a few times outloud. Consumer. Consumer. We consume. Consume. After a while, doesn't it start to sound just a little, I don't know, thoughtless, callous, selfish? Yet, for many Americans, consumerism equates with patriotism. We hear of supply and demand economics like there's no other kind. Advertisers seduce us and our kids from birth with images of glitzy gadgets or instant glamour. Necessities are rarely advertised. They don't need to be. Buy, buy and buy again. It will make you happy. It's good for the economy.

But the corporate armor is beginning to show a few cracks. The idea of enough is beginning—just beginning—to catch on. According to a Merck Family Poll cited in *In Context,* 82 percent of Americans agree that "Most of us buy and consume more than we need." Twenty-eight percent of Americans said that they had downshifted or voluntarily cut back their income in some way over the past five years. (And 35 percent said they had "upshifted." Oh well.)

Now is the time to introduce a book that can be a great boon toward helping you achieve the goal of a mortgage-free home, Charles Long's

Be Careful . . .

Perhaps you already live on a family farm, or your parents own country land which they'd be willing to share with you. Great. Count your blessings. In this case, you'll still need a grubstake for building materials, perhaps for a well and septic system. However, be sure to get and record a deed for the property prior to any construction. "But Mom and Dad wouldn't cheat their dear and loving only son!" No, no, of course not. (Although I know of such a case.) But there are two points to keep in mind here. One: Just as in the case of friends joining together on a land purchase, there is more at stake than just land or money or houses, so it is imperative to avoid misinterpretation of your agreement. Sometimes these family "understandings" are far too casual, and, after a few years, each party to the understanding remembers it just that wee bit differently. A family feud can then erupt.

Two: Problems could arise if a probate court gets involved in the case. Probate courts are only concerned with facts, such as written agreements and recorded deeds. Do it right. Never, under any circumstance, build a house, dig a well, or conduct any valuable improvements to property that you do not own by clear recorded title or some other airtight legal instrument. No one can foresee all the circumstances that could foul up a casual agreement. Based on my personal experience and observations of the experiences of others, the success ratio of nonbinding agreements is less than 50 percent. Buck the odds at your own risk.

How to Survive Without a Salary (Warwick, Toronto, 1996). The subtitle names Long's basic philosophy of life: *Learning How to Live the Conserver Lifestyle*.

If you consider Thoreau's economic philosophy to be inspirational, but intrinsically simplistic and impractical, you are not alone, although I found it to be quite workable when applied to individual economic problems. But along comes Charles Long, a living breathing twentieth-century student and teacher of what I call empiric economics, who shares very practical methods of achieving fiscal freedom. The thrust of his book is implicit in the title, *How to Survive Without a Salary*. And his point of view is not that of a nineteenth-century bachelor aesthete, but, rather, that of a happily married man with family, who has talked the talk and walked the walk for many years. Long says it best:

> Real poverty is not a laughing matter. It's destructive, depressing, and self-perpetuating. It's an economic state. It's also a state of mind. It's not the same as living cheaply. Our little family has lived quite happily and comfortably on a great deal less cash than the same-sized family might get on welfare. We aren't poor. We don't feel poor and don't live poorly. We have few of the material things that really poor people around us take for granted. No cable TV, instant foods, or fashionable clothes. Even if we wanted to, we couldn't afford to smoke. On the other hand, we enjoy drinking wine with meals, eat the finest of foods, and travel abroad more frequently than most. They are modest indulgences, but in our lifestyle they are vital (p. 28).

The book in your hands is about mortgage freedom, not living without a salary, although the former can easily lead to the latter. And Long says of his own work, emphatically, "This is not a back-to-the-land book." Rather, Long shares with us one of the most workable systems of saving money there is: the Conserver Lifestyle. Its essence? *Reduce spending.* Just as there is a kind of warped methodology built around spending, there is an enlightened methodology about conserving, and no one expresses it better than Charles Long. And his methods work. I know this because Jaki and I have been using them for twenty-five years. While I only discovered Long's book while researching this one in early 1997, by the time I finished his preface, I knew that Long was talking my language. I read through the book at a sitting, fascinated with the author's clear perception of the reality of personal economy, as opposed to the hyped muck called Western values which has put 43 percent of Americans in debt.

The strategies that Long details for achieving freedom from a regular job are just as workable for laying by a grubstake. "For the conserver household," says Long, "costs are more important than earnings."

Other Benefits of the Conserver Lifestyle

One good thing leads to another. We see this over and over again in life, and in the strategies of this book. Just as mortgage freedom can lead to a whole different set of economic and personal freedoms, so, too, a move toward the Conserver Lifestyle has other benefits, many of them as important as the economic benefits. Let's play the word-sound game again, this time with *conserver*. Conserver. Conserve. Conservation. Conserver. Whereas "consumer" brings to mind consumption of resources, energy, and planetary capital, "conserver" suggests taking care of our limited natural resources, protecting the environment, and living on a higher qualitative plane. It is conservation, not consumption, which equates with social responsibility.

Mortgage freedom will change your life for the better. So will the Conserver Lifestyle. Give it a try. Although everyone is different, I think there is a high chance that you will find that changing to the Conserver Lifestyle is more likely to increase quality of life than to diminish it, both for you, your loved ones, and your fellow passengers on Spaceship Earth. Accuse me of proselytizing, if you must, and I will have to return a plea of guilty. Sometimes I can't help myself.

It's not my fault.

My editor made me do it.

REEXAMINING NECESSITIES

To get on the savings fast track, you must be able to differentiate between necessities and luxuries. Let's examine the necessaries more closely, to try to determine the difference between that which is truly a "necessary of life" and that which is not.

Food

Without going into a detailed nutritional analysis (read John Robbins's *May All Be Fed* listed in appendix 3 for that), we can safely state that the more common form of malnutrition among American adults is obesity, not undernourishment. When youthful activity decreases, as early as the mid-twenties for many people, and the habitual diet is maintained, body weight will increase. The alternatives are increased exercise (building a house?), a decreased caloric intake, or a combination of the two. Just as forest management can yield firewood and an improved woodlot, a change in diet can yield dollar savings and improved health. Americans, for example, consume an inordinate amount of meat, especially fatty meats such as streaky bacon, sausage, and beefsteak. This is good neither for planetary nor bodily health and, as protein production, it is a wasteful use of agricultural lands. Americans consume two and one-half times the amount of protein recommended by the United Nations Food and Agricultural Organization. To accomplish this, we grow ten times as much grain to feed cattle and other livestock as we consume ourselves.

For many years, and certainly while grubstaking, Jaki and I bought very little meat at the market, although we were inclined to order meat, especially chicken, when eating out. More recently, we have cut meat out of our diets, although we still use dairy products and, occasionally, seafood. And, in the autumn of 1997, I was heartened to learn of the work of Dr. William Castelli, medical director of the Framingham (Massachusetts) Heart Study. According to Dr. Castelli, other societies don't have the problems with heart disease to the same degree as Americans, and four billion people don't get arteriosclerosis at all. "Our society is concerned about the symptoms of heart attacks, but not what leads up to the heart attack." He adds that one of the major contributors to heart disease is this country's love of red meat. "Vegetarians in our society outlive us by seven years," Castelli says. "If you can't be a vegetarian, eat a vegetarian from the sea. Oysters, clams, scallops— they are all low-fat foods" (Jeff Meyers, "American Diet Recipe for Poor Health," *Plattsburgh Press-Republican,* November 4, 1997).

Eating out is not food consumption for survival, but for entertainment. During times when it was necessary to save money for some purpose, dining out was one of the first items we scratched from our budget. According to *The Statistical Abstract of the United States* (1996), the average "consumer unit"—what a term!—spent $4,410 on food in 1994: $2,712 at home and $1,698 away from home. Granting that meals away from home still need to be eaten somewhere, the potential savings is still considerable.

Fuel

The standard suggestions for conserving fuel and cutting down on costs, which most people ignore, really do work: car pooling, organizing chores to avoid duplication of trips, and wearing a sweater so that you can turn down the thermostat to 68° Fahrenheit or less. Rooms in the home that are seldom used need not be kept heated while not in use. Water heaters should only be flipped on if a significant amount of hot water is required. I think it was Amory Lovins who said that the American predisposition for keeping the water heater on all the time was like keeping your car idling in the garage in case you might want to go for a ride. Plan hot water usage for specific times of need.

If the game plan calls for a couple of years of grubstaking, or more, it may be worthwhile to make some substantial energy-saving changes to your current living situation, such as replacing central heating with energy-efficient space heating, using gas or wood instead of electricity for cooking and water heating, and modern energy-efficient lighting that delivers equal lumens of light for about a third of the electricity used by standard incandescent bulbs. All of these changes help reduce fuel consumption as well as cost, which is good for the planet. And you'll learn by doing, which will help you to focus on energy efficiency in the home that you're grubstaking for.

Clothing

Clothing expenses can offer a tremendous opportunity for savings by eliminating fashion considerations and concentrating instead on insulating the body. We have found thrift shops and Salvation Army stores to be excellent sources for clothes and we sew on patches at worn but "strategic" locations.

Shelter

The big gain here will come later, which is the point to this book. In the meantime, be alert to opportunities for cheaper shelter cost, such as: finding a lower rent situation; taking on a house caretaker position; or sharing your accommodations expenses with someone else. When collective land purchase with others is being considered, time spent together in close quarters during grubstaking might help to confirm— or refute—the group's compatibility. If you can survive this intact, your chances of success on the land partnership are greater. As I write, my twenty-year-old son has a job at a hiking lodge in the Adirondacks. A strong hiker and skier himself, Rohan is just where he wants to be. Although the job doesn't pay a lot, he is saving most of his pay, because the job provides a small house which he shares with another employee.

Luxuries

While there is room to save even where the necessities of life are concerned, the real impact will come from cutting back on the luxuries. One young couple of my acquaintance, with a small child, each smoke a pack of cigarettes a day while complaining of being unable to afford some of the basic necessities. They don't even smoke the generic brand at $2.14 a pack, but a name brand at $2.50. A $5-a-day habit like this works out to $1,825 a year, a figure about equal to either the down payment or the annual land payment (plus property taxes) for most of the land parcels in our neighborhood. Ten years, of course, equals $18,250 (if the cost of smoking stays the same).

Smokers reading this should consider themselves fortunate. They are already budgeting a significant amount of the grubstake savings for something that is dangerous to their health, and perhaps to the health of other family members. Their good fortune is that, at a stroke, they can improve their health and begin transferring $5 a day, or whatever the habit costs, to the grubstake. Non-smokers are less fortunate.

Smoking can be dangerous to your house.

They're going to have to examine their spending much more carefully to find out where they can come up with the $5 a day that our neighbors somehow manage to budget.

Beer is my vice. When we're short of cash, Jaki and I brew our own beer, at a tremendous saving. As with most of the savings tips in this section, the gain is not only in dollars, but in quality. (You wouldn't put anti-freeze in your homemade beer, even though it is present in some of the national brands.)

Expensive cars and expensive toys, such as snowmobiles, large motorcycles, and fancy stereos, make grubstaking difficult. If you own any of these machines, appliances, or toys and find that they mean less to you than owning your own home, sell them now. Unlike economy cars and practical appliances such as a cast-iron cooking range or a fine set of tools, luxury items depreciate very rapidly. If the resale value seems low today compared to the original price, rest assured that it will be worse tomorrow.

Gifts

Department store companies rely on the American prediliction toward Christmas gift buying to generate half of their annual sales. It follows that average Americans—like you?—spend about half their annual department store "budget" between Thanksgiving and Christmas. My unscientific observation, based upon years of informal study, is that most gifts are unwanted, unappreciated, unneeded, or all of the above. They contribute more to wasteful squandering of resources than they do to family harmony and the spirit of the season. Most gifts are bought out of a personal sense of pressure. If this were not so, why isn't gift-giving spread out equally over the year?

Lest you think your author has outflanked both Ebenezer Scrooge and the Grinch, let me share an alternative gift idea that is more thoughtful, more loving, will be genuinely appreciated, and won't cost a cent. Make a "Gift of Time" to those you love. Hand write a certificate that says, for example, "I, Ebenezer Grinch, present to you (father, mother, brother, sister, loved one, etc.) a Gift of Time. I promise to ___." Here you fill in what might be appropriate for the giftee: Take you on a picnic, play tennis on Saturday, have you over for a home-cooked, candlelit meal, give three hours of undivided attention to do what *you* want to do, give you a half-hour massage, read you a book. . . . The test of this plan is very simple and you can do it right now. Ask yourself how *you* would feel about receiving such a Gift of Time yourself. If you'd really rather receive the polka-dot tie, food slicer, or Star Wars video trilogy, well, maybe you *are* more genuinely a consumer than a conserver. But, while everybody's different, anybody can change.

Fun

It could be argued that entertainment is a necessity of life. You know what is said about people who are "all work and no play." However, consider the many inexpensive—and even free—entertainment activities and social events that are available. As an added bonus, some of these offer the opportunity to make new friends and learn new skills. Instead of going to expensive rock concerts or buying record albums, why not learn to make music through local music clubs? The publicly owned television or radio station in your area may provide more satisfying entertainment than a disappointing but high-priced movie. Rent a film six months after it comes out at $3 for the rental makes five times more sense than a couple spending $15 at the theater. If babysitting and a meal are factored in, the movie rental might save $60 or more. Or get back into reading. You don't have to buy the books; that's what libraries are for. Appendix 3 lists some books that will help you along toward your goal of mortgage freedom. Later, when you're really ready to start building, you'll probably want to own those books that you have discovered that best explore and explain your choice of building or lifestyle. But check used bookstores first. For some of the books, that may be the only place you can buy them.

What? You don't smoke, you don't drink, you don't have expensive toys, you don't run around with the neighbor's spouse? You are disadvantaged. You are, as Mark Twain said, "like a sinking ship with no freight to throw overboard."

OTHER SAVINGS TIPS

Saving money is easy for some and difficult for others. While individual circumstances and responsibilities definitely impact people's ability to save, I feel strongly that the larger issue is the individual choices that people make. There are a few areas of spending—and remember that spending is the inverse of saving—where my point of view is a little different from that of the mainstream, and, at times, is in danger of seeming unAmerican. The last reason for buying anything is to "bolster the economy" or to "help sustain jobs." If a service or a product does not grace your life, do not buy it. Perhaps the people employed in these industries can find work where they can actually make a contribution to the planet. The green mantra—reduce, reuse, recycle—is not only good environmentalism, it is good personal economy. Contrary farmer Gene Logsdon says, with Yogian logic and wisdom, "Although few people seem willing to admit it, it is easier today than ever to save money. The more things go up in price, the more you save by not buying them" (*The Contrary Farmer*, Chelsea Green, 1994, p. 23).

Buy Used

Jaki and I have found it advantageous to buy used cars upon which the greatest depreciation has already been taken. Over the years, we have established a good working relationship with the local Toyota and Nissan dealers, two brothers. We actually bought our first pick-up truck (new) from their father in 1975 at a time when he was trying to win a sales promotion contest, a trip to Europe. We got the truck at the lowest possible price, about $3,000, he won his trip, and we began a long and successful relationship with the family. Now, when we feel it's time to replace an old car that is becoming more expensive and more troublesome to keep than it's worth, we let the brothers know well in advance. We tell them what we are looking for—sometimes a car, sometimes a truck—and ask that they let us know when something interesting comes through on trade. The vehicles always carry a sixty-day full guarantee, which pretty much protects us against any major hidden problems. Our trust in the family, and their strong desire to maintain their well-earned good reputation in the community, assures us that they would never hide a known defect. We've had great success with rust-free vehicles about five to seven years old, with relatively low mileage: fifty-five to sixty thousand miles is just broken in on the cars we buy, and we fully expect to get another hundred thousand (eight more years at our rate of use) out of them. We buy them at 30 to 40 percent of the price of the equivalent new vehicle. And we don't forget to bargain with the brothers. They expect it from us, and we always come away feeling good about the deal.

Other major ticket items like furniture and appliances can also be bought at great savings once they've been owned by someone else who has taken the new price depreciation. Buying appliances through the want ads is always a little risky, and it pays to try before you buy. But name-brand appliance dealers also have used machines that they take in on trade, service as needed, and resell. We bought our Maytag washing machine that way, at about half of the new cost and completely guaranteed by the dealer.

We've bought both used and new furniture, some was given to us by relatives who were getting rid of it in the name of change, and some we've made ourselves. We've even saved money buying new furniture. Our pine dining room table, part of a set with four chairs, was just what we wanted, but it had a quarter-inch-diameter gouge prominently displayed on the top surface. This was good for a couple of hundred dollars off the set, and our then two-year-old son, aided by the business end of a butter knife, helped disguise the gouge by creating several complementary visual distractions. We're glad we didn't buy that one in perfect condition. By the way, it is not an acceptable strategy to bring a two-year-old and a butter knife to the furniture showroom.

Auctions

You can get practically anything, including the kitchen sink, at a country auction. Furniture can be cheap or not, depending on how many dealers show up. If the item has antique value, and there is at least one knowledgeable dealer present, then that item will not go for a utilitarian price (except, perhaps, to the dealer, if no one bids against him). Some of the best buys at auctions go on ordinary household goods and on building materials. No young couple starting out should buy new dishes, cutlery, and the like. If they didn't get everything they needed as wedding presents, they should be able to make up the shortfall in two or three auctions. All kinds of building materials come up regularly at farm and country estate auctions: windows, doors, bathtubs, sinks, barn beams, lumber, nails, bricks, and useful tools come up all the time. They practically give toilets away, even new ones, so why would anyone spend $79.95 for a W.C. down at Home Depot?

If you're unfamiliar with buying at an auction—and, yes, it can be a little scary—then attend one as an observer only. Leave your wallet at home. Learn the ropes of the auction itself. You might kick yourself for losing a bargain, but you won't wind up with a car- or truck-load of useless whatzits because you got caught up in the excitement. There are bargains at almost every auction, the primary exception being when the auction has high prestige value (lots of antiques, estate of a well-known local luminary, etc.) and is attended by all the local muckety-mucks. The best auctions are out-of-the-way estate sales held on a rainy day.

The alert reader will say, "Wait a minute, I thought we were trying to save a grubstake here. How can buying something, even cheaply, help me to save money?" Great question. You've been paying attention. The answer is that, sometimes, we just really need something. The old clunker throws a piston rod. The puppy tears up the sofa. Your spouse threatens to leave if he/she has to do the clothes one more time on the washboard in the bathtub. Some purchases are either necessary or perceived as such by at least one of the partners. As for taking advantage of cheap building materials, this is not a violation of saving for the grubstake. It is a part of the grubstake's purpose.

Bargains

The best bargains are those that appear while you aren't out looking for them. Looking for them puts a pressure on to buy. Having cash money laid by to enable you to take advantage of bargains when they come up—for land, tools, materials, whatever—is a tremendous advantage. Borrowing to take advantage of the bargain might end up negating the bargain altogether. So get some grubstake cash laid by as quickly as you can. You can even seed your grubstake by selling off any expensive items that you no longer use.

Cultivate bargains. Bargains come from unexpected sources, and they can be cultivated in much the same way as James Redfield describes "cultivating coincidences" in *The Celestine Prophecy.* You can do this by letting people know what your needs are, by watching the want ads (and the little Pennysaver or Free Trader papers), and by stopping at garage sales. I'm going to give just one example of the kind of thing that I mean. Let's say that at an auction Fred outbids Mona and Lucille on a pile of windows and doors. Unsuccessful Bidder Mona walks away disappointed and no beneficial "coincidence" occurs. Unsuccessful Bidder Lucille wonders if maybe the winning bidder really wanted all that stuff. She chats Fred up and learns that he really just wanted the bay window, not the doors. Lucille winds up with good free doors, because Fred couldn't be bothered dragging the old doors home and storing them. Mona later hears the story and moans that Lucille was lucky. No, Lucille simply extended herself and gave a coincidence a chance to happen. The more events, the more coincidences. This is just plain Statistics and Probability 101. A mathematician once said, "The greatest coincidence of all would be if there were no coincidences." The upshot of the story is that Lucille wound up with the doors, the bay window, and with Fred, having just picked a fine time to leave her previous husband.

Get Out of Debt

Some readers, 43 percent if the readership is statistically average, will need to get out of the red before they can get into the black. Buying on time is the most common cause of going into debt, easily outdistancing medical emergencies and other personal tragedies. And it is a self-inflicted disaster. While it's easy to say, "Don't buy anything until you can pay for it," this was, in fact, the standard economic wisdom in my parents' generation. Nowadays, waiting until you can truly afford something before buying it would strike many as unAmerican. You're not contributing to the economy!

Little plastic credit cards have become the most common self-enslavement device. "Fewer than half of credit card holders pay up within 30 days," says Charles Long. "The other half carry an average balance of $1,000, and pay 18 percent interest (or more) on that." Department store cards are even worse. An obsessive-compulsive consumer with a credit card is worse than an alcoholic with a key to the wine cellar. The credit card actually brings about unnecessary spending by making it so darned easy. Long recommends a little test. He tells his readers to put the credit card away and return to a cash economy for one month. When the month is up, compare your actual cash spending with the normal charge card bill. "If the cash method has saved

The modern guillotine.

you money," he advises, "you can cut up the card and flush it down the toilet" (*How to Live Without a Salary*, pp. 71–72).

Debt has to be paid off. Bankruptcy is never a good strategy. The key here is to stop the rot. Stop going further into debt by buying only with cash, and use the various expense-reducing strategies in this book (and in Long's) so that money is released to pay off existing debt. You can't get ahead until you first break even.

THE MATERIAL FAST

One of the quickest ways to save money—or to get out of debt, the prerequisite—is to go on what Long calls a *material fast*, which he defines as buying nothing but essentials during a pre-determined interlude of Spartan discipline. Jaki and I adopted such a strategy in the early days, and, during that time, developed good habits which have served us well ever since. Every purchase was subject to one simple test. Is this purchase absolutely necessary? It is amazing how often the answer is no.

A new word has been coined to describe the American consumption pattern: *affluenza*. I don't think it requires further definition. The day when the most Americans contract affluenza is the Friday after Thanksgiving, the biggest shopping day in the year. Groups who are concerned about where unbridled consumption is taking us, as individuals, as a nation, and as a world society, have urged Americans to stay away from stores on the day after Thanksgiving. They call it "Buy Nothing Day," something like the Great American Smoke-out, the smoking-free day, also in November. Once you get used to it, it's surprising how easy it is to break the consumer spending habit. Just see how many Buy Nothing Days you can link together, and watch your grubstake grow. It's a sure-fire *get-rich-slow* scheme.

In our experience, the material fast works if three conditions are met.

Goal

First, there must be a clear and compelling goal that makes the whole thing worthwhile. For readers of this book, it is becoming free of shelter cost. For readers of Long's book, it is freedom from a regular job. As I've stated, these goals dovetail very nicely. Long tells of a freshly married couple who went on the material fast for six months, putting most of two small paychecks in the bank each pay period. Then they went on a three-month around-the-world tour. They traveled in comfort and paid cash, a great way to start their marriage together. Imagine how they'd grown after six months on the fast followed by three months of experiencing other cultures.

Time Limit

There must be an end in sight. Three months, six months, a year, whatever. If the savings goal is not met at the end of the specified time period, you have two choices: reward yourself with a minor splurge like a weekend at a country inn, and then renew the fast with a better idea of how long it should be, based on the results of the first period. Or, re-examine your goal and decide if it can be accomplished on less.

How Chelsea Green Publisher Stephen Morris Raised his Grubstake

In the spring of 1970, the world was a tumultuous place. The country was embroiled in a tangle of wars: kids versus parents, blacks versus whites, Americans versus Asians, students versus teachers, and everyone against the government. It seemed like an excellent time to head to the country.

My wife Laura and I set off for Nova Scotia, not as fugitives from the draft so much as fugitives from the insanity. It seemed exotic and primitive—plus, we were told that land could be had for as little as $10 per acre.

For our grubstake we sold my wife's 1967 orange Camaro, a graduation present from indulgent but well-meaning parents, and headed north. We didn't find $10-per-acre land, but pretty damn close. We fell in love with a 268-acre farm with 18 acres cleared, an abandoned farmhouse, and a distant view of the Bay of Fundy. The price was $8,000. We returned stateside where we convinced three friends to become our partners. They all agreed to contribute $2,000, but since we were the only ones with any cash, thanks to the Camaro, we footed the entire bill.

For the next five years, we played at homesteading, camping out in the house while working stubbornly on labor-intensive tasks such as rebuilding fieldstone foundations, then heading south when the weather turned cold, our money ran out, or our visas expired. These were great times, but gradually a different reality took hold, as we became entrenched in professions that decreasingly accommodated our homesteading inclinations. Our partners had never come up with their portion of the grubstake, so we owned the property outright. Reluctantly, we conceded to maturity and decided to sell.

Meanwhile, the real estate market in Nova Scotia had quietly entered the twentieth century, and we sold the property for $30,000. Also, the Canadian dollar was then quite a bit stronger than the U.S. dollar, so the money had appreciated even more when we promptly used it to buy our first year-round home in Scituate, Massachusetts. That home was subsequently sold for $55,000, which we reinvested in another home in Vermont.

I'm now pushing fifty and have never made a mortgage payment, and it can all be traced to my wife's orange Camaro.

Pulling Together

A couple needs to be mutually agreeable about entering into the fast together. Then, the partners can actually help each other keep to the fast. It can even become a game. How much can we save this month? Let's beat last month's record. Pulling in different directions is an exercise in futility, as when one partner wants to give up smoking and the other doesn't. I've never seen that work. If they have the same goal, pull together and support each other, however, the chances of success are very high.

The quality of life can go up as the "standard of living"—the accepted euphemism for material consumption—goes down. "Not surprisingly," says Long,

> many families who submit themselves to radical savings binges find their lifestyles permanently altered. Some find that walking feels better than driving, that evenings spent in conversation do more for a marriage than a television does, that old shoes are more comfortable than new ones. The material fast can actually start to become an attractive way of life in itself. The sense that less might actually be better is the beginning of becoming a conserver (p. 79).

CHOICES

I realize that some of the money-saving tips offered above might involve a departure from your current value system. But, I also know that if you really want to build your own home in the country, you'll find a way to tighten your belt and make the necessary choices. I prefer the word "choice" to "sacrifice." Most people who have already made the kinds of decisions discussed in this chapter report that they really weren't sacrifices at all, but were, in fact, qualitative improvements in their physical and spiritual well-being.

Aside from everything else, austerity budgeting is an education. The skills and self-discipline learned will help guide the way when economic impoverishment is not voluntary, particularly during house construction.

And when you get really sick of skimping and saving and watching every penny, there is no sybaritic pleasure to compare with giving in and indulging in a gourmet dinner with a bottle of fine wine.

3

The Land

At a certain season of our life we are accustomed to consider every spot as the possible site of a house. I have thus surveyed the country on every side within a dozen miles of where I live.

—Henry David Thoreau, Walden

The cost of the land may be the single greatest expense you'll incur in your mortgage-free home, so we'll examine how to obtain it at the best possible price. And we'll look into other economic considerations of the land choice: how the land affects construction costs (Shelter), energy costs (Fuel), and Food costs.

THE FIRST QUESTION

The first major question, the one that has to be answered before any land search can commence, is this: Do you intend to stay close to where you live now or are you open to moving anywhere that suits your wants and needs? This is a tough one. When I was a young know-it-all of twenty, fresh from two major world journeys living out of and under a backpack, I used to say that the chance of someone being born in the place that best suited their personality was slim indeed. This dubious wisdom might stem from that line of thought often expressed by kids just out of school, the idea that one's own hometown can't possibly satisfy the important ambitions, needs, and desires of life. For many, college helps them to find out if this is true. For me, it was backpacking around the globe. Footloose and fancy free, the world was my oyster. (There, two horrible cliches out of the way in one sentence.) I decided that moving to the northwest highlands of Scotland suited my introspective nature better than Webster, Massachusetts, home of my youth. How this revelation affected my life, and Jaki's, is recounted in chapter 6.

But, again, everybody's different. You may be equally sure that your hometown or the near environs thereof suit your personality just fine. You have strong family contacts, good friends, perhaps a job you really like.

If it happens that you really would like to move to a different area, how do you do that? How do you decide what area might suit?

Some self-examination is necessary. Large questions lead to smaller questions which are easier to answer. The small answers eventually gang together and help answer the big questions. For example: Are you a city or a country mouse? Mountain man or bijou queen? Snow bunny or sun worshipper? Redneck or tree hugger? Do you prefer the security of a regular job, or the security of not having a regular job? You'll think of other questions pertinent to yourself. This is good practice for the future. You'll ask slightly different kinds of questions when you come to design your house.

My oldest son loves mountains and snow. If you gave him one hundred acres in Florida or Kansas, he would politely decline, or sell it immediately to some flatlander for a land grubstake in the mountains.

RESEARCHING THE RELOCATION OPTION

Let's say that your small answers reveal that you lean toward hill country land and a climate with four distinct seasons. You have a profession or skill that allows you to work at home. You're not independently wealthy, so inexpensive land is a must. These considerations narrow the search quite a bit.

One tried and proven way to start is to get a copy of *United Country*, "America's Catalog of Country Real Estate for Sale." This catalog is published by United National Real Estate, formerly United Farm Agency. The chances are that you won't buy any of the properties listed, although you never know, but you'll be able to compare property values around the country. I bought a copy recently for $4.95 plus $2.50 by calling United National's toll-free number, 1-800-999-1020, but you might be able to get one at your local United National agency.

Your demographic preference profile (see previous paragraph) reduces the search to, say, ten or twelve states. Next, you'll need a national road atlas to get a sense of the lay of the land. Last year's atlas works just fine and can often be bought at discount stores for three or four bucks. The atlas will tell you what local towns are near properties that interest you, and what their populations are. The next step involves a trip to the library. Ask the research assistant for a copy of *Gales Directory of Publications*, which lists virtually every newspaper in the United States. Write to the newspapers in the areas that interest you and send them a couple of bucks for a sample issue of their paper. Get the entire paper, Sunday edition, if they have it. You'll have a lot of fun looking through these papers, and you'll learn a lot more about the area than simply what land is for sale. You'll get a sense of the political climate, the social life, job and business opportunities, cultural amenities, even a little about schools, churches, clubs, and other entities. You'll find out what local and state news is making the headlines. Here are a few headlines that appeared recently in our local paper. Imagine how much you would learn about our area from reading the articles themselves:

POPULATION DECLINING: CLINTON COUNTY RESIDENTS LEAVE IN RECORD NUMBERS (Plattsburgh Air Force Base was recently de-commissioned and the county's population went down 6.3 percent. One upshot is that property values have remained static or even gone down slightly.)

'SELLING' POLLUTION MAY CLEAN ADIRONDACK AIR ("In a bid to cut down on acid rain in the Adirondacks, the public may now buy so-called pollution 'credits' that otherwise would allow companies to emit tons of sulfur dioxide into the air.")

PLATTSBURGH DRAWS RAVES AS A GOOD PLACE TO LIVE (In Kevin Heubusch's "The New Rating Guide to Life in America's Small Cities," Plattsburgh, New York, ranked seventeenth in the nation out of 193 "micropolitan" areas. Plattsburgh, just 12 miles from our homestead, received high marks for its strong service and manufacturing economy, but low marks for weather!)

ENVIRONMENTALISTS MAY TRASH PRISON (A new state prison has been approved for Franklin County. Many people want it to boost jobs and the economy. Some folks are fighting it on environmental grounds.)

LOVE OF LLAMAS BECOMES FAMILY AFFAIR (A rural family raises llamas, more for fun than profit.)

MOHAWKS TURN DOWN SETTLEMENT (The Mohawk Indian Nation has turned down an offer from the state and federal officials of $54 million and two islands to compensate for violation of two hundred-year-old treaties.)

TRIANGLE OF EXCELLENCE: MAYORS OF THREE CITIES TO PROMOTE REGIONAL STRENGTH (Plattsburgh, New York, and Burlington, Vermont, have joined forces with St. Jean, Quebec to promote the Lake Champlain Basin region. They hope to improve the social and economic conditions of the people in the region.)

Obviously, reading a few newspapers won't tell you as much about your target area as you already know about the place you're presently living, but you'll learn a heckuva lot more than you knew before.

From here on in, the strategy for finding and buying land is similar whether you're buying locally or relocating, the major difference being that you will have to do some travelling if you are thinking of relocating some distance away.

CARETAKING

Why not try an area before you buy? It would be a shame to buy a piece of land, build (or start to build), and find out that you really don't like the political climate, biting insects, short summers, or whatever. One good way to do this is as a caretaker for a property in the area. A caretaking situation could arise in several different ways. You might answer an ad in the classifieds from someone who is looking for a caretaker while they go south for the winter or take that long-awaited world cruise. You might initiate the arrangement yourself by placing an ad saying that you are looking for a caretaking opportunity. Or, you might take a one-year subscription ($24) for *The Caretaker Gazette*, a bi-monthly publication that can put you in touch with folks all over the United States looking for a caretaker. Write them at 1845 NW Deane St., Pullman, WA 99163, or call 509-332-0806.

Besides introducing you to an area to see if you like it, the caretaking strategy enables you to take more time in finding the right piece of land. If you are not rushed, the chances are you'll get a better deal.

Whether you are caretaking, renting, or making use of some other temporary living strategy, there is a lot you can do to learn about the area other than simply reading the paper. Visit the Chamber of Commerce, the building inspector (town and county), and the utilities' offices. If you belong to a particular church or civic organization, or have a particular field of interest like music, sports, or drama, you've got instant friends to draw on for information. When I traveled around the world, I found water skiers in unlikely places. I was well looked after in El Salvador, New Zealand, Spain, Singapore, even Zambia, where we skied among hippos just above Victoria Falls.

TOWN VS. COUNTRY

Assuming you now know the region of the country where you want to live—it may be the one where you presently reside—we must narrow the parameters quite a bit more. The question this time will be, "In what sort of neighborhood do I want to live?" Central city? Suburbs? Countryside? Wilderness fringe? Consider future strategies as well as present factors. The economic benefits of leaving your job to build a house could be so compelling that you don't feel a need to limit your land search to areas within commuting distance of your present job. Perhaps you have skills, or a specific idea that will allow you to leave your job and work for yourself from home. On the other hand, while the economic and other personal benefits that come from living in your own house may be important to you, they may not be important enough to sacrifice a particularly satisfying position. Your job may tie you to commuting distance, and the possible extra cost of the land, if located conveniently, may be a favorable trade-off, particularly if your salary is sufficient to meet your needs and you like your job.

However, low-cost owner-built homes generally are situated away from population centers for three reasons. One, land prices near town are often prohibitive when compared to the cost of building the house. Two, stricter planning regulations and building codes control the areas nearer to town, adversely affecting some of the owner-builder's most valuable building strategies, such as the temporary shelter and the pay-as-you-go house. Three, other values, such as clean air and water, economic independence in food and fuel production, and peace and quiet, are almost always important considerations to a person who makes the philosophical decision to be responsible for his or her own shelter . . . and life.

Consider the targetlike illustration of figure 3-1. The "bull's-eye," Area A, is a circle of 10 miles in diameter, representing all the land within 5 miles of downtown Centerville, a town of, say, 40,000 people. A total area of 78 square miles, it has a population density of 512 people per square mile. Even within this area, of course, the density varies. A residential neighborhood near the center might have 3,000 people in a given square mile. Nevertheless, most of the businesses, schools, churches, and recreational facilities are found within the "bull's-eye" and all the people in this area are able to share the benefits of relatively close proximity to these amenities.

Here, land is sold in terms of lots and cannot even be considered on a per-acre basis. Owner-builders are limited by building and zoning regulations to constructing pretty much the same kind of home sold by contractors and developers.

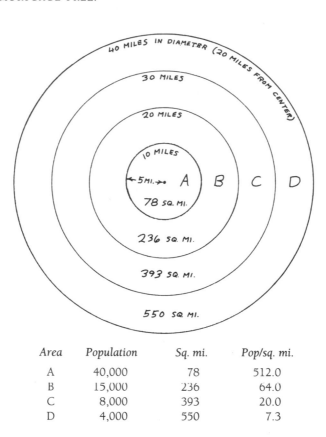

Area	Population	Sq. mi.	Pop/sq. mi.
A	40,000	78	512.0
B	15,000	236	64.0
C	8,000	393	20.0
D	4,000	550	7.3

3-1. The region surrounding the hypothetical Centerville.

Even here, however, there is a great potential for savings, as only about 40 percent of the selling cost of a contractor-built home goes toward materials. (The rest goes to labor, profit, and bank charges.) And there are ways that the owner-builder can save on materials that the contractor cannot. A contractor, for example, cannot justify the time and trouble involved in trying to knit some special door or window bargain into the housing design.

In the town scenario, the greatest savings available to you come in reduced labor costs, elimination of contractor and developer profits, and reduction or elimination of bank interest. The problems you'll encounter are bureaucratic hassles if you build anything even slightly different from "conventional standards"; severe restrictions on the add-on or pay-as-you-go strategies (temporary shelters are o-u-t!); high interim shelter costs during construction; and financing. More materials are generally needed, and more expensive materials at that, to meet town zoning and building code requirements. Even though a potential savings of 50 percent can be demonstrated, and a smaller loan is thus required, lending institutions will be reluctant to make mortgage money available to "inexperienced do-it-yourselfers." (A personal loan may be possible based on the strength of the borrower's reputation, but the interest on an unsecured loan will be higher.)

While I believe that building your own home under the conditions described above is preferable to the lifetime rent or mortgage situation, especially if you're happy with your job situation and life in the town, it is not as economically beneficial as building in the country. Complete or near-complete freedom from the shelter aspect of fiscal bondage requires an almost quantum leap away from the idea of an owner-built but conventional house in a subdivision.

I feel so strongly about this line of thought that I'm going to give it the status of a law. Roy's Third Law of Empiric Economics, then, can be stated thusly: The conventional approach to building a house presumes a conventional mortgage. Houses made from recycled and indigenous materials are often mortgage-free.

The conventional approach to building a house presumes a conventional mortgage. Houses made from recycled and indigenous materials are often mortgage-free.

My last comments on this topic are directed to people who want the typical suburban ranch, don't want to build it themselves, and think that the use of recycled or indigenous materials and alternative building styles is best left to hippies and beavers.

Frankly, I don't know how you've made it this far into the book, but you, too, "deserve a break today!" My advice is that you consider acting as your own general contractor. This does require some organization and research on your part, but 15 to 30 percent of the final cost can be saved in this way. Several excellent books on the subject of being your own contractor are listed in appendix 3. Further savings are possible by keeping the house shape and structure simple, as outlined in chapter 5. Otherwise, I can only invite you to read on. You may never put these strategies and philosophies to use, but then again, they might get you to thinking about alternatives.

OUT OF TOWN

The second ring, Area B in figure 3-1, is the rest of the land within 10 miles of downtown Centerville not included in Area A. Its area is 236 square miles and might typically provide habitat for fifteen thousand more people. In a community like Centerville, these people are often a combination of small farmers and overflow from the town. There will be individual home lots, mobile homes, and even some planned housing developments. The population density drops to sixty-four per square mile. Incidentally, the density of the United States as a whole—city, farm, and arctic tundra all factored in—is about seventy per square mile. It's a kind of meaningless number, with Death Valley, Peoria, and Manhattan all factored together, but interesting nonetheless.

Planning and zoning restrictions are not likely to be as severe as in Area A, although building codes may be, depending on where actual town boundaries fall and whether or not state building codes are in effect. Keep in mind that this belt will be very much in demand for all kinds of development, as Area A is already nearly saturated and Area B is still within comfortable commuting distance.

Proximity to town makes the prospect of settling here attractive to the owner-builder, too, although land prices are likely to be quite high because of the pressure from the expanding town. Even though the density is only one-eighth as great, building lots tend to be much bigger and much of the land is likely to be agricultural, so the net effect is still a lot of people chasing comparatively little "spare" land.

Area C is very popular among owner-builders. Population density is down to twenty per square mile, and the greater distance from town eliminates much of the buying pressure on land prices. The proximity to employment opportunities is acceptable, although it's probably worth assessing the economic and time trade-offs involved in commuting. An economy car is the usual strategy for owner-builders in this area, although this can mean different things to different people. One friend's idea of an economy car is a big old American gas guzzler. Since they have very low book value, he picks them up cheap and just runs them into the ground. They're roomy, usually start in the winter, and, yes, burn inordinate amounts of gas, and possibly oil. But the capital cost and the lower insurance—who needs collision?—makes this a fairly economical strategy. Jaki and I take a different approach. We buy small, reliable, warranteed used cars (usually Japanese, I have to admit, but my political allegiance is to the planet), after the major depreciation has occurred. Our latest purchase was a like-new eight-year-old Toyota Corolla with 63,000 miles for $5,000. New, the equivalent car today costs $16,200. But we expect to get another 100,000 miles of economic transport out of the car, which comes to only about 5¢ per mile, about a third of the capital cost component of buying the same car new. We bought a pick-up truck the same way, and a pick-up is one of the most valuable tools you can have when it comes to building a low-cost home.

Building and zoning regulations are becoming more and more prevalent in the Area Cs of the country, even where I live in northern New York. This trend will continue as time goes on. We're all going to have to learn to live with them, and enlightened planning is better than no planning at all. Zoning is like a shock wave resembling figure 3-1. In our area, Plattsburgh (Area A) started with building and zoning regs about thirty years ago, and it has taken about ten years for the wave to hit each successive area. I still get lots of phone calls from rural Midwesterners who tell me that building codes and planning regs are nonexistent in their areas. Part of your homework is to find out if and how such regulations might affect you in your chosen area, keeping in mind that the trend is for more regulation, not less. Twenty years from now, this discussion will probably be moot in 99 percent of the United States, as well as in the provinces of Canada.

Area C is commonly devoted to agricultural use and, if it is prime farmland, it will not be cheap. In hilly or wooded areas, however, the price of land may be favorable. Earthwood is located in just such country. Other, smaller towns often are found in this belt. When this is so, the population density for the area as a whole is higher than indicated, but not in the spaces between the small towns or villages.

Area D includes all the land between 15 and 20 miles from downtown Centerville, as a determined crow flies. Population density is down to 7.3 people per square mile in this hypothetical model. Land will be quite a bit cheaper, barring special features such as lakefront, village land, and so on. Roads do not run "as the crow flies," of course, and commuting to a regular job in Centerville might be unacceptable in terms of time and money. If you want to maintain a job in town, you'd be advised to weigh up this trade-off very carefully, keeping in mind that an extra ten minutes of commuting time could take you out of the expensive land belt and into truly economical country land.

Very often, owner-builders this far from town sever themselves from urban employment. They find work in the country closer to home, or they adopt a lifestyle in which they are able to support themselves with a home-centered business or part-time work. Here are to be found true homesteaders and farmers, living on low budgets by providing all their own firewood fuel and a significant amount of their food from their gardens and livestock. Usually, they pay less for property taxes, as well.

If there are building codes here—sometimes there aren't, but this is very rare in the 1990s—building inspectors are likely to be more flexible. But don't take this for granted. Before buying land to build your straw bale earth-roofed yurt, try to find out from others in the area how flexible the building inspector really is.

Other important considerations in this area are proximity to schools, doctors, and fire departments; snow removal and road maintenance; cost of power and telephone; and nearest neighbors. Alternative energy sources, such as wind, solar, and water power, all become potentially more economical. Land without access to commercial power starts out with a lower value, because there aren't many people willing to live "unplugged." Clustering of like-minded families is a good strategy, one that will be illustrated in other parts of this book.

Beyond the twenty-mile ring—remember, this could be a much greater distance from town by road—the land may be cheap, but life is spartan and lacking in human companionship. Commuting is impractical, especially in the wintertime. Building here on the edge of the wilderness (social, if not actual) requires a certain pioneer spirit (possessed by the very few), and an already established independence of the need for much human interaction. Living in such a rural environment is both good for the kids and very hard on them. They will be better educated in nature and the fundamental realities of survival, but may be somewhat lacking in the humanities, even if they watch television on their 12-volt set (especially if they do!)

We Have a Responsibility . . .

Out beyond Area D, and perhaps in parts of Areas C and D themselves, another responsibility confronts the homesteader (for inhabitants of these areas are now more truly homesteaders than simply owner-builders). It is their responsibility to husband the land and protect the existing flora and fauna. We may *legally* own the land (although this concept is foreign to many of the world's indigenous peoples), but can we ever *morally* own it? The question can be argued philosophically, but trying to find an answer, if one exists, would take a larger volume than the one in your hands. As a writer, my primary responsibility is to report the truth as I see it, knowing that it is only *my* truth, and might even change as I change. And my truth, here and now, is this:

To "legally own" is vastly different than to "morally own." Once upon a time, it was possible to legally own another human being in the United States. But legal slavery could never imply moral slavery, and the day will have to come, sooner or later, when we will look at land ownership in the same way. Passing through Earth for eighty years out of an eternity does not give any of us the right to destroy the land and, wantonly, the resources of the land. And yet we do it all the time, the primary difference among people being, simply, a matter of degree. At best, we can only be—*morally*—stewards of the land. As stewards, we must take care of the land in such a way that our children and our children's children forever will find it in as good or better condition than we found it ourselves. Stewards are entitled to a living in return for our stewardship, but we are not entitled to destroy the trust for which we are responsible. We must think of our responsibilities as stewards before we clear the forest for our homesite, before we dig great holes and pour a lot of energy-intensive cement into them, before we create elaborate trenches and underground piping systems to dispose of valuable and biodegradable human waste, before we spread poisonous chemicals on the land, *before we do anything*. Having thought as stewards and not as consumers, now we can intelligently design living systems that will impact the land as minimally as possible.

INFLUENCES ON PROPERTY VALUES

If land were all the same, an equal concentric development around a centerpoint might well occur, as shown in figure 3-1. Einstein tells us that space is warped by gravity. In the world of real estate, topography warps the theoretical development to something more closely resembling figures 3-2 to 3-5. These illustrations show that smaller towns and settlements, satellites to the main town in the area, also exert an influence on land prices, as does the proximity of a more distant city (figure 3-3). Government statistics tell us that towns and cities with twenty-five hundred to ten thousand people are the fastest growing population centers in the United States. Grand City, with one million people, is assumed to be 75 miles from Centerville. This not-too-distant population exerts an influence on property values in the Centerville area, too, because of the desire of many Grand City people to own a vacation cabin or retirement home in the country.

The denser the cross-hatching in figure 3-4, the greater the demand for land. Of course, quality of access is just as important as distance. If an interstate highway exists between Centerville and Grand City, the "gravitational influence" is greater, as shown in figure 3-5. Similarly, properties on secondary roads and dirt tracks will be proportionally lower in cost than properties on state and county roads. Taken to an extreme, land without access at all can be bought very cheaply indeed, but of what use is it to the owner-builder if it can only be reached by helicopter, parachute, or pogo stick? Never buy land without deeded access. A seller may tell you that you can get an "easement by necessity." Technically, he might even be right. In reality, the easement could cause you much grief and thousands in legal fees.

Like figure 3-1, figures 3-2 to 3-5 are greatly simplified because they do not take into consideration landform, quality of schools, quality of the existing development, or details of access and utility availability. Generally, land quality and topography will influence the degree of effort that municipalities have undertaken to supply access to services and utilities. The resulting development and its proximity to various population bases will dictate the demand for, and cost of, the land. My examples are meant to illustrate some of the influences on land prices in an area developed to the extent suggested by the population figures for a place like Centerville and its surrounding towns.

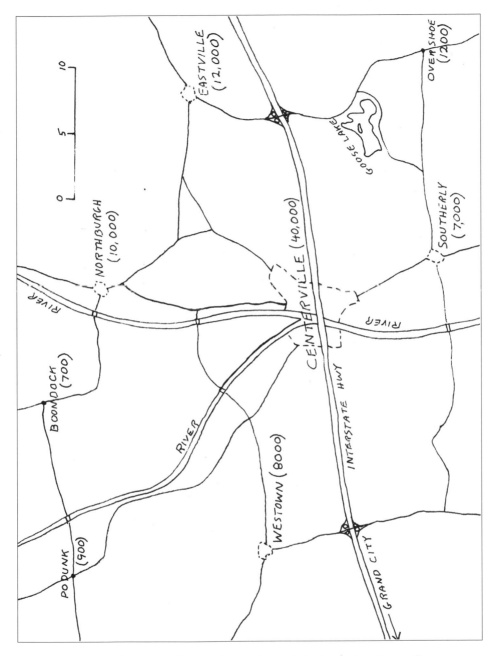

3-2. A map of the Centerville area. Grand City is 75 miles west of Centerville. Town and village population estimates are in parentheses.

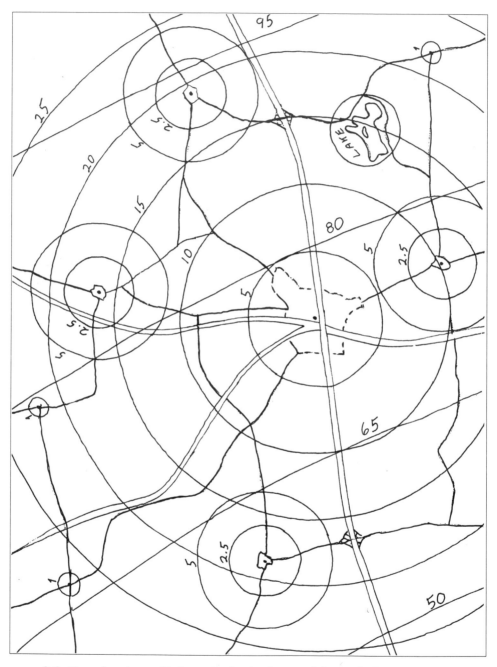

3-3. Here, the spheres of influence on land values are delineated. The numbers
indicate distances to population centers.

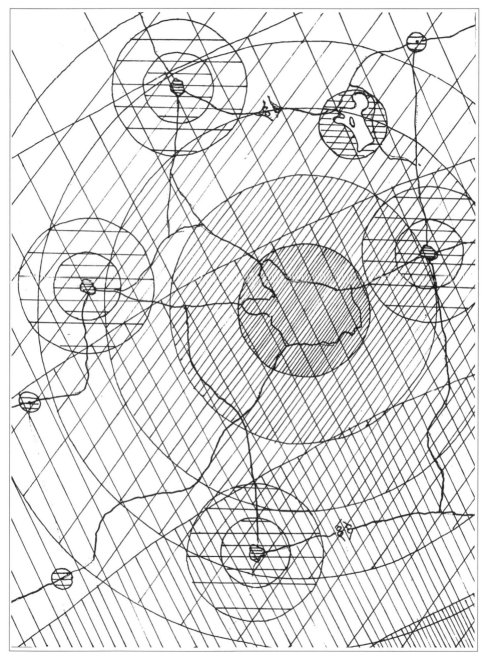

3-4. Here we see the effects of population centers on land values. The most expensive land can be found in those areas with the most cross-hatching.

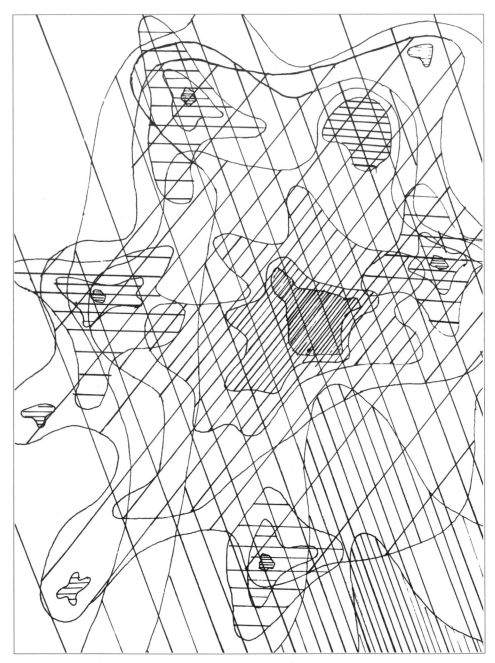

3-5. This diagram is a more realistic rendering of fig. 3-4, taking into account ease of access along roads, as well as proximity to rivers and lakes.

FINDING LAND

We'll assume that you've made a decision on the general vicinity where you hope to find land. The distance to town is acceptable, either for commuting or for access to other important amenities, such as school, church, commerce, or recreation. The land in the chosen zone seems to be affordable to you, based upon preliminary research through want ads or real estate agents. Now what?

You can find out about specific pieces of land for sale in several different ways, some obvious, some not so obvious.

Real Estate Agents

These professionals earn their commissions. They can smooth a lot of the paperwork involved in the land transaction. They know the available land in the area. The most important thing to remember is that the agent works for the seller, not the buyer. Do not appear overly enthusiastic about a piece of land in front of the agent. Never reveal

---

A VALUABLE RESOURCE

Les and Carol Scher's excellent book, Finding and Buying Your Place in the Country (Dearborn Financial Publishing, 1996) has been the bible for land buyers since 1974. The book is continually updated. My latest copy, the fourth edition, bears a 1996 copyright. The Schers put the reader in touch with almost every consideration in the land search: climate, water, soil, topography, evaluating existing structures, and so on. Les Scher, an attorney specializing in country property, then guides the reader through all the legal considerations of buying land, including the ins and outs of surveys, easements, water rights, the contract for sale, abstracts of title, the kinds of deeds, and a whole lot more. He even gives useful advice on bargaining to buy the property at the lowest possible price. The $26 investment in the Scher's book prior to conducting your land search will pay for itself many times over, and could save you a bundle in legal fees. It is one book that is probably better owned than borrowed, because you will want to refer to it constantly during the land purchase phase of your journey.

how high you're willing to go to buy the parcel. This information will be relayed to the seller and will make future bargaining more difficult. There is one way that the seller/agent relationship can work to your advantage. If you make a written offer to purchase the property, the agent is legally bound to deliver this offer to the seller. The agent may tell you that your offer is way too low and not even to waste everyone's time with it, but don't let this deter you. Remember that the agent works on a percentage commission. He or she wants to see a large selling price, not a small one. The owner may have been trying to sell this parcel for a while and might look favorably on your offer.

A word of caution, whether or not you are buying through an agent. While most real estate agents are honest professionals, some are not. Never sign anything that can even remotely be deemed a binding contract. Attorney Les Scher cautions:

> The deposit receipt is the most infamous example of this practice [pushing the buyer to sign without caution] throughout the United States. Any document that is dated, contains the name of the parties, states what is being sold, and for how much, and is signed by the parties is a legally binding contract, regardless of what it is called (p. 272).

Classified Ads

Many parcels of land are sold directly by the owner, without an intermediary. You deal directly with the owner. Sometimes such land is cheaper than similar listed properties, sometimes it's not. With direct purchase, you will miss some of the expertise in paperwork which is second nature to an agent. Agents, of course, also advertise in the classified ads.

"For Sale" or "For Sale by Owner" Signs

If an agent is handling the property, the agency sign will be prominently displayed. A handpainted sign with a phone number can lead to bargains. A couple owned land across the road from Earthwood and put a sign up on the corner of the property. My neighbor took the sign down, called the sellers and negotiated purchase of the property at a very low price. By the time I called, within twenty-four hours of the sign's appearance, a verbal agreement had already been reached. Finding signs like these involves a lot of driving around country roads, but so does following up on an ad. You're just doing it in reverse. And you get to know those country roads. Keep a notebook handy, with detailed notes on each property, no matter how you learned about it. After seeing several, it is very difficult to remember details that might be important. Was that nice barn on the Smith property on Jones Road, or was it on the Jones property on Smith Road?

Prospecting for Land

While you're driving around the countryside, try a little land prospecting. This is how Jaki and I found our land. Years ago, fresh from Scotland and searching for land for our homestead, Jaki and I passed some pretty acreage on a country road near Plattsburgh, New York. Gently rolling meadows were framed by a beautiful, mature, mixed hardwood forest. We observed that most of the land was posted against hunting by a single landowner. Soon, we came to a mailbox bearing the same name. We stopped and asked the man, a semi-retired farmer, if he had any land for sale. He said, no, he was saving the land for his family, but knew of some abandoned farm land "up on Murder Hill" that was for sale by a gentleman of his acquaintance. (I swear he said "murder" and locals still call Murtagh Hill by that name today.) The farmer even took us to see the land, a mile up a rough dirt road. Pleased with our first impression, we phoned the owner, arranged a meeting to view the property together, and wound up buying it. The land was not marked "FOR SALE," nor did the owner bother with very much advertising. He bought land as an investment and enjoyed walking it and showing it to people.

The lesson: In an area that appeals to you, stop and ask the local people if they know of any land for sale. If they like you, and the time is right, they might even offer you a part of their own land. Stranger things have happened. Some country farmers will not put up a "FOR SALE" sign, lest their neighbors think they are being forced to sell because of some failure in their farming enterprise, or, perhaps, for some other reason. Since moving to "Murder Hill" almost twenty-five years ago, we've seen much land near us change hands without even knowing that it was for sale. One might think it would be good common sense to tell nearby owners that a property is being offered for sale.

Surprisingly, this often doesn't happen, and an enterprising visitor to the area buys up the property. Well, that's what we did.

You might spot a burned-out or abandoned house on a piece of land that you like. Ask the neighbors about it. They might get you on the trail of finding the owner, who might just like to dump the mess at a bargain price. If the building is far gone, you might have to factor in demolition costs. Or the building might yield lots of good materials for building your own place. With a little fixing up, the abandoned house might even provide a place to live on-site while you build the house you really want. Later, when you've settled into your dream home, you might really fix the old place up and derive a rental income. Don't dismiss these kinds of scenarios as unrealistic or idealistic. Keep open to all possibilities. A derelict property may be your key to the future, and you'll be doing a kindness to the countryside at the same time.

Tax Sales

Buying land at a tax sale is a controversial subject, and there are moral considerations that each individual must decide for him/herself. These sales, usually in the form of an auction, are conducted by counties or towns that sell off land that has been taken for failure to pay a certain number of years of property taxes (a number that varies from state to state). After the sale, a "redemption period" begins, during which the original owners can redeem ("buy back") their property for payment of back taxes plus penalties to the municipality plus interest to the tax sale "buyer." During this redemption period, typically one to three years, the high bidder is issued a "tax certificate." Only when the redemption period is over will the municipality issue a deed, usually a Tax Deed. Counties don't normally take the time or go to the expense of hiring an abstract company, lawyer, or surveyor to research the title, so they aren't about to warranty that the title is good and clear.

Purchasing such lands involves risks. The obvious one is that you might not ever get the land. The original owner could redeem it at the eleventh hour. (Unless, of course, the owner is deceased, in which case he or she is unlikely to redeem the land, although heirs might.) Less obvious risks include liens on the property, other prior claims, in short all the risks involved with the purchase of any piece of property, except that the risks are not in any way ameliorated by the security of

The tax sale.

a Full Warranty Deed. In short, do not bid on tax lands unless you have researched them to as great an extent as possible. This means not only visual inspection of the property, but conducting at least a rudimentary search among the book of deeds at the County Clerk's office. The clerks there can point you in the right direction.

We know a fellow who buys a lot of land at tax sales, usually at bargain prices. My sense is that he has made quite a bit of money buying and selling such land. Some he has kept for himself or his family. However, another friend, who happens to be a licensed surveyor, thinks that buying tax sale land is, at best, a shady practice. He can cite cases where unscrupulous land barons from out of the area buy lots of tax sale land, and local people lose their homes or their family farms. This ambiguity puts us on the horns of a moral dilemma. Some properties are up for sale because the owner died and left no heirs (called escheated land), but in other cases, people might lose their homes simply because they have fallen on hard times.

The best way to avoid this dilemma is to track down the owners of the land and negotiate a deal before the auction. There is no law against this. It eliminates the possibility of being outbid on a property at auction. And the owner might come out the better for it, too. If it's a large parcel, he or she might even be willing to deed you the part of the land you want in exchange for your paying the back taxes, a win-win situation.

Edward Preston, in his little book *How to Buy Land Cheap* (Loompanics Unlimited, 1996), devotes his longest chapter to buying tax land from counties. If this is a strategy that you can feel okay about, you might want to get a copy of Preston's book. He tells how to research such land, and talks about other potential land bargains, such as "leftover land" (land not bid on at auction), federal land (such as foreclosed land from Rural Development or from the Internal Revenue Service), state land (foreclosed land, unused government property, abandoned estates, etc.), and even city land. Such bargains are becoming less common all the time, and title might be murky. At best, a lot of research and legwork is required to find these kinds of land bargains.

A final word on tax sales: If you have satisfied your own karma on purchasing such land, don't even think of bidding at a tax sale until you have spent some quality time at the county real property department, so that you can learn all the rules, ramifications, and repercussions of such a land purchase.

Other "Bargain" Land

Edward Preston goes into all sorts of other "cheap" land available from federal and state agencies, banks, and quasi-governmental agencies. Success in this sort of endeavor will take a lot of legwork, patience, and luck. Your chances of finding your ideal land this way is slim, but people have done it. See Preston's book for more information.

One of the most promising agencies of this ilk is the Federal Deposit Insurance Corporation (FDIC), which is now responsible for cleaning up a lot of the mess left by the collapse of savings and loan associations (S&Ls) in the 1980s. According to Preston, writing in 1996, the FDIC "now sells just about every kind of land or structure imaginable: houses, apartment buildings, condominiums, commercial buildings, mobile homes, building lots, agricultural land, mining properties, etc. Prices range widely, from a few hundred bucks to millions of dollars per asset" (p. 50). You can get listings of available FDIC properties by calling one or more of the five regional offices. I checked each of the following toll-free 800 numbers in April of 1997, and they can all lead you to FDIC land listings: Northeast Region, 873-7785; Southeast Region, 765-3342; Midwest Region, 944-5343; Southwest Region, 319-1444; West Coast Region, 234-0867.

Distressed Sales

Land is sold under duress for all sorts of reasons: foreclosures, divorce settlements, estate settlements, business bankruptcy. The trick is finding out about them. Preston says, "You can find out about foreclosure actions by reading the legal notices in the newspaper serving the county seat. Banks are required to give several weeks of printed notice before they can foreclose. This is your chance to find the owner and make him an offer he can't refuse." Do not "pack a piece" during these negotiations. You won't need it. As with purchasing tax sale land, some of the "moral dilemma" element is associated with this strategy, but, hopefully, by dealing with the owner instead of the foreclosing agency, both seller and buyer can come out better off. With complications like impending foreclosure casting a heavy cloud over the transaction, you should secure legal help to prepare the closing documents.

Sometimes banks hold land that they've foreclosed upon. This recently happened here on good old Murder Hill. A bank had been trying to sell a foreclosed property, a house and two acres of land, for a couple of years at $50,000. A friend of ours made what many would consider to be the ridiculously low offer of $18,000. He eventually bought it in 1997 for $20,000. The bank was just sick of this property, which had been a thorn in its side through several owners who had all paid too much for it in the first place. Granted, the house needs a good $10,000 in repairs, but it's good enough to live in now, so our friend's shelter cost (presently rent) will take a big drop when he moves in. He can fix the place up while he's living there.

The lesson: Ask around at the local banks, credit unions, or mortgage corporations.

Squatting

No, I'm not seriously going to suggest that you go occupy some abandoned property for the number of years (called the "statute of limitations") specified by your state's law, after which legal access to property can be gained by adverse possession (the period varies greatly from state to state). But, for fun, I'll share a couple of inspirational stories with you, and then speak of a related strategy that is much more common and practical.

Our old friend, Henry Thoreau, built his house at Walden Pond on property that he did not own. It was owned, you may remember, by his friend and mentor, Ralph Waldo Emerson. The economics of land ownership is a matter given short shrift by Thoreau. When he lists the purchases of materials for his house (the sum total was $28.12½), he adds, "These are all the materials excepting the timber, stones, and sand, which I claimed by squatter's right." In one sentence, Thoreau speaks to the economic benefits of using indigenous materials as well as building on land that you don't have to pay for. A few pages later, he tells us, "As for habitat, if I were not permitted still to squat, I might purchase one acre at the same price for which the land I cultivated was sold—namely eight dollars and eight cents. But as it was, I considered that I enhanced the value of the land by squatting on it." A true steward!

When we lived in Scotland, Jaki and I enjoyed the personal acquaintance of a modern-day eccentric bachelor who made good use of the squatter's strategy. This individual, a dark bearded English poet with deep-set and piercing eyes, was something of a mystic. He would pick up "messages" in unlikely places, such as cemeteries. One day, in London, he "picked up" the vibe that he should go to the North of

Divining a homestead.

Scotland, where he would find the place that he was meant to be. He arrived at Findhorn, one of the first dozen settlers in a New Age community that has now become legendary. After a while, the spiritual head of the community, herself sensitive to mystical messages, decided that it was time for the poet to move on. Two strong personalities, perhaps, were at odds with one another. Our hero moved on, arrived on an abandoned 70-acre croft (smallholding) near Loch Ness, and moved into an empty stone cottage there. One day, he asked the local constable whose property this was. The reply, we were told, was, "It's yours, if ye want it." Our friend has been there ever since, over twenty years now. It is a wonderful, magical, secluded property.

Modern squatting is fraught with risks. Not only must the squatter persist on the land for the required period of the local statute of limitations, but the occupation must be "hostile, actual, open, notorious, exclusive, continuous and under claim of title." It also helps, and might even be a requirement, to pay the taxes on the property. It is always possible, if not likely, that just before the statute of limitations runs out, someone (the true "owner?") will obtain a legal eviction against the squatter, although this, too, can be difficult. It seems that nothing involving legal action is easy.

Gifted Land

Much better than squatting—safer at least, if not quite as emotionally satisfying—is the strategy of building on free land that someone has given to you. Thoreau was not really as much a squatter as he was a guest on Emerson's land. In our part of the world, it is common for farming families, or even non-farming families with woodlot acreage, to deed parcels to sons or daughters for the purpose of building their homes. A young couple from the Toronto area, students at our Earthwood Building School, were discouraged about the high cost of land in their community. A relative owned a large piece of land in a sparsely populated area a couple of hundred miles to the north, where land prices and the cost of living were both very much less. After a frustrating land search, our former students were offered a substantial tract of land for free. As the couple were both artists, they were free to accept, and they are now building their homestead in a beautiful but remote part of Ontario.

Now, it doesn't seem like a proactive strategy, getting free land. You've got to be born lucky, it would seem. But maybe some gentle nudging can help to actualize the situation. James Redfield, in his novel *The Celestine Prophecy*, speaks of cultivating coincidences. After reading the book, many people report an increase of seemingly mystical coincidences occurring in their lives. I observed the same phenomenon. What is really happening, I think, is that we can learn to latch on to connections with others. We extend ourselves. We become more active, mentally, spiritually, and physically (proximity to opportunity, for example). Perhaps old Aunt Minnie has forty acres on the wilderness fringe of town, for example, in which no one else in the family seems even vaguely interested. Before Aunt Minnie departs the planet for points unknown, a nephew or niece just might make it known that he/she would really make good use of such a piece of land. An extension of this kind can be made, thereby cultivating favorable coincidence. Or—the other possibility—no one says a word, Minnie passes on, and the property winds up in probate. Perhaps the old dear would have been delighted for her young relatives to use the property, which may have had some special place in her heart. Those who do not extend themselves will never find out. Two of the case studies in chapter 7 tell the story of young couples who built on land provided by the mother of one of the partners. The mother gets the benefit of keeping some of her family close by. Lots of mothers really like that.

So, if gifted property comes along, remember the old saying: "Don't overlook a gift house in the south." Or something like that. Maybe the place isn't exactly where you would have liked it to be, but check it out. If it's really not your cup of tea, keep looking. Free land is too expensive if it takes you further from, rather than closer to, your dreams. This goes for cheap land, too.

EVALUATING THE LAND

The criteria for evaluating land are as varied as there are people because, after all—horns and fanfare please—*everybody's different*. In the next few pages, I want to discuss criteria that either contribute to building a mortgage-free home or help keep other costs of living down. Why go after one and ignore the other? The first consideration that can greatly impact the cost of your home is . . .

Building and Zoning Regulations

Building codes were originally devised as an honorable attempt to prevent and prohibit the very unhealthy living conditions imposed upon people by unscrupulous builders and owners of shoddy tenement houses. According to Rudolph Miller, founder of the Building Officials Conference of America (BOCA) in 1915, the intent and purpose of the building code is as follows:

> The building laws should provide only for such requirements with respect to building construction and closely related matters as are absolutely necessary for the protection of persons who have no voice in the manner of construction or the arrangement of buildings with which they involuntarily come in contact. Thus, when buildings are comparatively small, are far apart, and their use is limited to the owners and builders of them, so that, in case of failures of any kind that are not a source of danger to others, no necessity for building restriction would exist (Kern, Kogon, and Thallon, *The Owner-Builder and the Code,* Scribner's, 1976, p. 14).

Today, the codes have evolved to the point where they can present a very real obstacle to the owner-builder, financial and otherwise. But, with a little care, patience, and common sense, you can overcome these obstacles. For over twenty years, I have promoted a building method called *cordwood masonry*. (If you don't know what it is, don't worry. You'll find out in chapter 6.) For now, suffice it to say that cordwood masonry is a technique that is unknown to most building inspectors. It is not mentioned in the Uniform Building Code (UBC), upon which roughly two thousand of the three thousand–plus U.S. counties base their codes. But in all these years, I am not aware of a single instance where someone who wanted to build a cordwood house has been flat-out refused by code enforcement officers to the extent that they didn't build it. Some had to jump through a lot more hoops than others, and some had to incorporate expensive but necessary systems (such as extra foundation rebar in seismic 3 earthquake zones), but all, to my knowledge, eventually managed to build something close to the house that they wanted.

Zoning (or planning) regulations are meant to protect inhabitants of a residential neighborhood from a factory moving into their midst,

European vs. American Village.

and other similar kinds of land use problems. Although it is true that zoning regulations can restrict individual property rights somewhat, sensible planning and zoning has become a necessity. And, generally, thanks to "grandfather clauses," people don't lose existing-use rights when zoning is implemented.

About 80 percent of counties in the United States have zoning regulations, and some zoning boards are a lot more enlightened about the environmental impact of zoning than others. For example, a town near us has a zoning ordinance requiring that houses be built "parallel to the road." It is well known that the orientation of a house—any house, energy efficient or *inefficient*—can mean up to a 35 percent difference in the cost of heating and cooling. The roads of the town were laid out with regard to access, not solar orientation. A new house in this town, or even an entire subdivision, may have an annual fuel cost 35 percent higher than if thoughtful siting was employed. There are rays of sun on the planning landscape, though. The city of Davis, California, pioneered building codes and regulations that, among other measures, *require* new houses to have a southerly orientation.

Democracy is alive and well in small-town and rural America (although I'm beginning to have my doubts on the state and national scenes), so get involved in local zoning decisions. In my experience, zoning boards are made up of conscientious citizens. Good planning is better than bad planning, and always better than no planning, and I admit that this statement reflects a change of view on my part over the past twenty years. I'm still against bad zoning, that which is not environmentally sound. The carrying capacity of this planet is already being stretched to the limit, for all species, without exacerbating the problem with bad laws. For example, in some municipalities, regulations have been established calling for expensive and rather wasteful minimums of two to four acres for lot size and 2,000 to 3,000 square feet or more for houses. With ever more people chasing less land, and with the new reality of energy costs, such regulations are ecologically counterproductive. Besides promoting wasteful use of the planet's resources, such laws help to drive the cost of living beyond compatibility with personal freedom.

Be sure that you are allowed to build on a particular piece of property before you buy it. We have a summer cottage on a nearby lake situated in the Adirondack Park, an area of restrictive zoning larger than New Jersey. Even on the privately owned land (half of the park's area), the right to build depends on where the land is located. On land zoned Resource Management, for example, only one house can be erected per 42 acres. My intent is not to criticize these regulations. In the long run, the animal world, humankind, and Planet Earth in general all benefit from sound environmental planning. But you had better be aware of these laws if they are in conflict with your personal dreams for the property.

Building codes can be equally hard on the owner-builder's pocketbook. Before buying land, find out what special building code requirements are in force that might drive the cost of building up unnecessarily. Check with both town and county officials. Find out how strictly the regulations are enforced. Here is just one example of an unnecessarily expensive building code. In the name of frost protection, a municipality near us requires that every wall foundation be built down to a level of 48 inches. While this method works quite well in our area, the code will not allow other less expensive frost-proof methods of construction, such as the floating slab (one of Frank Lloyd Wright's favorite methods), the rubble trench foundation (another of Frank's favorites), pier-and-grade-beam foundations, or building on 48-inch-deep pillars. Other codes might prohibit the low-cost alternative building method that you have in mind, particularly if the local code enforcement officer is the kind who plays strictly by the book, and just can't be bothered learning about some new way of building, even though the new way may be both less expensive and more energy-efficient than the old way.

There are still a few places where building codes are either not in place or are not strictly enforced, although these are becoming rare and will probably become extinct before long. There are potential savings in such areas. The land will be cheaper in the non-coded area. The construction costs will be less. The trade-off is that you will be responsible for the safety of your own house, which is as it should be. Use the codes as guidelines and as aids to problem solving. But also tap the wealth of literature in libraries and bookstores, which is often easier to understand than codes because it explains the *intent* of the recommendations. Codes do change, however, and even some of the alternative methods are being recognized. California, for example, a state known for particularly tough codes, now has a section on straw bale construction. The National Electrical Code has a section on alternative energy systems.

We often hear the argument: "If you don't build your house to code, you will adversely affect its resale value. Banks won't finance houses that are not built to code." But the argument is flawed. First, this is not strictly true. In rural areas, where codes are not so likely to be found, or where many homes were built before the introduction of codes, banks finance homes all the time. Second, owner-builders have imparted a tremendous "sweat equity" into their houses, the fruit of their own considerable labor. They will derive far more than their initial investment, even if they sell their place "below market value." Third, you might owner-finance the sale of the property to the new buyer, a situation that can be financially beneficial to both buyer and seller.

Water

Perhaps Thoreau should have included Air and Water among his necessaries of life. Air supplies the oxygen required for the internal combustion that keeps our temperature up to snuff. All land has air above it, at least on this planet. Only the quality is suspect. You'll know in one or two visits if the land you are thinking of has poor air quality. Is it downwind from an incinerator or refinery? Adjacent to a landfill? At the bottom of a temperature inversion?

Water is much more of a concern and even more necessary than Food, since we can't go nearly as long without it. Potable water can come in many forms: deep (drilled) well, shallow (dug) well, spring, municipal supply, private water companies (primarily in the West), purified lake or river water, even rainwater collection. The latter option is dicey, at best, but is the only source on 4-acre Tobacco Caye off the coast of Belize, where I helped dig for the collection cistern.

The problem of water is of particular import in the West, where the water table is deep and getting deeper. Drilled wells are expensive at best, and can be dry holes at worst. "Land for Sale" advertisements in the West will sometimes include the words "water shares available," perhaps specifying a quantity. This designation is found in areas where water is supplied by a private water company. Sometimes water rights are based upon owning stock in a company, which could be quite expensive. Know where your water is coming from before you buy the land.

Drilled wells are more common now than dug wells. Usually, banks won't even give a mortgage on a home that gets its water from a shallow well. Even if the water tests great, they will often insist on a drilled well, citing "policy." Out in the country, at least in the East, a dug well may be a viable option. Perhaps there is an existing well on the property that you're thinking of buying, as was the case at the first property we bought on The Hill, but don't assume it is good water. Have it tested. Sometimes, a snake or frog or worse has fallen into the well and made it unsafe to drink. And sometimes these wells can be cleaned up with a gallon of sodium hypochlorite solution (common bleach). Get advice where you have the water tested. If the source of pollution is identified as human fecal coloform, watch out. The strong indication in this case is that the well's catchment area is too close to the leach field of a septic system. There is virtually nothing you can do except to dig or drill a different well much further from the source of pollution. In New York, state health code requires that the well be at least 100 feet from any part of the leaching field.

If there is no well on the property, the best source of information might be a local well driller who keeps logs on all the wells that he has dug in the area. If the nearby property owners have wells, find out about the depth and quality of the water. Be very careful about this, because securing a good water supply could add greatly to the cost of making the land usable.

Septic System

Installation of a septic system is another potentially expensive problem. Don't think that you can get around this with a composting toilet. While most states will allow the use of a toilet for making compost, they'll still insist upon a septic system approved by the health department. In New York, for example, virtually all counties follow state health code regulations. You need either a septic system or connection to a public sewer. Lands in a special sewer district are almost certainly going to be more expensive, and taxpayers within the district might be paying for the system over the next thirty years.

We commonly hear the expression, "The soil has good perk," or "The soil perks well." When I first heard this, I envisioned water bubbling out of the ground. Wrong. Perk, short for percolation, refers to the ability of soils to percolate water into the ground. In my years as a housing rehab specialist, I conducted dozens of perk tests. Basically, you dig a hole in the ground, usually three feet deep, saturate the area with a few buckets of water, and then time how long it takes for water

A bad perk test.

to drop one inch in the hole. I'll prop up a yardstick as a guide, fill the hole to the 12-inch level, and, with my wristwatch, time how long it takes the water to drop to the 11-inch level. The county health department will tell you how many feet of leach field you will need based upon the perk test results and the number of bedrooms in the house. It's like a mileage chart. You intersect perk and bedroom figures on a grid and a number tells you how many feet (meters in Canada) of leach field you need. In New York, for example, a three-bedroom house built on land with a ten-minute percolation requires 250 feet of drain field. Four bedrooms and twenty-five-minute soil require 500 feet of drain field, a considerable expense. Ideally, the perk would fall into the three- to ten-minute range. If the perk is over an hour, you should consider looking elsewhere to build, as the system could wind up being extremely expensive, or might not work at all.

I once saw very sandy soil that perked in forty-five seconds, test after test. This is a bit worrisome, suggesting that the septic tank effluent may be leaching into the ground *too* fast, with the danger of polluting the water source. A well even 100 feet from any part of the drain field might be too close. In a properly designed system, most of the water is carried away by transpiration and evaporation out through the ground, not by percolation into the ground. This is why the grass is always greener over the drain field.

Appendix 3 lists a good book about water and sewage systems, *Wells and Septic Systems*, by Max and Charlotte Alth. For those of you who realize the eminent good sense of a composting toilet and plan to build in an area with minimal health code requirements, congratulations. Your heads are screwed on right and you are planetary patriots, the best kind. But, as you only represent a tiny percentage of potential builders, and my own experience is limited to a composting toilet in an outhouse that has been in use less than a year, I will defer to *The Humanure Handbook*, by J. C. Jenkins, also listed in appendix 3. The book is thorough and a lot of fun to read.

Availability of Indigenous Materials

Both the dollar cost and the energy cost of transporting building materials over a long distance are unfavorable trade-offs. Suppose, for instance, that a load of chipboard is carried 1,000 miles in a large truck.

Indigenous materials can help a house blend in with the landscape.

A considerable amount of oil is used to manufacture and transport this material. Pollution is created during the transportation from the oil field, during the oil refining, during the manufacture of the chipboard, and again, during the burning of the diesel fuel by the truck. The air gets dirtier. Oil becomes a little bit more scarce. Prices rise.

As we use more and more petroleum, the remainder becomes increasingly difficult to extract from the ground. The term "energy cost" can be understood in another way when you consider that if there is an estimated 100 million units of energy in a field, but 90 million units are required to get it to its usable state (this is the energy cost), the reserve is effectively 10 million units, not 100 million.

To varying degrees, any manufactured product embodies energy cost: plywood, chipboard, finished lumber, concrete blocks, insulating materials. The advantages of using these products should be weighed against the disadvantages, in terms of dollar cost, the long-term effects of the energy cost, and most importantly, the environmental cost.

I am not saying that manufactured products should never be used. They will frequently be necessary, at least for certain kinds of houses. I am advising you to look for indigenous alternatives whenever and wherever possible. Using rough-cut lumber from a local sawmill, for example, is cheaper in both dollar and energy cost compared to buying finished lumber originating hundreds of miles away. Other favorable byproducts from this strategy are that the local economy benefits to a greater degree and you will generally have a better product. A rough-cut, two-by-four stud has a full 8 square inches of cross-sectional area, while the dressed stud has only 5¼ square inches of cross-sectional area.

The use of indigenous materials has other advantages outside of economics. Aesthetically, a house will be in greater harmony with its surroundings if it is constructed of the same materials. A log or cordwood house blends into a wooded area just as an adobe house seems to grow naturally from the dry, treeless, Southwestern desert.

We Americans are relative newcomers to this continent, and perhaps that's why so few of us look at the long-term impact of housing on the environment. In older societies, housing is an integral part of the environment during and after its life as shelter.

In my opinion, the book that best illustrates the use of indigenous materials is Bernard Rudofsky's *The Prodigious Builders* (Harcourt Brace Jovanovich, 1977). With regard to building permanence, he says:

> These days, buildings have a shorter life span than the men who build them. The thought that a house might serve a family for several generations, and serve it well, has no currency. We accept premature architectural decrepitude as a matter of course. The culminating point in a building's life is reached the moment it is finished and its photograph is taken for publication. In a way, this parallels the once popular belief that a person's days of youthful exuberance and venturesomeness end with marriage (p. 271).

Rudofsky points out that even animals do better than people in this respect (the term "owner-builder" would seem redundant to a honeybee):

> Beavers' consolidated bulk of work will stand up to the ravages of time for thousands of years, a record rarely matched by man-made constructions, perhaps because beavers are eager to provide constant supervision and labor for repairs, while man is not (p. 58).

Rudofsky's explanation for the success of animal "architecture" hits close to home:

> Granted, animal builders work under enviable conditions. Unhampered by red tape, and innocent of profit motives, with an incalculable backlog of practice at their disposal, they often attain perfection by simply following their instinct (p. 59).

The master builder.

Again, regulations and profit motives (often one and the same thanks to successful lobbying) surface to complicate the relatively simple matter of shelter. But natural building skill and lack of building codes by themselves are not sufficient to explain the quality of ancient dwellings, their beauty and their durability. The use of local materials is important. When you, like the animal, simply reshape materials at hand, you stand a good chance of long-term success because these materials have the intrinsic ability to survive the local conditions of sun, wind, rain, and frost. With materials, even *natural* materials, brought in from somewhere else, this intrinsic durability may or may not be present, and the chances of long-term survivability are diminished. An adobe house makes as little sense in Alaska as an igloo in New Mexico. Neither is likely to last very long.

The construction of the "soddies" of the American North-Central Plains during the last century is a good example of the use of indigenous materials. Lacking any other building materials, settlers in this region built comfortable houses out of the very ground itself. Years later, when transportation made cheap wood available, cheap enough that barns, fences, and outbuildings could be made of it, many perceptive builders continued to use sod because it made more sense in terms of comfort, energy efficiency, and durability. Sod house historian Roger L. Welsch says, "The frame house was painfully vulnerable to prairie fires, severe weather and wind. Wood burns, shrinks, swells, rots and can be eaten by insects and rodents. Sod resists all of these" (*Shelter*, Shelter Publications, 1973).

With regard to the selection of land, consider the kind of house you want and the suitability of the available materials to your design. If the most practical of the indigenous materials in your area is wood, but all of the woodlot was clear-cut a year before the land came up for sale (a common occurrence), it should be obvious to you that its value is greatly diminished for building a log cabin. On the other hand, the logging slash left behind might be suitable for a cordwood masonry house. This could prove a bargain all around if the land price was greatly reduced as a result of the clear-cutting. And you have the opportunity to help bring this spoiled land back to bio-diverse forest again.

Here's another example. A new method of construction (but based on very old and sound construction principles) is being promoted and popularized by architect Nader Khalili and the Cal-Earth Institute in Hesperia, California, listed in appendix 2. Students and apprentices of Cal-Earth learn to build beautiful, earthquake-proof, and energy-efficient homes of whatever earth happens to be on site. The house is built of sandbags, filled *in situ* with a coffee can, so there is no heavy lifting. To create a vaulted or domed roof, consecutive courses are corbelled inward an inch or so, until the arch shape meets overhead. Although the $2,000 tuition is considerably higher than other building schools, Cal-Earth claims that they will teach you "how to build your home, your school, your career, or your entire community, without being forced to cut a single tree; by using the earth under your feet and utilizing the elements of sun, wind, water, and fire." Khalili's methods may well provide safe, low-cost housing to many of the world's people living in substandard housing, particularly in tropical and sub-tropical parts of the world, including desert lands. And, while I am unsure about the thermal performance of the houses in northern climates, the work at Cal-Earth is impressive, and shows that indigenous materials are, indeed, everywhere. NASA is carefully considering Khalili's methods for building shelters on the moon: sandbags filled with moondust.

Indigenous Energy Sources

Fuel is one of the "big three" on Thoreau's list of "the necessaries of life," along with Shelter and Food. The availability of Fuel, including the potential for generating electrical energy, can be a valuable bonus on your land. This potential may or may not be reflected in the price of the parcel, depending on the seller's degree of perception in these matters.

Firewood. Wood is the obvious fuel source for burning. In the case of clear-cut land, the logging slash left behind might be of considerable value as firewood, but the question is whether or not it will last until the new growth is ready for harvest. This will depend on the degree of "clear" cutting, and the energy efficiency of the home to be built.

A well-managed hardwood lot can yield a half cord of wood per acre per year. If the house requires three cords of wood per year for heat, six acres can perpetually fulfill the need and the woodlot will actually improve in quality! For fuel, hardwood has a higher value than softwood, whereas softwood is generally preferable for building. Many people in the West heat with softwood, however, due to the unavailability of hardwood, and many a fine home has been built of oak and even poplar.

If you plan to use wood as the primary source of heat, be sure to burn it in the most efficient manner possible. Wood should never be allowed to smolder. Either reburn the wood gasses in a secondary combustion chamber—stoves with a catalytic converter can help a great deal—or, better yet, burn the wood hot and fast in a masonry stove, as discussed in chapter 5.

Wind power. Wind is a potential energy source that rarely influences the selling price of land, probably because people who use windpower are still so few and far between. Good wind sites are not as common as you may think.

Years ago, I cofounded a company that sold and installed wind machines. I would often hear people say, "I've got a great wind site; there's always a breeze." They didn't realize that the potential power in the wind increases as the cube of the wind speed. For example, a 20-mile-per-hour wind has eight times the potential of a 10-mile-per-hour breeze. The bulk of the power made by any wind machine, therefore, occurs during the time of the "power winds." The "steady breeze" experienced at certain sites, such as at the edge of a small lake, may not help very much in supplying power. One good frontal storm, on the other hand, might be sufficient to charge a small battery system. For a few years, particularly during the 1980s, photovoltaic (PV) cell systems were actually cheaper than small wind energy systems, and several small wind machine manufacturers went out of business. In the 1990s, though, new technologies have brought the cost and size of wind machines down, and they are now cost-competitive with PV cells.

If wind power is an important consideration, make sure that the site will meet your needs. At the very least, get a visual analysis from someone who is familiar with wind power. If he or she says, "Forget it," then forget it. I know of no dealer in wind machinery who will tell you that you have a good site if you don't, just to sell a wind machine. In a borderline case, you might be advised to do a three-month analysis with a recording anemometer to find out the average wind speed at your site. The figures derived from such a short test should be compared with the figures for the same period recorded by the nearest meteorological station or airport. Then the two sets of figures should be compared to the average for those three months over the last twenty years. This double comparison method should make up for the gaps in an abnormal testing period.

Some wind machine dealers will deduct the cost of the analysis if you buy a wind machine. The problem, obviously, is doing a wind analysis on a property that you do not own. In many cases, you'll have to rely on visual observations and local data. Does the area in general have high average wind speeds? Can you get the windplant forty feet higher than any obstruction within 400 feet?

I do not advise building your own wind machine from scratch unless you are the kind of person who would be quite happy building your own motorcar from scratch! Reliable, relatively inexpensive wind machines are available now that can't be beat by the backyard tinkerer. It's the old reinventing-the-wheel scenario: a loser.

There are two different kinds of systems for making and using electricity from the wind. The best system, economically and philosophically, is the battery storage application, also called the "remote site" system, although it is not limited to remote sites. With these systems, users are responsible for budgeting their own supply of electricity stored in large banks of deep-cycle batteries. The home is not connected to the national electrical grid.

The other kind of wind system is the "utility interface" system, also known as the "on line" or "reverse feed" system. With this approach, the wind machine makes electricity that is synchronous with that made by the power company. Some machines do this right in the generator, while others require a "synchronous inverter" to do the same thing. When power is made, it can be used directly in the home without affecting your monthly power bill in any way. When the windplant is making power in excess of the household draw, an electric meter records how much power is being put into the power grid. When the wind is not blowing, which is most of the time at most sites, you must pay for your power at the regular rate. Unfortunately, in most states, consumers are credited at wholesale rates for the power they supply and charged regular retail rates for the power they consume. Sometimes a rental is charged for the second meter. *And* the consumer's windplant cannot be used—in fact, the blades will not turn—during a power outage! (This safety feature prevents a line repairman from being zapped with a surge of someone's homemade power during an outage.)

In general, power companies don't like dealing with small power producers, and even where state law seems to side with the small power producer, many power companies do everything they can to avoid compliance. Minnesota and Wisconsin are two states with more enlightened attitudes and regulations. There, small producers, defined as those with 40-kilowatt (40,000 watt) machines in the case of Minnesota and 20-kilowatt ones in Wisconsin, are on the "net metering" system, which is the best deal for the homeowner. When the windplant makes power, the house electrical meter actually turns in reverse. An acquaintance in Wisconsin consistently makes more power with his 20-kilowatt unit than he consumes, and he gets a check from the power company each month.

As I write, there is talk of deregulation in the power industry and it is hard to say how this will affect small wind, hydro, and solar producers. The only sure advice I can give is: Don't buy land on the basis of selling power to the power company without first checking both state law and with the power company involved. If you already have the land, don't buy utility interface equipment without answering the same kinds of questions.

Photovoltaic panels. The potential gain from photovoltaic (PV) solar electric panels is largely a function of geographical region, but we have been very happy with them at Earthwood in northern New York, one of the poorest regions of *insolation* (solar gain) in the United States. Without getting into the science or magic of PV panels, the bottom line is that light enters the panels on their top side and the light energy is miraculously converted to direct current (usually 12 volts or 24 volts) in the molecular layers just below the surface. The panels are just giant versions of the little solar-powered calculators that you can now buy for $6.95. Photovoltaic panels continue to come down in price, and are comparable to (if not cheaper than) wind power on a dollars-per-usable-watt basis, but with a lot less trouble. You have no tower climbing, regular maintenance, or mechanical problems with PV cells.

As with wind, you can set up a utility interface system between solar panels and the utility-provided power. But again, it doesn't make a lot of sense economically. Photovoltaic power, like wind power, is several times more expensive on a per-kilowatt-hour basis than the cheap power provided through the national grid. Selling power back to the power company just doesn't make any kind of economic sense to me, except perhaps in states where net metering is in effect.

Although photovoltaic power (and small wind machine power) is more expensive on a unit cost than readily available grid power, there are circumstances in rural areas where the economy tips in favor of the independent power producer. This happens when the cost of bringing power to your site is high. It is quite common nowadays for power companies to charge $25,000 in line-extension fees to bring power just a quarter mile to your home, whether along a hitherto unsupplied road or along your private driveway. Twenty-five thousand dollars is a lot of squabbish, to say the least. For less than $5,000, you can install a darned good starter system of PV panels, safety equipment, and batteries that will provide your basic electrical needs (but not big-draw luxuries). Then, instead of paying power bills, a homeowner can add extra panels and batteries to the system, until, in just a year or two, based upon typical American electrical bills, a system has been built up that should satisfy all but the most energy-greedy electrical consumers. That's the nice thing about photovoltaic power: it's modular. This, to me, is a compelling advantage over wind power.

Michael Potts, author of *The Independent Home* (Chelsea Green, 1993), likes to make the "operating cost" argument with regard to photovoltaic power. In recent correspondence, he used the example of someone who would have to pay $25,000 for a quarter-mile of line extension from the local power company, and commented that:

> A lovely home-sized converter electrical system can be had for $20,000. In this example, one individual purchases for $25,000 the right to pay monthly electric bills, while the unhooked neighbor wipes the birdshit off his panels four times a year, replaces his batteries once a decade, and has time to mind the roses.

Remember, land prices will be lower wherever the cost of bringing in power is high. And savings on the cost of the land might be enough to pay for a good wind, hydro, or photovoltaic system.

Water power. Water power potential will usually be reflected in the cost of the land, even if by way of other criteria, such as a river or stream's value for fishing and recreation. Small turbines are more and more common nowadays and can be bought at a relatively low price per usable watt compared to wind and solar energy. The catch is that there are comparatively few good small hydro sites. I personally know three families who derive the bulk of their electrical energy from water power. Their systems produce power quietly, cheaply, and steadily, to the tune of a constant 300 watts, 600 watts, and 1,000 watts respectively. The 600-watt producer's system makes use of a 50-foot drop in his stream over a 500-foot distance. A 4-inch-diameter pipe runs along the stream from the catchment area (an oak barrel) to the Pelton turbine. The pipe is always full of water, and every drop borrowed from the stream is returned.

The national grid. If commercial power runs right by your property, and there is no extraordinary cost in tying into it, the most economical approach is to hook into it and use energy-conserving measures in the house, such as energy-efficient lighting and appliances. Do not use devices with heating coils, such as electric ranges, clothes dryers, space heaters, and water heaters. The functions of these appliances can be accomplished more efficiently with other fuels, such as gas, wood, or passive solar systems. Try to get consumption down close to what it would be with an alternative energy system, and your actual life-cycle electrical cost will be lower than with wind, solar, and possibly even hydro power. A lot of people don't like to hear this, but the reality is that electricity made by the power companies is still a lot cheaper on a unit cost basis than power made by wind or solar, and is likely to remain so for the next twenty years. Small hydropower systems, given a good site, can be competitive with commercial power, but such sites are rare. So stay unplugged, if you like, for environmental, spiritual, or philosophical reasons, but not for economic reasons, unless the cost of bringing in the power is $5,000 or more.

With regard to the price of land, remote sites (those not near power lines) will be less expensive. In this case, off-the-grid alternative energy can be an economical as well as a spiritually satisfying mode of existence. Of course, the remote site system places greater responsibility on the householder to conserve, but this is as it should be. As long as we're going to all this trouble to save on Shelter, why not tackle one of the next biggest living expenses, Fuel, at the same time? And the most economic "fuel" we have is still conservation of energy, which Amory Lovins calls *negawatts*.

Food Production

If you are one who sees a strong connection between homesteading and mortgage-free living, you will be very concerned about potential food production as you conduct your land search.

Vegetables. Besides providing a decidedly healthier diet, growing your own veggies can potentially reduce the cost of living—or it can be a time-consuming hobby with a break-even bottom line. Our personal experience might be of benefit to those without previous gardening experience. One of the reasons that Jaki and I left Scotland in 1975 and moved to northern New York was that we had only one-quarter acre of land, less than half of which was fit for growing vegetables. We didn't know then that one-tenth of an acre is more than enough to grow all the vegetables required by a family of four, if the raised bed (also known as bio-dynamic French intensive) method of gardening is employed. Using this method, we now grow lots of vegetables in a space smaller than what was available to us in Scotland. Sometimes, people looking for land insist that they must have "some cleared land, an acre at least, for a garden." We said the same thing in 1975. Now we realize that even wooded land can be prepared for vegetable gardening at little expense. Clear a space in the woods for a garden—not too big—and you obtain at least seven other benefits by the effort: building materials, firewood, natural light, passive solar orientation for the home, air movement to diminish the number of biting bugs, recreational space, and an angle to the sun for PV electrical production.

One of the prettiest gardens I have seen, as well as one of the most productive, was virtually carved out of the edge of a recently harvested

THE ADVANTAGES OF RAISED-BED GARDENS

French intensive or "bio-dynamic" gardening involves the use of several "raised beds" of about 4 feet in width—the maximum width allowing the gardener to reach the center from either side—and virtually any length, although 8 to 12 feet is common. We once built a raised bed 32 feet long with occasional "crosswalks" to facilitate moving around the garden. Ideally the beds should have at least 12 inches of good soil to turn each year, although that varies somewhat with the crop. Beds can be either permanently framed with stone or wood, or shaped with a rake and a spade each season. We like the "permanent" beds, but we've also seen many excellent gardens of mounds reshaped each year at the time of turning. The advantages of raised beds are:

1. Less land is needed. Intensive planting is possible since no space between rows is required, yielding much more produce per square foot of garden.

2. Seeds or seedlings are spaced so that the young plants form a living "green mulch" over the bed, discouraging weeds and helping to retard moisture loss through evaporation.

3. Gardening is three-dimensional: leafy vegetables are alternated with root vegetables so that both the surface and the subsurface spaces are productive.

4. Each bed can be tuned to the proper pH factor (acidity vs. alkalinity) for the particular vegetables to be grown in that bed.

woodlot. Using stones, logs, and the natural contours of the property, our neighbor built dozens of small, easy-to-manage beds, connected by a winding path. Land that had been quite badly scarred became beautiful and productive.

The length of the growing season is an important consideration when buying land for growing food. Find out at the local cooperative extension office or gardening club what the first and last frost dates are in your chosen area. Land at altitude generally has a shorter growing season than lowlands, but be cautious about lowland valleys which can trap frost for lack of air movement. Sometimes we escape frost

Lettuce likes sweet soil, for example, while strawberries prefer acidic soil. Certain special mineral requirements can also be economically satisfied by concentrating them where needed.

5. Much less watering is required because of the lack of runoff and reduction of evaporation. This advantage is greater with the permanently bordered raised beds, as opposed to the mounded method. In combination with drip-irrigation watering methods, the advantage is compounded.

6. Much better use is made of mulch and compost with intensive gardening. Good soil is built up faster.

7. No rotary tillage is needed. The beds are easily maintained with a spade, rake, and small hand tools. The raised beds are easier to work on because they are 10 to 12 inches above the permanent walkways.

8. Pest control is simplified because the growing area is contained and compact.

9. Raised beds are aesthetically superior. They stay neat and tidy with the permanent walkways. Very little weeding is required.

10. In combination with a built-on protective cover and the use of rigid foam insulation around the inside edge of the bed, growing seasons can be greatly extended. Jaki and I use a plastic sheet over a light bamboo frame to extend the season or to grow vegetables that require more heat, such as peppers.

damage on the top of The Hill at 1,200 feet, where neighbors' gardens in more sheltered areas are adversely affected.

Livestock. If sheep, goats, or cows are a part of your food production or income-earning plan, the land will have to provide pasture. In the case of cows, you'll need additional land adequate to grow winter hay. Growing winter feed for goats and sheep is a dubious economy for the homesteader. Buying winter feed from a local farmer is probably the better strategy.

Converting a genuine woodlot to a hay field is not recommended as a sound economy, either, and it is counterproductive in terms of maintaining the planet's biodiversity. Reclaiming formerly cleared lands that are being encroached by saplings is somewhat more viable. Just make sure that encroaching tree stalks do not exceed an inch or so in diameter unless a tractor is available (and it will have to be available if growing winter hay and grain is a part of the plan).

In any case, the land must be evaluated for such considerations as depth and quality of the soil, frequency and size of stones, and drainage. In northern New York, a good meadow will support about six sheep or goats per acre as pasture. Cows will require from one to five acres of pasture each, depending on the quality of the land. Beef cattle will require an additional acre of good hay field (per head) for winter feed, two acres each for dairy cows. Obviously, these figures are different in areas with longer growing seasons. If you are an inexperienced owner-builder but find the farmsteading lifestyle appealing, have a long talk with the local county agricultural agent or cooperative extension agent or a neighboring farmer prior to buying your land.

Pigs and rabbits do not require very much land at all and are considered by some modern homesteaders to be the best livestock for economical meat production. The manure from these animals is particularly effective in the garden. Chickens supply meat, eggs, and strong manure, and they can be raised on a wooded lot.

Having said all that, I would be remiss if I did not point out that raising livestock for food production, even protein production, is tremendously inefficient. Ten times as much food (including protein) can be grown in the form of grains and vegetables than in the form of livestock. Livestock, like pets, also tend to tie a family to the land.

Travel is hard to arrange, because of the great responsibility of looking after the farm animals. Yes, we have pets, but it is easier to arrange care for them than for livestock. Since we like to travel, this is an important consideration.

My oldest son, Rohan, influenced by the writings of John Robbins and conversations with vegetarians on three continents, became a vegan vegetarian at the age of 18. Vegans don't even use fish or dairy products. Jaki and I were never heavy carnivores, at least on an American scale, but we did eat poultry, the occasional pork chop, breakfast sausage and bacon, and beef (rarely). Rohan spoke to us for a year or more on the benefits of vegetarianism, from the standpoints of improved health ("Elimination of animal products from the diet reduces the risk of heart disease by 90 percent"), more sensible land use ("35,000 square feet is returned to forest for each American who adopts a meat-free diet"), and decreasing world hunger ("80 percent of U.S. corn and 90 percent of U.S. soybeans are consumed by livestock"). He asked us to read John Robbins' pivotal book *May All Be Fed: Diet for a New World* (William Morrow, 1992), and, finally, we did. Our New Year's resolution for 1997 was to become vegetarians, and, although we are only about a year into this new lifestyle, I can report definite health benefits (due mostly, I suspect, from greatly reduced fat consumption) and I feel better about the way my eating habits impact society and planetary ecology.

Trees, Fruit, and Berries. Maple syrup production is particularly viable in our area, and thrives as a cash crop in northern New York and New England, Wisconsin, Michigan, and the Appalachian Mountain region. A mature maple grove, or sugar bush, adds considerably to the value and price of land. It can also be a source of income, either by producing the syrup and sugar yourself or by letting out the bush to a commercial boiler. If there are young sugar maples in your mixed hardwood forest, they may not have increased the land price yet. However, with proper woodlot management, they may produce a viable sugar bush in a very few years, a good investment of time and money.

On the other side of the coin, sugaring equipment is expensive, unless you are fortunate to find a bargain situation in which someone is either closing down a sugar house or moving up to a bigger boiler.

Producing maple syrup is a strong New England tradition.

And sugaring is lots of hard work. You may think that $30 per gallon for maple syrup is expensive, but be assured that sugaring is not a get-rich-quick scheme. We do it for the syrup, which we use at home and give as Christmas gifts, and, yes, we do it partially for the romance of it. After a long and tedious North Country winter, especially in March when "cabin fever" can reach epidemic proportions in our area, the first sap run is a joyous event. That otherwise dismal month of cold rains, mud, and wind is cheered by the cozy atmosphere of the sugar house with its blazing wood fire and the sweet smell of boiling sap.

Beekeeping is probably a more economical proposition for the production of sugar than mapling, and suited to a wider variety of landforms and climates. Producing honey consumes far less energy than boiling off 97 percent of the water in maple syrup. The bees provide the energy. We do not keep bees, for no particularly good reason except, perhaps, that we do have bears in the forest fringe of our community.

A producing orchard—apples, pears, peaches, whatever—will add tremendously to the land price, but a few abandoned "scrub" apple trees or the like will not, especially when the fruit looks small, scabbed, and wormy. Hopefully, what the seller doesn't realize is that these old trees and their offspring can be very valuable to a homesteader. They have strong, long-established root stocks and it isn't difficult to learn how to graft scions of McIntosh, Golden Delicious, or any other desired apple onto these established trees. This is a fast way to establish good fruit production and has the advantage of using an established, hardy root stock. (See appendix 3, Country Wisdom Bulletin A-35, *Grafting Fruit Trees*, Storey Communications). And one of the first things you should do upon purchasing the land is to plant fruit trees hardy to the area. Dwarf varieties are often a good choice. They produce faster and the fruit is easier to pick.

Wild berries and natural herbs on a property are a bonus that you might not even notice unless you look at the land at just the right time of year, but they make a welcome surprise when they show up, which, on most acreage, is more often than not. And you can plant both berries and herbs on a permaculture basis, if they are not already there or if you want different varieties.

Marginal Land

Sometimes land comes up for sale that has been denuded of its resources: wood, topsoil, gravel, and so on. Most people think poorly of land that looks such a mess and seems so barren of possibilities, and this prevailing attitude is often reflected in a very low asking price.

"Right," you say, "and I don't want it either." But don't dismiss this land too lightly, especially if your primary goal is to find a cheap building lot, and not to produce the various food, fuel, and indigenous materials just discussed. So often we see heavy machinery turn a pretty lot into a wasteland before construction of the house anyway. This is an example of the typical North American approach of fitting the site to the house, instead of the more thoughtful and gentler attitude of fitting the house to the site. Bulldoze, build, landscape. Trees are destroyed. Topsoil is homogenized with subsoil. Additional expense is imparted to already expensive land in order to get it to the point where "convenient" building can take place. Using already decimated land may enable you to afford property closer to town and at a lower price than for "prime" land. The estimated cost of land reclamation must be subtracted from the savings of the land cost, but if the work is done by you yourself—sweat equity—this tradeoff should be economically favorable.

This future typically American housing development is just a mile from the road where we live.

There is another positive aspect to buying marginal land. For so many years, American corporations and individuals have taken from our land, and given back little in return. Instead of pillaging more of the planetary capital for convenience and short-term gain, let's reverse the trend whenever and wherever we can. A lot to build a house on need not start out as a part of Eden; we can accomplish the transformation ourselves. A house requires, first and foremost, space to build it on, not scenic views, not waterfront, not prime agricultural land. Friend and advocate of "gentle architecture" (as well as illustrator of this book) Malcolm Wells tells about the building site of his first underground office back in the seventies:

> Cherry Hill, New Jersey, is a lavishly rich, trashy suburb of nearby Philadelphia. My office is a tiny place on a tiny lot, wedged between a freeway and a sewer. When I bought the property (for $700!) all I could see were a few scabs of old asphalt on a patch of barren subsoil. It was dead; all the way down the scale from forest to woods to farm to suburb to abandoned highway construction yard. Now, five years later, it's almost a jungle, even though no topsoil and no fertilizer have ever been used, and a building now underlies almost half the root space. The secrets: plenty of mulch and a few key starter-plants . . . Now, when we tell our

clients how to find choice building sites, we always urge them to pick the worst ones, not the best, as we were always taught to do. Now people can see for themselves how easy and how gratifying it is to restore a bit of this trampled continent ("Underground Architecture," *The CoEvolution Quarterly*. Fall 1976, p. 87).

Jaki and I built Earthwood on the same hill where, in 1975, we joined with others to start an intentional community of owner-builders. It is a beautiful hill, with woods, meadows, springs, and streams. If there was an eyesore in the neighborhood, it was a 2-acre piece of land from which gravel was removed many years ago. The excavation of gravel ceased when sand was struck, at a depth of about four feet, so the extraction proceeded laterally, turning the two acres to waste, where almost nothing grew and the sand was whipped up by the wind; not what you would think of as the ideal building site. But, just as the repair of the one weak link in a chain is more beneficial than strengthening all of the other links combined, so, too, the restoration of this one piece of devastated land, a work in progress, will mean more to the visual and ecological character of the hill than any amount of landscaping where Nature has already set the standard. In our seventeen

Believe it or not, the ideal building site is dying land that is just waiting to be restored. The prospects: silence, privacy, wildlife, clean air and water, more topsoil, less erosion, and lower fuel bills.

years of occupation on this property, and inspired by the admonition of the Gentle Architect so many years ago, we have reclaimed about two-thirds of the wasteland. Where once was lifeless moonscape, we now have gardens, oxygenating grasslands and wildflowers, even a megalithic stone circle; but that's another story.

Adapt the house to the site, not the site to the house.

The main story here calls forth Roy's Fourth Law of Empiric Economics: Adapt the house to the site, not the site to the house. This law has more to do with ecology than money; but after all, economics is fundamentally about how people interact with the natural environment.

Natural Disasters

If the area where you intend to live is prone to tornados, earthquakes, or high fire danger, such as wooded hilly western lands, consider an earth-sheltered house, the safest kind in these conditions. See appendix 3 for books on the subject.

Don't build in the hundred-year flood plain. This is land that the government projects will flood about once every hundred years. Especially don't build an underground house, the worst kind in a flood. 'Nuff said.

Buying Land Cooperatively

In 1974, Jaki and I bought 64 acres of land in northern New York, and the seller gave us an option on an additional 180 acres at the same time. A year later, a number of families from around the United States joined in with us on this land. While we all own our own individual parcels, we did benefit from buying a large tract together at a good price per acre, and then subdividing it. The full story is told in chapter 6. In chapter 7, Chelsea Green Editor Jim Schley tells of the successful co-ownership strategy employed in the intentional community where he lives. Here, I will outline some of the various methods of co-ownership.

Tenancy-in-common. Each buyer shares an undivided interest in the land. In the case of the death of one of the co-tenants, his or her share is passed on to any heirs.

L. John Wachtel's P.L.A.N.E. Plan

In his book *How to Buy Land* (Sterling, 1982), L. John Wachtel shares a formula that he uses when helping clients to evaluate land. For convenience in helping them remember the formula, he has organized the first letters of his criteria into the word *plane*. Every parcel of land under consideration is plugged into a detailed evaluation sheet, and is numerically judged on a one-to-ten scale in the five criteria.

Price. Can you afford the property? Can you stretch your budget for something really exceptional that is being sold at a reasonable price?

Location. Consider proximity to the things of importance in your life: job, school, church, friends, commerce, recreation, etc.

Access. Access includes access to the property and access into the property, if indigenous resources are important. Is the land on a town road? How is road maintenance, particularly snow removal? Do not confuse an easement with access. The property might have an easement (a right to get to the land), but no access. Building a road could cost more than the land itself.

Natural features. Topography, plant and animal life, soil quality, well water.

Everything Else. E.E. includes all the other things that might impact life on this piece of land. In the negative, E.E. might include bad smells, loud noises, or ugly sights (such as a nearby junkyard). In the positive, there might be streams, ponds, a nice view, or a particularly wonderful old oak tree.

Wachtel's method involves filling out detailed checklists to help you rate the various criteria. Then you average it all out on a summary sheet to get a final score. This strikes me as a good method of narrowing down the search to two or three strong candidates. You might not end up deciding on the very highest ranking parcel, particularly if numerical differences are not very great. Ultimately, rightly or wrongly, heart has a big part to play. If the P.L.A.N.E. Plan appeals to you, you might want to find Wachtel's out-of-print book at a library ot through inter-library loan. He devotes about forty pages to the Plan, and discusses lots of valuable considerations.

Joint tenancy. Similar to tenancy-in-common, but the co-owners have the "right of survivorship," which means that the interest of a deceased member of the joint tenancy passes to the other owners.

Tenants by the entireties. Applies only to a husband and wife, and only in certain states. Each marriage partner automatically has the right of survivorship. Jaki and I are "tenants by the entireties."

Corporate ownership. A group can form a corporation solely for the purpose of owning land. Agreements can be made among the owners of the corporation, which has all the legal status of a single person. This strategy should be entered into very carefully and I would only consider it if subdivision were not possible. Any business dealings should be conducted precisely, clearly, and legally.

The unincorporated nonprofit association. This is not a rock group! The land is purchased by a not-for-profit group, the members of which which might have religious, social, educational, or even philosophical affinities. No individual actually owns any part of the land. Usually, members pay a kind of rent to the association for living on the land. One of the members is appointed the trustee of the association in order to take title, but the association retains liability. (For example, see chapter 7 for Jim Schley's story about cooperative governance of a community by a "board" comprised of the residents.)

Casual co-ownership. Emphatically *not* recommended, especially among relatives or casual friends. Maybe even close friends! More than land and money is at stake. Friendships and relationships are at stake. The passage of time has a way of changing recollections of very important conversations and understandings. Get it in writing. Signed. Better, notarized!

For more information on co-ownership possibilities, consult a lawyer in the state where the land is to be bought and read Les and Carol Scher's *Finding and Buying Your Place in the Country*, chapter 31: "Types of Co-Ownership." The book wisely suggests that an owners' agreement be drawn up and signed by the several parties and it even provides an excellent "Model Owners' Agreement," which can be adjusted to meet the needs of particular communities.

BARGAINING

At last, after an extensive search, you've found the piece of land you want. All you have to do is buy it. And at the best possible price.

Rule One: Never fall for pressure, like, "If you don't close on this bargain right now, I have another client who will buy it tomorrow." Balderdash. All the real estate agent cares about is getting the best price. Period. Same with the owner. They don't really care who buys it. Exception: If the owner is going to keep living next door, he or she might well care about who buys the property. If you are a member of a minority group, and practically everyone is nowadays, of one kind or another, remember that anti-discrimination laws are on your side.

Rule Two: Never accept the seller's asking price without bargaining. This is how many people wind up paying more for land than is necessary. Do not accept out of hand an agent's admonition that the seller will not come down on his price. Never feel embarrassed, or worry that you are being insulting by making a counter-offer. "Get into a bargaining posture," says L. John Wachtel. "The expectation of bargaining is implicit in the words 'asking price'," say the Schers. "Think cheap," says Roy.

And don't expect that your offer will be accepted, either. The point is that you've entered into negotiations, and these negotiations will either lead to a sale that you'll both be happy about, if not ecstatic, or you'll reach an unresolvable stalemate, in which case this wasn't the right piece of land for you.

Your first offer will depend on a lot of things. Is the seller's asking price very high, about average, or very low for similar properties in the area? The answer to this question could lead you to starting with an offer of 60, 75, or 90 percent of the asking price. Your offer should be in writing, and should express any conditions you might have. In Britain, a common condition is that an offer is made "subject to planning approval." If title is suspect, you might specify that you want to be provided with a clear abstract or title insurance. Perhaps easements and access need to be guaranteed. Now is the time. Your offer should also be for a specific—short—time period. Two or three days is sufficient. Any longer, and the seller might use your offer to leverage other potential buyers to a higher offer.

Chapter 20 in the Schers' book, "Bargaining to Get the Seller's Asking Price Down," is full of great bargaining tips. In chapter 27 the Schers provide a "Model Contract for Sale," which you can use to make your offer. Or you might use a form provided by the broker. Just make sure that it includes all of your conditions. Include a small deposit, called *earnest money*, that shows that you are serious.

When the buyer and seller finally meet together at an agreeable price, a contract for sale is drawn up. All conditions must be in the contract. Only signed written documents have any legal value. Don't sign until every last question or doubt you might have is satisfied. Oral promises are carried away by the wind.

DRY STUFF YOU SHOULD KNOW

Before closing on a property, there's a lot of stuff you need to know. It's dry and boring stuff, but important just the same. You don't need it right this minute, though, and the next chapter about the Temporary Shelter is really exciting, so rather than put you to sleep with a discussion of things like abstracts, title insurance, land contracts, and types of deeds, I'm going to put it all together for you in one easy-to-access place, appendix 4: Before Closing.

This chapter on land has been long, and necessarily so; you can't build a house without land, even if it belongs to someone else. We've talked about the pressures on land that affect its value. We've considered the possibility of relocation, and ways to learn about different potential places to live. We've spoken of building and planning regulations, and the influence they may have on your project. We've talked about how to find and evaluate land, with ideas about indigenous energy and materials resources that can save lots of money down the road. We've considered the very important concept of land *stewardship* as a prerequisite to land *ownership*. We've talked about how to bargain for the land.

Once you have the land, what then? Well, if the grubstake and current Shelter situation allow, you might be ready to build (but not without reading chapter 5: The Low-Cost Home). If the building grubstake isn't ready, or if you are simply ready to make the move, then the Temporary Shelter strategy will be the key to taking miles off the road toward mortgage freedom. Turn the page.

4

The Temporary Shelter

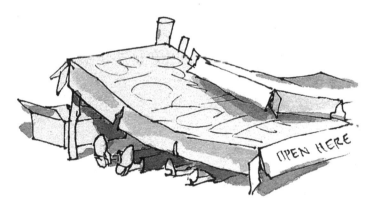

*I had three chairs in my house: one for solitude,
two for friendship, three for society. When visitors came
in larger and unexpected numbers, there was but the
third chair for them all, but they generally economized
the room by standing up.*

—HENRY DAVID THOREAU, WALDEN

Obtain the land at the earliest possible date. It's the best hedge against escalating real estate prices. Equally important, land acquisition can immediately accelerate your rate of savings—perhaps by 100 percent—so that you can accumulate the house grubstake much faster. The key is the temporary shelter, or TS.

THE STRATEGY

In its classic form, the temporary shelter plan involves building a small, low-cost structure on the land, and living in it while you build your permanent house. There can be variations on this strategy, as will be seen, but essentially, its potential advantages are these:

1. You gain building experience.
2. You eliminate interim shelter costs.
3. You learn about the land itself.
4. You gain a useful outbuilding for extended use.

Gaining Building Experience

Most owner-builders start with a common background of inexperience in construction, which, of itself, is not really that great a handicap. Unfortunately, many people have an unwarranted *fear* about their lack of experience, and this can evolve into a lack of *confidence*, which *is* a problem. But, by methodical application of building techniques to a small project based on a simple set of plans, the novice will soon find that, "yes, I really can build a structure in which I could survive." Psychologically, this is a quantum leap. In a month or less, the neophyte moves from dependency on others for shelter to full equality with builders, birds, bees, and beavers, who skillfully provide their own. Later, the construction of the home itself is not a difference in kind, only of degree.

Jaki and I fondly remember our first days in our TS, a 12-by-16-foot shed. Our sense of accomplishment has remained unsurpassed through any of our subsequent building projects. Although I'd acted as my own general contractor for the cottage renovation in Scotland, my actual building experience was virtually nil. I'd done a lot of the destructive work, but I subcontracted the skilled carpentry, masonry, plumbing, and electrical work to tradespeople.

My late father designed two houses and had them built by professional contractors. "You have to build two houses to get one right," he would say. What he meant is that you get the mistakes out of your system with the first house—90 percent of them, anyway.

My experience is that some mistakes will continue to be made as long as new techniques are tried. Because we keep experimenting, we've had to build three houses to get one totally right. I don't want to scare anyone off by this admission, because all the houses we've built, and both of my father's, were unqualified successes for providing comfortable and pleasing habitat. One keeps improving, however.

My father also used to say, "We should learn from our mistakes, of course, but the wise man learns from the mistakes of others." If you want an error-free home, buy a set of building plans for a simple framed structure that has been built hundreds of times without problem. Lumberyards have stacks of such plans. The result will be a well-built, somewhat functional, antiseptic home. Sometimes these plans can be adapted fairly easily to the use of rough-cut or recycled lumber, which will introduce a little more scope for individuality into the home. I list a few sources of plans in appendix 3.

My father may have been right with his two-houses theory, but who but a confirmed building addict (like his son) is willing to build more than one house? Hardly anyone, which is why the Temporary Shelter strategy is so important.

Build two to get it right.

You should give some thought to the final house design, even during construction of the TS. Practice the building techniques that you will employ on the main structure. Why build a cordwood masonry temporary shelter if a straw bale house is the desired permanent home? Your TS can be post-and-beam, adobe, stone, underground, timber-framed, cordwood, log, or any other type that you desire for the main house. While any building experience is useful, the full advantage of the strategy incorporates practice of the very techniques to be used in the future. Better to make a $500 mistake on the TS than a $5,000 mistake on the home.

Staying with the same building technique is particularly important architecturally if the temporary shelter is to be recycled as a part of the main structure later on. And even if the final purpose of the shelter is as a useful outbuilding—office, shed, sauna, or the like—it is important that this outbuilding be in architectural harmony with the home, particularly if it is in close proximity.

Eliminating Interim Shelter Costs

Usually, the temporary shelter can be built in two to four weeks, or a little longer if work is limited to weekends and spare time only. The cost, typically, is similar to paying for a month's rent in town. Upon completion of the TS, you can move to the land and the portion of your budget formerly devoted to shelter costs now can go toward materials for your new home, minus any increase in commuting expenses resulting from the move. Even if you've already laid up the full grubstake, the TS provides rent-free accommodation during construction. In this case, eliminating the additional cost of traveling to the building site is a further savings, a safety margin.

The convenience of living on-site during the construction of your permanent house cannot be over-emphasized. We enjoyed this advantage while building Log End Cottage and again at Log End Cave, 50 yards away from the Cottage. Earthwood is a half mile from Log End, which was no great inconvenience during construction. If you fancy working for an hour after supper, you're there to do it. If you have to drive 10 miles to the site, time and money are lost and you're less likely to make the effort.

Learning About the Land

So often people decide where to build their house, even the exact alignment of the structure, after only one or two visits to the land. A certain view, the location of the road, or some other seemingly obvious factor make other considerations inconsequential. Frequently, the choice involves romantic, rather than practical, decision-making. There's nothing wrong with romance, but it lasts longer if coupled with the stuff of substance, like respect for sun and wind direction, ease of construction (can a concrete truck get to the site?), and integration with other living systems (to be discussed in chapter 5). These considerations will become much clearer after even a couple of weeks of actually living on the land.

Bob Easton, writing in *Shelter,* says:

> It would be ideal to camp out on your site for a year and watch the changes before building anything. An alternative would be to build a small shed to the side of your site and live there for a year before deciding what to do next. You could watch the angle of the sun change throughout the year, learn where the winter storms come from, and figure out how to have the morning sun at your breakfast table. You could see how to catch cool breezes in the summer and see the stars at night. Also, you'd have time to meet the neighbors, study their houses, talk to the old folks about elements peculiar to the area: special winds, drainage problems, sources of cheap materials: local wisdom about local problems (Shelter Publications, 1973, p. 40).

Mr. Easton's advice is sound, if you have the frame of mind to take advantage of it. For many, a year in a small shed prior to starting the house might be a bit too austere. We spent eight months in our shed, and although we were sad to leave the first home we'd actually built ourselves, this was more than compensated for by the pleasure of having a few hundred more square feet in which to move around, especially as a North Country winter was about to heap its fury upon us. We know other families whose time spent in the TS was just too long— two years and more, for example—so that the initial high of moving to the land turned to dissatisfaction with the cramped living conditions. And apart from psychological disgruntlement, it is very difficult to maintain a steady temperature in a small structure, unless it is earth-sheltered. The place oscillates from sauna-like to freezer-like conditions, day and night, summer and winter.

Gaining a Useful Outbuilding

The buildings discussed here may be temporary shelters insofar as human habitation is concerned, or they may be incorporated into the final house plans, but they need not be short-lived structures. Give some thought to that seemingly far-distant day when you move to the permanent house and the TS becomes empty. It may have fifty useful years of life left as a garden or wood shed, workshop, playhouse, studio, sauna, guest house, chicken coop, barn, or even root cellar, if built underground. The building's anticipated future use is just as important as its temporary job of providing human shelter, so you should tailor siting considerations and structural details to the long term plan.

Scandinavian immigrants settling in the Midwest during the last century often adopted the strategy of building their sauna first—such were their priorities—and living in it until the house was finished. By the time the house was finished, they were pretty dirty, and it was handy to have a bath ready.

Another common strategy, involving a different set of priorities, is to build the garage first, and live in it until the house is completed. I have heard of one instance where local codes forbade the temporary shelter strategy. The family moved into their owner-built garage and that was okay as long as they did not have a "kitchen," defined by

The temporary shelter.

"permanent cooking facilities." They trotted out a Coleman gas cooker each time they wanted a meal, and that apparently satisfied the building inspector.

TENTS, CAMPERS, VANS, AND TRAILERS

Temporary shelters are not limited to built structures. You can live several months in tents, tepees, vans, and small house trailers while building your permanent dwelling. In fact, Jaki and I lived in a small camping trailer while building our shed, a truly *temporary* TS. In certain circumstances, the time gain and economic advantages of staying in a van or a tent might make this the correct strategy, especially if you already have building experience. Some of the case studies in chapter 7 illustrate variations on this theme. Two of the four benefits of the TS strategy are missing, though, if you don't actually build the shelter: you don't gain the building experience and you don't wind up with a useful outbuilding.

I do not recommend bringing in a full-sized mobile home as a temporary shelter. The cons of such a strategy outweigh the pros. An old mobile home can be a trap in many ways. Before embarking on such a plan, please read Michael Potts' sidebar on mobile homes. The exception is if you are already living in a mobile home on the property where you are planning to build. You've already got your TS and might as well make use of it.

THE SHED

The common shed or one of its variations is the building most often used with the temporary shelter strategy, and it is particularly recommended if you desire a standard framed construction in your final home. We built the 12-by-16-foot gabled shed drawn by Bob Easton in *Shelter*. Easton's drawing was detailed enough to supply us with the information required to build, yet simple enough not to overwhelm us. Figure 4-1 is based upon Easton's original drawing and reproduced here with permission.

We built our shed on six cedar posts set about three feet into the ground. Pressure-treated timbers would last even longer than cedar, although our original shed and posts are still in good condition after twenty-two years. We cut the tops of the posts to the same level and

MOBILE HOMES

From an energy standpoint, it is hard to imagine a more miserable shelter than a mobile home. Using aluminum for lightness (a material that embodies enormous energy because it is refined in electric furnaces from bauxite, and is further cursed with good heat conduction properties), these thin-walled, barely insulated, single-glazed monstrosities are serious warts on the face of our nation. They are independent in the sense that their occupants can, at a whim, pump up the tires, kick out the blocks, and be gone, but they are horribly wasteful. In fact, their impermanence commits the occupants to a life of unwitting disconnection from the land their mobile hovels infest.

To heat or cool a trailer requires roughly triple the energy used by a properly insulated house of equal size, and trailer residents, who invariably pay the energy bills, are condemned to perpetual slavery to the energy mongers because of this inefficiency. In a trying environment, it is practically impossible to operate anything but the smallest mobile home on an alternative energy system, because it takes too much energy to keep them warm or cool. Furthermore, they are firetraps and they are containers for a horrifying collection of toxic vapors.

Evaluated by the [most basic criteria], the mobile home is a mistake from beginning to end. Significantly, elsewhere in the world, not even the most disadvantaged people consider them remotely habitable.

Champions of the mobile home offer the excuse that these may be the only kind of habitation affordable to low-income folks. That's absurd. So much goes into making the damn things mobile that equal energy and equal care put into a stable dwelling would provide a much more functional and beautiful home at much less cost to the environment. It's also important to ask—to what extent have the lax health and safety standards applied to trailers made their existence possible, while similar relaxations have not been applied to solidly constructed low-income housing?

The advice of many who had moved onto undeveloped land and lived in a trailer while building their home is, "Don't waste your time and money." Camp in a tent, and build a guest cabin to weather the first winter in, while you learn about your site first-hand (Michael Potts, *The Independent Home,* Chelsea Green, 1993).

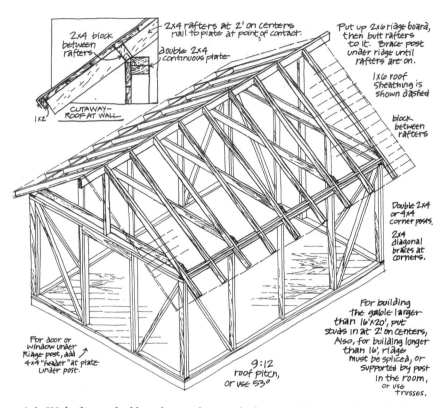

2x4 block between rafters

2x4 rafters at 2' on centers, nail to plate at point of contact.

double 2x4 continuous plate

CUTAWAY—ROOF AT WALL

1x2

Put up 2x6 ridge board, then butt rafters to it. Brace post under ridge until rafters are on.

1x6 roof sheathing is shown dashed

block between rafters

Double 2x4 or 4x4 corner posts.

2x4 diagonal braces at corners.

For building the gable larger than 16'x20', put studs in at 2' on centers, Also, for building longer than 16', ridge must be spliced, or supported by post in the room, or use trusses.

For door or window under Ridge post, add 4x4 "header" at plate under post.

9:12 roof pitch, or use 53°

4-1. We built our shed based upon this simple drawing. (Excerpted from Shelter, *©1973 by Shelter Publications, Inc., PO Box 279, Bolinas, CA 94924. Distributed in bookstores by Random House. Reprinted by permission.)*

installed a 2-by-10-inch girder along each side of the structure. We fastened a 2-by-4-inch nailer alongside the girder, as shown in figure 4-2, to support the 2-by-6-inch floor joists. The thirteen floor joists were placed 16 inches "on center" (16" o.c.), which means that the spacing from the center of one joist to the center of its neighbor is exactly 16 inches. We floored our shed with ½-inch exterior grade (CDX) plywood, so the 16-inch joist spacing worked well with the 48-by-96-inch plywood, and was frequent enough that the floor didn't sag, as it would have done on 24-inch centers. As it was, our floor had a little spring to it, because we used only six posts instead of the nine recommended by Easton. My drawing, figure 4-3, shows the use of nine posts and three girders, a better method than what we actually did in 1975.

Another strong flooring option is 2-by-6-inch tongue-and-groove planking, but it's quite expensive, unless the local sawmill has planer knives that will shape this sort of material. Several people on The Hill, including ourselves, have successfully bought up old wooden silos that were rotting out at the base, but still had lots of good tongue-and-groove planking above ground level. The cost of these recycled silo staves, often spruce or cedar, can be less than a third of comparable new material. And keep the silo hoops! They make excellent reinforcing bars for the footings of the permanent house, saving another hundred dollars or so.

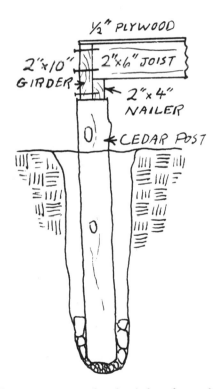

4-2. Set cedar posts (or pressure-treated timbers) three feet in the ground with gravel and jamming stones at their bases. Fasten the girder and nailer together and toenail as a unit to the posts, ready for floor joists. Check all dimensions. The foundation can be checked for square by seeing that the two diagonal measurements are the same. As the 12-by-16-foot dimensions form two sides of a 3–4–5 right triangle, the diagonal measure, conveniently, is exactly 20 feet.

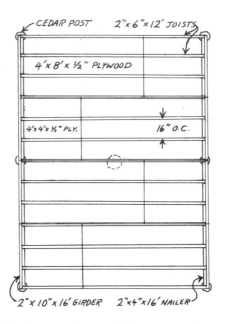

4-3. *The location of the thirteen 2-by-6-inch floor joists is shown, as well as the six sheets of plywood. Two sheets are cut exactly in half for staggered jointing.*

Old Tom, from whom we'd bought our land, showed us how to frame the first wall. He was certainly qualified to teach us, having built ninety houses in one nearby village alone. He also made three sash windows for us, bartered for an old hand-cranked sharpening stone that we'd picked up at an auction for $3. Steve, one of the people who joined in on the land purchase, shared his roof framing experience with us.

Fresh from Scotland and really needing a place to stay in a hurry, we bought finished framing lumber and new plywood, both from a discount yard. Scrounging around for bargains on materials can save a lot of money, but it does take time. On Log End Cottage, we did more scrounging and used a lot more recycled materials. Still, we built the shed in three weeks for $350, which wasn't too bad for beginners, we thought, although Steve or Tom certainly could have accomplished the same in three days.

We successfully employed one unusual innovation on our shed that could save you the price of this book several times over if you use the idea on your own project. Our shed roofing is composed of aluminum offset printing plates, like the ones used to print your local paper. These heavy-gauge plates are used once and thrown away or sold for scrap. Although some papers have started selling them to the public, it's still possible to get them for nothing or next to nothing if you ask around print shops. We left the printed part exposed to the weather, so the roof looks like it is made of newspaper! The plates, nearly 2 feet by 3 feet, go on very quickly, but be sure to use aluminum nails with neoprene or rubber washers. Ordinary galvanized roofing nails will promote leaking, and create the added danger that electrolysis between the different metals will eat away the aluminum around the nails. Nail the plates at frequent enough intervals that the wind won't work them loose, or, better yet, use one-by-two or two-by-two wooden battens to hold the edges down, as we did.

We stapled 15-pound builders' felt (sometimes called *tarpaper* as in "tarpaper shack") on the exterior walls, as a temporary measure to protect the plywood. Later, we applied the cedar slabwood seen in

4-4. This 12-by-16-foot shed, with its cedar slab siding and printing plate roof, was our temporary home for eight months while building Log End Cottage. Later, we added the 8-foot-square greenhouse.

figure 4-4. We were given this slabwood when Steve had his cabin logs cut, but local sawyers still sell it very cheaply and will often "throw it in" if you buy other sawn material from them. By all means, get to know your local sawyer(s). Even the byproducts of lumber milling are valuable. We use sawdust quite extensively in cordwood masonry, for example.

We added the greenhouse two years later. During the winter of 1979–1980, the shed even served as a peaceful office while I wrote a book. The building has proven valuable as a storage shed, garden shed, and greenhouse, and is still in use by the new owners of the property twenty-two years after it was built.

Thoreau's house on Walden Pond, incidentally, was 10 feet wide and 15 feet long, even smaller than our shed. He built it for $28.12½ in 1845. "I thus found that the student who wishes for a shelter can

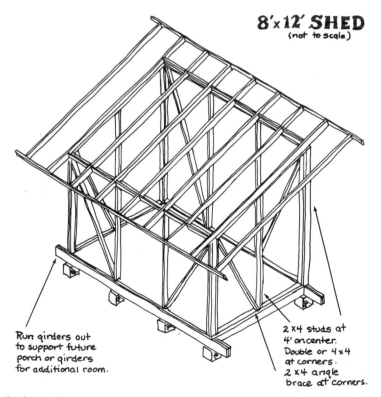

8'x 12' SHED
(not to scale)

Run girders out
to support future
porch or girders
for additional room.

2 x 4 studs at
4' on center.
Double or 4x4
at corners.
2 x 4 angle
brace at corners.

4-5. The frame for an 8-by-12-foot shed. (Excerpted from Shelter, ©1973 by *Shelter Publications, Inc., PO Box 279, Bolinas, CA 94924. Distributed in bookstores by Random House. Reprinted by permission.)*

4-6. Susan Warford Seguin, with the help of her dad, built this 12-by-16-foot A-frame temporary shelter.

obtain one at an expense not greater than the rent which he now pays annually." Students paid $30 a year for a room at Cambridge College at that time. (It is interesting to note that a kit based on Thoreau's cabin design was being offered in 1983 by Roland Wells Robbins, the archaeologist who discovered the Walden homesite just after World War II. Cost? $3,856 plus shipping, fourteen years ago.)

A smaller 8-by-12-foot shed with the traditional single-pitch "shed roof" is shown in figure 4-5. This structure is quick, easy, and cheap to build and would supply adequate temporary shelter for a single person. Six pillars or posts would be plenty for this size of shed.

Susan Warford Seguin felt that the A-frame style would be the easiest for her to tackle (figure 4-6). She and her father built the basic shell of her 12-by-16-foot shed in a week and Susan moved in. As the weather was mild and she did not plan to build the main house for a year or two, Susan took her time "winterizing" the shed. Although the little place was difficult to keep at a steady temperature, Susan did brave one hard winter in the A-frame, after a total outlay of $550, including

4-7. Friends lived in this gambrel-roofed shed while building a log house. The shed, made from a recycled hen house, was returned to its original duty upon completion of the home.

insulation and stove. She bought most of the materials new. The platform for the building is the same size as our shed's, but the immediately receding walls greatly decrease the useful floor area and the practicality of shelves. Still, Susan found the construction to be quick and easy and recommends it as a short-term shelter.

The temporary shelter seen in figure 4-7 is the classic case of a building coming full circle in its function. In 1975, one of the original Hill families bought a chicken coop from a local farmer for $50 and transformed its materials into the barn-shaped structure that became their home for three years while they built a large octagonal log house. Later, their temporary shelter returned to duty as a chicken coop!

THE STUMP HOUSE

A number of years ago, Pat, a North Country native, returned home after several years in Texas. He stayed with a brother in town while building a rather interesting house on The Hill. One day, while working together on a deck for his brother, Pat and I came up with the idea. After digging several holes for the pressure-treated posts, Pat decided that he did not want to repeat this exercise through the roots and stones of his Murtagh Hill property. "Well, then," I suggested, "why not use tree stumps for posts? You can use the rest of the tree for girders and floor joists." I made the suggestion thinking that Pat was really after a low-cost TS to spend a few years in while accumulating the materials for a larger and more permanent home. We decided that if the stumps were barked and treated with creosote, they'd last at least five years. Later we learned that our idea was in no way new, that many Adirondack cabins had been built on stump foundations and lasted for twenty years or more. Pat's lasted twenty.

Pat spent several hours looking over his woodlot for the right clump of trees, and, when he found it—a tightly knit stand of 6- to 8-inch-diameter balsam firs—plotted their location on a scaled diagram. Armed with this information, he worked out the best girder and floor joist system and site orientation, all on paper. The deck and house shape that evolved from this was, of course, irregular, which pleased Pat's artistic temperment.

Pat was beginning to take in a little money as a freelance commercial artist, and, with enough for gas and oil for his chainsaw, he began his Stump House. His schedule allowed him to work three or four days each week on the foundation, cutting trees, barking the logs, barking and treating the stumps, fitting the larger logs as girders connecting the stump posts, and installing a parallel system of floor joists over the girder system. So far, the entire support structure came right from the original clump of balsams, Pat's only expenses being gas, oil, and creosote.

The stump house.

4-8. Pat's preliminary drawing of the Stump House.

For $100, Pat purchased an old, leaning wooden silo from a farmer, which yielded 2,000 board feet of good 2-by-6-inch tongue-and-groove planking. This provided an excellent floor for his house, and, by leaving gaps between planks for rain runoff, a pleasant sitting deck outside the house walls.

At this point, in my view, Pat made a mistake. He abandoned the Temporary Shelter strategy, or, perhaps, decided that he would make the house bigger and more comfortable than is common for a TS. I think he figured he'd be living in the structure for three years or more while he built his real house, and he wanted room enough to be comfortable. In the event, instead of building fresh, he added on to the Stump House, this time by building pillars where he wanted them next to the original structure, and, eventually, tying the two parts together. After living ten years on The Hill, he sold the property to some people from Montreal who were looking for a getaway cabin in the woods. They, in turn, sold it to a young couple who have added on yet again, and are faced now with doing some major foundation work, as the stumps have reached the end of their useful life.

To me, the Stump House story has two important lessons. First, the stump foundation method *does* work. It provides a strong, low-cost foundation framework in the woods, ready for decking. A small TS can be built upon this deck in the woods, perhaps making use of the smaller logs provided by the original trees. Keep in mind that the stumps will last anywhere from five to twenty years, so the advantage of a permanent outbuilding is somewhat diminished.

The second point is so important that I am going to give it its own little section, because it introduces key design principles of the TS strategy.

Comfortable, but Not Too Fancy

No matter what structural form the temporary shelter is to take, make it livable. Not fancy. Not too comfortable. But livable. The temporary shelter should not be so comfortable that the builder never gets around to building the actual house. I have seen this happen more than once.

4-9. *Barked balsam fir stumps support the girder and floor joist system, made from the cut trees. Pat Duniho photograph.*

The dream house, the place that the individual or family really wanted from the outset, is never realized. The family ends up feeling kind of stuck in the TS.

Some discomfort—not misery, which is a different thing altogether, and is generally counterproductive—can be a great motivator. Chapter 7 provides some examples. I see a parallel with making guests comfortable enough that they enjoy a short stay, but not so comfortable that they never want to leave.

The unsuccessful temporary shelter is usually found geometrically between the small sheds already discussed, and a full-sized home. It doesn't know which one it is supposed to be, and neither does the owner. You should know from the start of the TS strategy that the building will provide only temporary living space while you build, and that it will serve some other useful purpose as an outbuilding when its initial use is no longer required. The exception to this is a carefully planned building intended from the outset to be an integral part of the final house design. The strategy now dovetails with the Add-on House strategy discussed in the next chapter. The TS, for example, might be earmarked as the eventual master bedroom. In this case, a stump foundation is not recommended.

Livability

Invariably, owner-builders are obliged to spend a longer waiting time in their TS than they thought they would. I cannot recall a case where this has been otherwise. So, spend an extra day or two to get the place comfortable: extra shelves, a sink with gray water runoff, a good light, and so on. Organize the space carefully to maximize its efficient use.

Sleeping. The sleeping loft is by far the best sleeping system for the TS. Ours was big enough that we could store a lot of stuff up there, too. Most of the people we know who have used the TS strategy have incorporated lofts into their structures, usually accessible by a homemade ladder. Some have used a tent just for sleeping. A regular bed in a TS seems an awful waste of space, but for Pat and Chuck Potter, now building an "Earthship" (rammed tire house) in Ontario, their TS is a tiny one-story, one-roomed cabin that was already on the property and it didn't have a loft. Their bed takes up about a quarter of the space.

Bathroom facilities. Where do people—you know—while they're living in their temporary shelters? Lots of strategies have been employed, some rather dubious that I will not share. Many builders have returned to the old-fashioned outdoor privy approach, and some of these have been very pleasant places in which to contemplate for a while. Jaki and I took this approach while we lived in our shed. When the cold weather came, we discovered that it was a good idea to store the toilet seat indoors next to the wood stove, and to carry it out with us as required.

Another good strategy, if the grubstake allows, is to actually install the well and septic system first, and to hook the TS into the system right off the bat. The key here is to put the septic tank and leachfield in a sensible location with respect to the house site. Septic tanks are normally installed within ten to twenty feet of the house, but if the house drain is a straight run and care is taken to get the slope right, there is no reason why the tank can't be as much as forty feet away. This makes for quite a bit of leeway with regard to connecting more than one building to a septic system. House drains can enter the tank from different sides, too. (But not different ends!)

Our indoor water system consisted of a plastic sink. We'd wash dishes in it, and, positioning it on the floor, ourselves. (And we'd go swimming a lot.) Some people set up a sink with a plug and a downspout leading to a 5-gallon bucket below the countertop. When the bucket is three-quarters full, it is taken outside and the "gray water" spread out on the landscape, or, better, used to water the garden.

Cooking and eating. Jaki and I made great use of a little three-burner propane gas stove, bought for $3. We hauled water from a neighbor's outdoor hand pump 400 feet away. This was no problem, as I am born under the sign of Aquarius, the Water Carrier. A table is a must in the TS, as well as the same number of chairs as inhabitants, no more. On fine days, we liked eating outside, usually on the Log End Cottage construction site, but the table provided a place to eat during inclement weather, as well as a surface upon which to draw plans, read, play games, etc. Countertop is as appreciated in the TS as in a home, maybe more so, since dishes might get done a little less frequently. We used a big old heavy table which we bought at an auction for a couple of bucks. It was solid and just the right height for a countertop, and it has become my workbench at Earthwood.

Storage. Plenty of storage is very important in a TS. Again, buy functional shelves and old cabinets at an auction. They don't have to be pretty. Cheap is nice and often homey. You can make solid shelving from planks and concrete blocks, the same kind that you think you might need later on your house, of course: Nails in the studs—above eye level, please—make great cheap hooks for hanging hats, coats, tools, pans, almost anything.

Food storage. We used a little propane gas refrigerator in the TS, the kind you see in recreational vehicles. In fact, an RV supplier is a good place to find such a refrigerator. New ones are expensive, so reconditioned units are often a good option. We bought it knowing we'd use it later at the Cottage. Dry bulk foods can be stored on shelves. We ate a lot of fresh food while living in the TS, including some we grew ourselves.

Light. Maximize the free and clean natural light provided every day by that big round bright spot up in the sky. Our shed featured a couple of 10-foot-long panels of translucent corrugated fiberglass. I think our TS was the brightest I've ever seen, even in the loft, which would have been quite dark without the long skylight. At night, we used a gas light, an Aladdin kerosene lamp, and, sometimes, candles. Some people who live near commercial power lines have managed to get a temporary hook-up to their property for using power tools during construction, and have been able to have electric lights, refrigerator, etc., right in the TS. If solar electric is in your future, buy one or two PV panels and a charge controller and hook them up to a couple of golf cart batteries. The wonderful thing about photovoltaics is that it is a modular system. You can start small, and, instead of paying monthly electric bills, add to your system with more panels, batteries, an inverter, whatever. And, just as building the TS gives you the practice to build your house, starting with a small and simple PV system teaches you the basics of solar electricity, a valuable education for later on.

For the benefit of my loyal readers and students interested in cordwood masonry and underground housing, the alternative building techniques in which we specialize at Earthwood Building School, I conclude this chapter with TS strategies involving these methods.

CORDWOOD MASONRY
IN A TEMPORARY SHELTER

Cordwood masonry construction, in which short logs are laid up widthwise in a wall like a rank of firewood, offers excellent opportunities for a low-cost TS. In *The Sauna* (Chelsea Green, 1997), I describe the construction of a post-and-beam cordwood masonry sauna with outside wall dimensions of roughly 10 feet by 15 feet. The original structure cost us about $600 in materials in 1978, of which $125 was for the stove and insulated stovepipe, and $50 was for reusable footing forms. It was never used as a TS, as were many saunas built by Finns in the upper Midwest during the nineteenth century, but it could have been. More recently, we built a guesthouse at Earthwood, following the same general plan as the sauna, and it serves very well as accommodation. It cost about $900, but does not have a stove. Full construction details for both of these buildings, as well as some circular designs, appear in *The Sauna*. Just think, when your house is Finnished, your sauna will be ready.

The Guest House is only used for a few days at a time. For a TS that will be used for several months, I'd suggest increasing the dimensions to the 12-by-16-foot size, which we used on our shed, because considerable floor area is lost in the cordwood walls themselves. This slight increase in dimensions actually adds 33 percent to the useful floor area. Later, the sauna will be proportionally bigger, too, giving more room to the saunees. Incidentally, the sauna took about 250 person-hours to build, a little longer, perhaps, than a simple framed structure of similar size, but it's built like a small fortress and should last a century or more. And if cordwood masonry is the intended building method for the house, you get invaluable practice on the little building. Maybe you'll find that cordwood is for you. Maybe not. Better to find out now.

For house construction, cordwood should be seasoned before use, the length of time depending on the species of wood. But if the temporary shelter's ultimate purpose will be unhampered by slightly drafty walls—a garden shed, wood shed, or small barn, for example—there's no reason why a building of green log-ends will not suffice as human

4-10. The Earthwood Guesthouse, built in 1996, is a slight modification of the Log End Sauna design. It is open-planned inside, but is easily converted to a sauna after it has served as a temporary shelter. Just build an internal cordwood wall, separating the stoveroom at the rear from the changing/relaxation room at the front.

shelter for a few months, even a year or two. How to build a cordwood house is the subject of my earlier book, *Complete Book of Cordwood Masonry Housebuilding* (Sterling, 1992), listed in appendix 3.

FROST PROTECTION

If you want the TS to last more than a few years in northern climates, where frost heaving is a potential problem, the foundation is extremely important, especially for masonry construction. Our sauna is built on a floating footing or "ring beam," but it could just as easily have been built on a floating slab. (See figures 4-11 and 4-12.) Some terminology needs to be clarified here. *Floating* means that the entire foundation floats or moves as a single entity on the compacted pad upon which it is built. If the foundation settles, it settles equally. The *pad* is different from the *slab*. The slab is made of reinforced concrete. The pad is composed of layers, called *runs*, of good percolating material, such as coarse sand, gravel, or crushed stone. A ring beam is a closed ring of

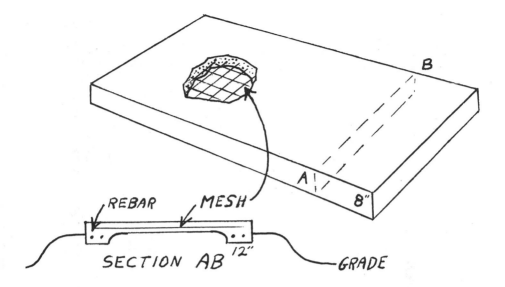

4-11. The floating slab can be made in one pour. The radius curve between footing and floor decreases the likelihood of shear cracking around the edge of the floor portion. The floor is four inches thick.

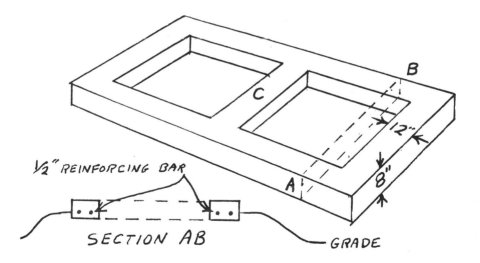

4-12. The floating ring beam foundation. The grade beam "C" is necessary only for load-bearing walls. The reinforcing bar—often called rebar—should be placed approximately three inches from the sides and bottom of the footing.

foundation footings, as in figure 4-12. Finally, in the same drawing, the letter "C" indicates an internal footing for a load-bearing wall. This is called a grade beam.

There will be a quiz.

In either case, the foundation must be poured on a pad of percolating material, such as coarse sand or gravel. Organic material and topsoil are first scraped to the edge of the site. The pad is built up about 18 inches above the undisturbed subsoil. All parts of the foundation should have at least a foot of compacted sand or gravel below. The pad thus created does not retain moisture, so the building is protected from frost heaving. No moisture, no freezing. No freezing, no heaving. At our sauna, I ran a piece of 4-inch perforated drain tile through the center of the sand pad and away to a dry well (or "soakaway") filled with stones. (Note: Since it is possible for a soakaway to freeze, an even better plan, if topography allows, is to run the 4-inch perforated drain tile out above grade and to cover the opening with a rodent proof screen, such as ¼-inch mesh hardware cloth.) This drain is further protection against water build-up below the structure and doubles as a shower drain in the sauna's stoveroom. The floating foundation is discussed in greater detail in *Complete Book of Cordwood Masonry Housebuilding*.

THE TEMPORARY EARTH-SHELTER

Underground housing should, perhaps, be more accurately called "earth-sheltering," as very few houses are truly built totally below grade. The advantages of earth-sheltering are compelling. The homes are energy efficient, require less maintenance than other homes, and have the potential to harmonize with the environment better than surface dwellings. I must qualify this last point, about aesthetics. Every house is an imposition upon nature to some degree. The earth-sheltered house, when done correctly, can minimize the impact.

Novice builders often assume that the technologies involved with earth-sheltering must be very complicated. They hear talk of prestressed concrete beams and exotic waterproofing techniques and, whoa, they're off to the woods with their "How to Build a Log Cabin" manual. Instead, they ought to consider the temporary earth-shelter, gaining familiarity with the various products and techniques involved.

If the small structure leaks, it's not the end of the world, and the builder will have a pretty good idea of what the problem is and how it can be corrected in the house. In the pages that follow, I offer plans for a simple earth-sheltered cabin of 125 usable square feet, utilizing the same surface-bonded block wall technique and plank-and-beam roof that we employed successfully at Log End Cave. The plans are intended to supplement the material in my book, *The Complete Book of Underground Houses: How to Build a Low-Cost Home* (Sterling, 1994), which is beyond the scope of the book you're reading now (see appendix 3). The step-by-step drawings that follow, however, do not appear in *Underground Houses*.

In addition to all the normal uses for the temporary shelter when the main house is finished, the temporary earth-shelter, with slight modifications, could be used as a root cellar, bomb shelter, or, again, a very effective sauna. In fact, the earliest saunas probably were underground, and a few of these still survive in Finland today. Figure 4-30, at the end of the chapter, offers a suggested floor plan for a large sauna, based upon the temporary earth-shelter plans that follow.

This temporary earth-shelter would cost about $1,700 to build at this writing, $300 more if the entire structure is wrapped with an inch of Dow Styrofoam™ insulation. The Styrofoam™ would only be necessary if the building is to be used for human habitation during a northern winter, or if conversion to a sauna is desired. Think about this prior to construction; it is virtually impossible to retrofit an earth-sheltered structure with insulation, since it is properly placed on the outside of the waterproof membrane and under the floor. As a sauna, it may be necessary to sheathe the inside walls with an inch of unfinished wood. Otherwise, it might take a long time to bring the air temperature up to the required heat.

The rough plans for the temporary earth-shelter conclude this chapter. For construction details and a full discussion of the techniques involved, see *The Complete Book of Underground Houses*. To get an idea of where these plans are heading, you might like to jump ahead and have a quick look at figure 4-29. Architecturally, the building will look a lot like our own Log End Cave, shown in chapter 6. The site is a south-facing slope, just ideal for this kind of building, at least in northern climes. In the Deep South, where cooling is the main energy consideration, you might actually look for a north-facing slope.

FIRST WEEK

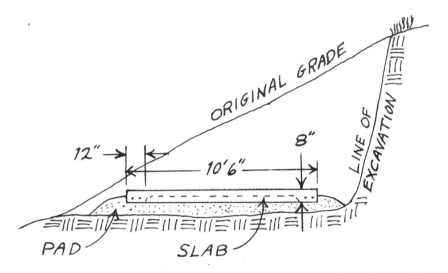

4-13. SIDE SECTION. *This page and those that follow document the week-to-week process of building an earth-sheltered TS. Above, a side section view of the first week's work: excavation, footing, and floor.*

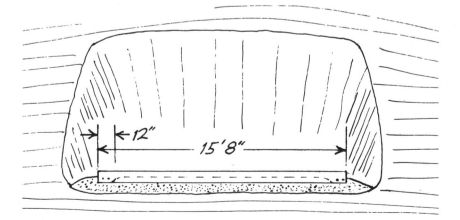

4-14. FRONT VIEW. *A front view of the excavation and slab.*

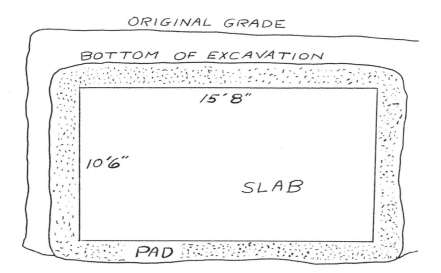

4-15. PLAN. *Plan or bird's eye view. Allow at least two feet of space to work around the wall. The footing and floor can be poured separately or together (see figures 4-13 and 4-14).*

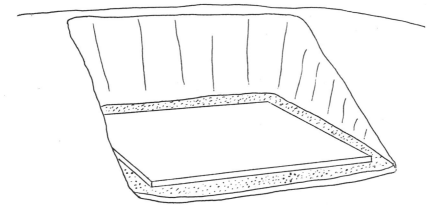

4-16. PERSPECTIVE. *A tamped earth floor with a sheet of six-mil polyethylene and a used carpet upon it is another option, recommended by Mike Oehler, author of* The $50 and Up Underground House Book *(Mole Publishing, Bonner's Ferry, Idaho, 1992). Perhaps a good inexpensive option for the temporary earth-shelter.*

SECOND WEEK

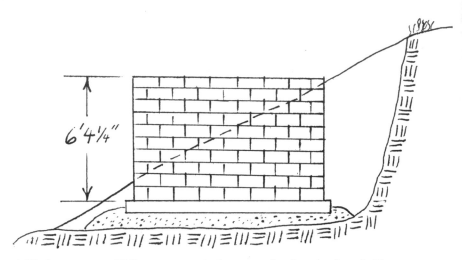

4-17. Side section. *Wall construction is the project for the second week. The east, north, and west walls are stacked without mortar in preparation for surface bonding. The first course only is set in mortar to establish level.*

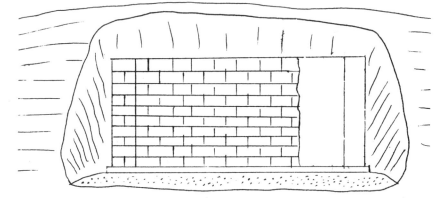

4-18. Front view. *Surface bonding is the application of a ⅛-inch membrane of cement and fiberglass to concrete blocks, 8-inch blocks in this case. Against lateral pressure, surface-bonded concrete-block walls are at least twice as strong as conventionally mortared walls. After the bonding mixture has cured, it becomes a good base for the application of a waterproofing membrane.*

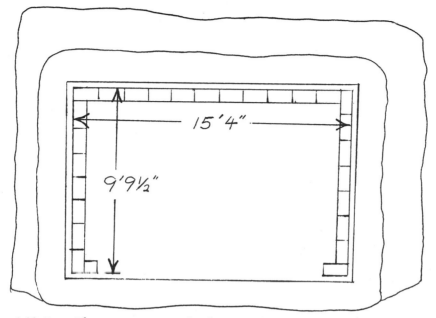

4-19. PLAN. *The measurements in this diagram take into account the fact that concrete blocks are actually 15⅝ inches long, not a true 16 inches. The ⅜-inch difference allows for the mortar joint used with conventional block construction.*

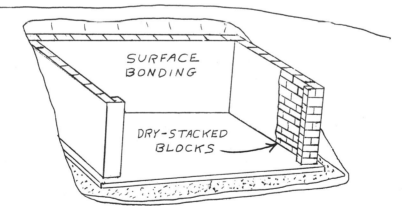

4-20. PERSPECTIVE. *Made by several companies, including Surewall, Conproco, Quikrete and others, surface-bonding cement comes dry-mixed in 50-pound bags. Water is added and the mix is prepared according to instructions on the bag. The dry-stacked blocks are soaked prior to application of the mix. The cement is applied with a plasterer's flat trowel.*

THIRD WEEK

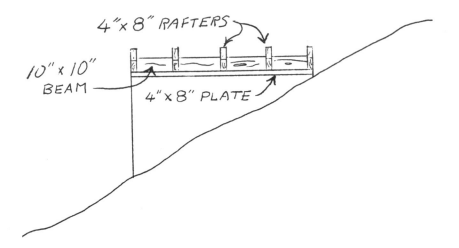

4-21. *Side section. Framing and planking the roof are the projects for the third week. First, the 4-by-8-inch wall plates are fastened to the block wall with anchor bolts.*

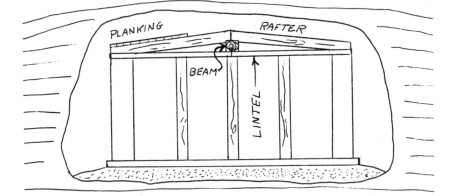

4-22. *Front view. The three temporarily braced posts on the non-earth-sheltered side are the same height as the block wall and are 8 inches square in cross-section. Old barn beams of similar dimensions are suitable, if they have suffered no deterioration.*

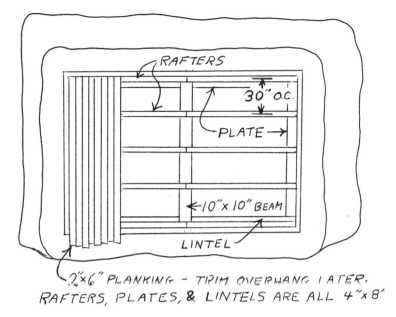

RAFTERS

30" O.C.

←PLATE→

←10"x 10" BEAM

LINTEL

2"x 6" PLANKING - TRIM OVERHANG LATER.
RAFTERS, PLATES, & LINTELS ARE ALL 4"x 8'

4-23. PLAN. *Now is the time to install the two 4-by-8-inch window and door lintels, which abut each other over the center post. A single 10-by-10-inch girder (10 feet, 9 inches in length) spans from the center of the north wall to the center of the south wall, over the middle post. If a strong hardwood girder is used, such as oak or ash, an 8-by-8 will suffice. Otherwise, the girder can be built up of four 2-by-10-inch planks.*

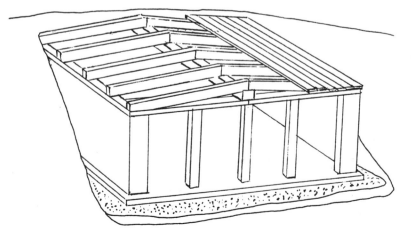

4-24. PERSPECTIVE. *Roof framing consists of ten 4-by-8-inch rafters. Planking is 2-by-6-inch material.*

FOURTH WEEK

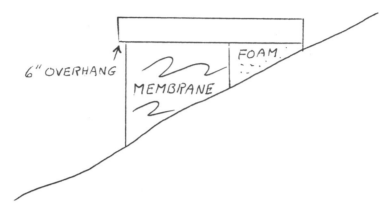

4-25. SIDE SECTION. *The TS is closed in during the fourth week. Apply the waterproofing membrane to the surface-bonded block walls and the roof planking. Waterproofing options are discussed in detail in chapter 9 of the* Complete Book of Underground Houses. *Next, apply an inch or two of extruded polystyrene over the membrane, depending on climate and whether or not the building will be heated during the winter. In southern climes, an inch of extruded on the roof is enough.*

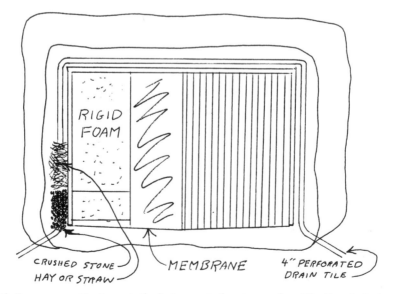

4-26. FRONT VIEW. *Drainage is the better part of waterproofing. The French drains consist of 4-inch perforated drain pipe set in crushed stone and covered with a hay or straw filtration layer.*

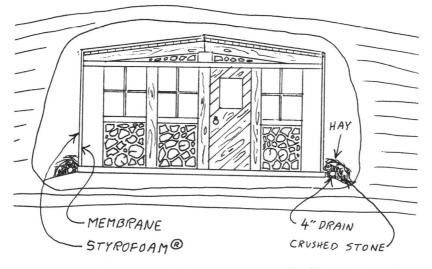

MEMBRANE

STYROFOAM®

HAY

4" DRAIN

CRUSHED STONE

4-27. PLAN. *Install windows and doors. Almost any wall infilling can be used between posts on the south wall and north gable, such as bricks, boards, straw bales, adobe, stone, and so on.*

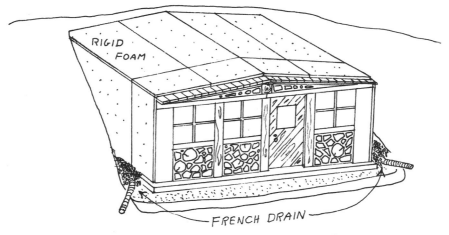

RIGID FOAM

FRENCH DRAIN

4-28. PERSPECTIVE. *This illustration shows cordwood masonry infilling, which is what we used for our second house, Log End Cave. Note: For a long-lasting building, a drainage layer (not shown) is now installed. It consists of a layer of 6-mil black polyethylene laid over the rigid foam, followed by 2 inches of crushed stone, and a layer of 2 to 3 inches of loose straw, which will eventually be compressed under the earth load and form a natural filtration mat, keeping the drainage layer clean. Rain percolates through the soil and is carried away quickly to the edge of the building by this drainage layer, taking most of the pressure off of the waterproofing membrane.*

FIFTH WEEK

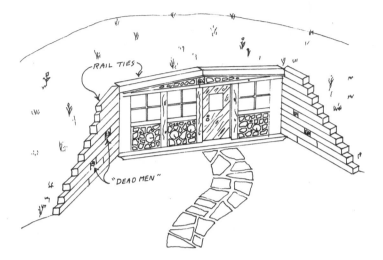

4-29. PERSPECTIVE. *Backfilling and landscaping occupy the fifth week. Old railroad ties or pressure-treated landscaping timbers can be used here to retain earth on the south side. The north "gable" is completely earth-covered. You can build retaining walls of stone, blocks, rail ties, or pressure-treated landscaping timbers. The "dead men" are timbers set perpendicular into the bank to help resist lateral pressure on walls. If soil has poor percolation characteristics, such as clay, a percolating backfill of coarse sand or gravel should be brought to the site. To prevent hydrostatic and frost pressures, insure good drainage behind retaining walls as well as behind the walls of the building. The roof supports an 8-inch earth load and a 50-pound snow load, if red pine or equivalent is used for the rafters and girder.*

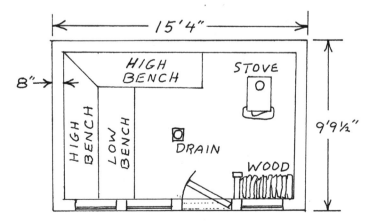

4-30. FLOOR PLAN. *The temporary earth shelter can be converted to a sauna after the home is completed. Here is one possible floor plan. It may be necessary to line the inside walls with planking to bring the temperature up to 160° Fahrenheit easily.*

#
5

The Low-Cost Home

There is some of the same fitness in a man's building his own house that there is in a bird's building its own nest. Who knows but if men constructed their dwellings with their own hands, and provided food for themselves and their families simply and honestly enough, the poetic faculty would be universally developed, as birds universally sing when they are so engaged.

—HENRY DAVID THOREAU, WALDEN

The more expensive the home is to construct, the more difficult it will be to own it yourself mortgage-free. "Well, duh!" my twelve-year-old, Darin, would say. But despite this most obvious piece of fiscal wisdom, it is amazing how many people trap themselves into a lifetime of economic servitude at the earliest stages of their project, by designing a home that they can't truly afford. There are many reasons for taking the expensive route—peer pressure, over-reaction to current crowded living conditions, greed, simply not knowing any better—but none of the "reasons" will keep you from the roster of wage-slaves. In this chapter, we're going to talk about affordable housing. We'll start right at the beginning, even before design.

RESEARCH

Building your own low-cost home involves the integration of many strategies, but, just as a house requires a strong foundation, building plans require the strong foundation of advance research. If you already have your land and know what kind of house you want to build, your job is much easier. Using the subject index at a good library, you can find out what has been written on the required building techniques for your design choice. Many libraries today have computerized subject indices. Often, a research assistant can head you in the right direction if you are unfamiliar with the library's system. The *Reader's Guide to Periodical Literature* will put you in touch with current and not-so-current magazine articles about the subject. Magazines with regular articles on building are listed in appendix 3. Bookstores, both for new and used books, often have a section devoted to building, although sometimes this section is intermingled with a more generalized do-it-yourself department. You will probably want to own any books that are important to the particular house you want to build. The library won't want them back after they've been on the construction site for six months.

A reference work on building should be clear, precise, and well illustrated. Good illustrations are often worth more than the accompanying text. Figure 4-1 is an excellent example. A drawing from the book *Shelter*, this illustration is really good enough to build from. As a technical writer, I would require several thousand words to explain the construction of this simple shed, but the illustration does the job more easily.

Research your subject on the Internet. It's incredible what's out there.

Videos can actually show you how to do things. Everything from plumbing to roofing to drywall to cordwood masonry can be found on video. This type of video is sometimes available at the library, and can also be found at many building supply stores.

Research should not be limited to reading. Observing, helping, and talking with experienced builders are all valuable methods of learning. In fact, book knowledge alone is rarely sufficient preparation, as books cannot adequately impart the human side of construction. Fine, but what if you're new to an area, and don't know any builders? Drive up and down country roads and keep your eyes open for signs of building activity. Very likely, there are others in your area starting out on the same adventure. Or perhaps you know of or notice a local farmer who's adding a shed or barn extension. Don't be shy. You're their new neighbor, and here's a way to make the acquaintance. Usually, folks will be

I don't say it enough in this book, but home-building can be fun! Especially if you build a house of straw, like Ki and Judith Light (chapter 7).

glad to accept a helping hand, especially if you are pursuing a common goal. You're doing each other a good turn. It is true that some farmers are too independent to allow a stranger to help, but they might not object to your stopping by every few days to take note of the progress and construction techniques. And they might allow you to study the construction of some of the older buildings on the farm.

Another possibility for gaining experience is to take a job as a laborer on a construction crew.

Seminars, workshops, conferences, and building schools are all excellent sources of useful knowledge. They cost money, but almost invariably they are worth more than the investment. The flow of information and ideas is very intense. Appendix 2 provides a list of American building schools.

WHAT KIND OF HOUSE?

People ask me, "What's the best kind of house to build?" and I'm sure that they expect me to say either cordwood masonry or underground, because of my special interests in these fields. They really want to see which of the two I will name. My reply is always this: There's no universal answer to your question. The right construction method for me is not necessarily right for you. You can build excellent houses of stone, timber framing, logs, straw bales, even earth. Use indigenous and recycled materials. Satisfy your own sense of comfort and aesthetics. Unless you've got lots of ability or lots of money, or both, keep it small and simple.

Often this answer is unsatisfactory. "No, no, I mean, which is better, cordwood or underground?" they persist.

I won't let them pin me down. I tell them that cordwood masonry is the cheapest way of building a house in this area (northern New York), but it's not without its problems—finding good cordwood, for example. As for underground, I wouldn't live in anything other than an earth-sheltered home. This does not restrict the builder to any particular construction technique, however. Poured walls, surface-bonded block, even stone masonry are all viable underground modes. The roof surface can be earth or something more conventional. Finally, I tell them that many of our students combine earth-sheltering with cordwood masonry, as we have done ourselves at Earthwood.

PLANNING

In their enthusiasm, people often begin planning their house—usually floor plans—before doing the research outlined above. And they almost always plan their houses before they've even bought their land. I advise against both of these approaches, although my advice on this will probably be ignored. Jaki and I were guilty of both mistakes ourselves twenty-three years ago, but we've learned since.

Prior to actual house design, you must have an idea of the building technique that you intend to employ: stick-framed, straw, stone, cordwood, whatever. This choice most often will be a personal value judgment based on the aesthetic, practical, and economic considerations of the techniques appropriate to the area. Prior research into the cost and availability of materials can help you avoid dead ends and disappointments later on. This is one of the reasons why the site is so important to planning. There may be materials right on hand.

As population increases and suitable building land and natural resources decrease, the choice of building style has got to be balanced with the environmental impact. Minimize energy-intensive manufactured materials. (They're energy-intensive to transport, too, and trucking is easily the worst offender among common transportation choices.) Avoid poisons and unnecessary chemicals. Keep the shape small and compact. (I discuss these points in detail a few pages hence.) Take stock of available indigenous and recycled materials, and knit their use into your design. Design the home for minimal fuel consumption; in this regard, several suggestions discussed later in this chapter could save you hundreds or even thousands of dollars each year, while you do a kindness to Spaceship Earth and your fellow passengers.

You might be a young couple with a romantic vision of a little log cabin in the woods, for example, and you plan accordingly. Then you find that the only wooded land that you can afford has softwoods averaging only six inches in diameter. The two possibilities here are (1) building a cabin with insufficient wall thickness to keep you warm or (2) you end up buying a pre-cut kit or logs from another lot to satisfy your romantic vision. In the former case, the energy cost may prove to be unacceptable, even though the romance might keep you warm for a while. In the latter case, the dollar cost of the home takes a big jump and most of the economic advantage is lost, particularly the potential that derives from the use of one's own indigenous materials. Of course, you could always switch to cordwood . . .

Sometimes the strong desire for a particular type of home can influence the land search by narrowing the pool of pertinent properties; still, the results can be well worth it if good use is made of the property's natural resources. Lovers of stone houses can really do well in this instance, as stony land is usually priced lower than nonstony land.

Another example of too-early planning often occurs with underground housing. Every kind of house has its limitations, and the primary limitation of earth-roofed houses is that large, internal spaces are extremely expensive due to the structural cost of supporting tremendous roof loads on long spans. People whose limited knowledge of earth-sheltering is that it contributes to energy efficiency will come to me with plans including an 18-by-24-foot living room, and the intention of placing three feet of earth on the structure. I tell them, "Well, if you cut your earth load down to six or eight inches, the minimum necessary to maintain the green cover, and put a stout post in the center, you could have a room of this size at reasonable cost."

"Oh, but we can't possibly have a post in the middle of the room! And we know it can be engineered, because we just saw it in *Better Homes and Gardens*."

"The calculations are not that difficult," I say. "But the elimination of that single post and the use of thirty inches of superfluous earth on the roof will double, and possibly triple, the cost of your home."

Long faces usually result from this expostulation. They (the long faces) can be avoided if the building style is researched and the building plans are tailored to the structure and not the structure to the floor plans. (See the sidebar on page 158 for more on earth roofs.)

A similar kind of mistake is made by people who design their house, then find their land, then set out to tailor the site to the house plans. This is a violent course of action. The more gentle, harmonious, and ecological strategy is to shape the house plans to the site. Western architects and builders can learn from their Oriental counterparts here, and also from the examples of folk architecture down through the ages.

In Support of the Earth Roof

Houses do not absolutely have to have earth roofs, even earth-sheltered houses, but the advantages are compelling and worth illuminating.

1. *Energy efficiency.* While earth is not a particularly good insulator, the vegetation does provide extra R-value, and holds the snow better than any other kind of roof. Light fluffy snow is worth R-1 per inch, so a fresh two-foot snowstorm can add a free R-24 to your roof insulation, like manna from heaven.

2. *Aesthetics.* Of all shelter designs, an earth-sheltered house has the greatest potential to minimize the visual impact of housing on nature. It would be a shame to fall just a few inches short of the goal line with a conventional roof.

3. *Cooling.* An earth roof stores moisture. The evaporation of this moisture on a hot day keeps the house cool, thanks to a phenomenon called, appropriately, "evaporative cooling." Try this experiment: put a cool six-pack of beer in an empty bucket. Drape the open top of the bucket with a wet towel. The evaporation of the water will keep the beer cool . . . until the towel dries out.

4. *Ecological harmony.* Here's the choice: One, a black lifeless moonscape of asphalt shingles; or, two, green oxygenating habitat for billions and billions of tiny little life forms.

5. *Longevity.* Build it properly and forget it. In a properly built earth roof, both the soil and the insulation are on the top side of the waterproofing membrane, protecting it from the two things that break down almost every other roof: the sun's ultraviolet rays and constant freeze-thaw cycling in the winter.

6. *Drainage.* On an earth roof, drainage is slow and natural. During an Arkansas frog strangler, other roofs need systems to deal with thousands of gallons of water in very short order.

7. *Protection.* What kind? All kinds: sounds, tornados, fire, radiation, U-2 spy planes . . .

If Malcolm Wells had his way, all new construction would have to go underground: houses, industry, parking lots, even bridges. I'm not kidding. To give you an idea of how this guy thinks, he's the same one who drew all the funny little cartoons in this book.

BASIC PLANNING PRINCIPLES

Okay, assuming that you have made the proper investigation into the chosen building style and you own the building lot (and it is in harmony with your chosen building style), truly beneficial planning can commence. There are four important guidelines that the first-time owner-builder should keep in mind throughout the planning stage.

1. Keep it small.
2. Keep it simple.
3. Tailor the floor plans to the structural considerations and the available materials, not the other way around.
4. Consider all the living systems at the design stage, not just the shelter requirement.

Keep It Small

It's kind of interesting, as well as instructive, to examine how the size of a new one-family house has changed over the past thirty years. The figures below are in square feet.

Year	1970	1980	1990	1995
Average Size	1,500	1,740	2,080	2,095
Median Size	1,385	1,595	1,905	1,920

Some banks are reluctant to loan money on "small homes" (less than 1,500 square feet), fearing a low resale value. Although this won't affect the mortgage-free home builder, it's amazing how often the "resale value" enters the decision-making process of owner-builders, as well. Sometimes, they are dissuaded against anything slightly unconventional by well-meaning relatives or friends who warn them that they'll never be able to sell a particular kind of house.

When people start harping on "resale value," I can't help thinking of my friend, Russ, who found himself on a beach in Morocco without shelter. He gathered together some sticks, stones, and banana fronds; set up a tentlike framework of the sticks; roofed the structure with the fronds; and covered the whole thing with a sheet of plastic, for which he'd paid $2. The stones kept the plastic from blowing away, and Russ bermed the little house with sand (to the extent that the framework would allow) in order to take advantage of the "coolth" below the hot beach surface.

After living in comfort in his $2 earth shelter for a month, Russ decided that it was time to move on. Wishing to leave the environment in the same condition as he'd found it, he decided to dismantle the structure. A fellow beach dweller, who did not have a place of his own, said, "Don't knock it down. I'll buy it from you." Russ sold the shelter for $6, a 200 percent appreciation in a month. Not wanting to take advantage of the buyer, Russ threw in a frying pan for good measure!

Sweat equity adds value to materials. Even if the palm frond shelter doesn't have the resale value of a fancier place a mile down the beach, it's worth a lot more than it cost to build. And, as it is owned by the builder, and not by a bank, all of the proceeds from the sale go to the right person. People ask me about the resale value of cordwood homes. It is true that there is not a lot of resale history on these types of homes, but I've yet to hear of an owner-builder actually losing money on a cordwood home. We sold Log End Homestead (both houses) with twenty-four acres for about $43,000 a few years ago, a bargain for the buyers. It was not an easy place to sell, not because of the building styles, but for two other reasons. First, not many people could see any reason to have two houses. (The layout of the houses on the lot was not conducive to selling them separately.) And, second, there aren't many people with the imagination to live unplugged from commercial power, maybe one or two percent of American homebuyers. Nevertheless, we didn't lose money on the sale, and while our hourly "wage" while working on the two houses turned out to be well below minimum wage, it was all "profit" when the sale was finally completed.

Over three hundred years ago, Thomas Fuller said, "Better one's house be too little one day than too big all the years after" (as quoted in *Shelter II*, ed. Lloyd Kahn, Shelter Publications, 1978, p. 74). This is still true today. But building small just for the sake of building small serves no purpose, either. A family's space requirements fluctuate. Young couples with a low budget can live comfortably in a small house which would not be suited to a family with three teenaged children. A small house can be expanded as need dictates and personal economy allows.

Although economics is the obvious reason for building small, it is not necessarily the most important one. The important reason for building small is to get the thing completed! Inexperienced builders, even those with plenty of money, should not tackle a house larger than about 1,000 square feet. There is a very real danger that the place will never get finished. I have seen couples break up over incompleted houses, and an overambitious project is one of the major causes of an incompleted house.

There is, of course, another obvious reason for building small. The ongoing life-cycle costs of the home will be correspondingly lower in a small house. Given similar construction, the small house will be proportionately easier and cheaper to heat compared to the large one. Similarly, the smaller home will require less maintenance. And property taxes will be less. All this adds up to a significant impact on the yearly operating costs of the home.

There are lots of reasons why people think they need to have a big house, aside from bank propaganda and outmoded zoning regulations. Two of the more prominent I call "the overreaction syndrome" and "bedroom mania."

The overreaction syndrome. Jack and Jill have been cooped up in their little apartment or house trailer for so long that all they can think is, "When we build our house, there's gonna be plenty of space!" They've got lots of time to plan; paper and pencils are cheap. They finally get started on their 3,000-square-foot masterpiece. The possibilities from there, in descending order of probability, are: (1) At first they have great enthusiasm. After about six months, money, energy, and patience run low, then run out. Jack and Jill split up. (2) After a while, Jack and Jill perceive that they've really bitten off too much. They move into one-third of the place. "Someday we'll finish the rest," they say. (3) They pull it off, as planned. I have heard rumor of this, but have yet to witness it first hand.

They moved into a third of the house.

Bedroom mania. The functions of a bedroom are to supply a peaceful venue for horizontal resting of the body and to supply storage, generally for clothes. Other uses you may think of generally don't require any more space than for sleeping. The bedrooms in most American homes could be divided in two and each would still serve the purpose. Sure, lots of other considerations come into the planning: building codes again; an adjustment, perhaps, of the individual value system; planning a small bedroom to accommodate furniture. One thing is certain: the larger the bedroom (or house, for that matter), the more unnecessary "stuff" one accumulates.

As for number of bedrooms, this is largely a function of individual thinking. Americans seem particularly concerned with the issue of privacy. Every kid has got to have his or her own bedroom and then we throw in one extra for the pot: the ubiquitous "guest room." In the reality of most family situations, the guest rooms are used less than 10 percent of the time. The living room of our house has a convertible sofa, so the room functions nicely as a guest room, too. A side benefit of this strategy is that guests are less likely to overstay their welcome than if conditions are made just too comfortable.

I realize that the above views are highly personal, but it is my intent to show that there are many trade-offs when it comes to building a mortgage-free home. As children get older, and the need for privacy becomes more genuine, you can build an addition to meet the changing circumstances, and it is likely that your family will be better able to afford this extra space a few years down the road.

The Add-on House Strategy

One of the most popular and successful strategies open to you is to build a small, affordable core—typically in the 500- to 700-square-foot range—and then to build affordable additions as they become truly necessary. Several of our neighbors on The Hill have employed this strategy successfully.

Sometimes the temporary shelter will serve as the core for the completed house, either by plan, or by evolution. However, get one part of the house completely finished before moving on to the next part. Living in a house under construction puts tremendous strain on a relationship. If you can retreat to a clean and uncluttered living area, this "refuge" may prove invaluable on all living fronts.

There are two schools of thought with regard to add-on houses. One is to have some specific expansion plan in mind at the initial design stage. The other says to let the house grow organically as such needs arise. My observation is that both plans will work, and, therefore, you should tailor your strategy to your personality. If you have an organized, analytical mind you may be happier knowing that you're working toward some specific end or goal, while a more spontaneous individual might feel cramped by such a plan, preferring creative freedom throughout. My own approach is a kind of hybrid of these two ideas. I allow myself to be locked into certain structural requirements, largely because I lean toward the use of massive timber framing, cordwood masonry, and heavy earth roofs, but I give my spontaneous creativity its outlet by using special design features within the structural framework. Rather than feeling restricted, the use of stone and wood masonry gives me the freedom to create special textures, alcoves, and designs.

Although I have not used the add-on strategy myself, I offer one strong caution, and it may be that my not using the strategy is a direct result of not having been so cautioned myself. All four houses that Jaki and I have built would be quite difficult to add on to, both structurally and aesthetically. They were all designed to be complete in themselves, and, therefore, no thought was given to expansion potential. When Log End Cottage became too small, thanks to a small new member to the family, we had two choices: attempt a difficult addition, or build a

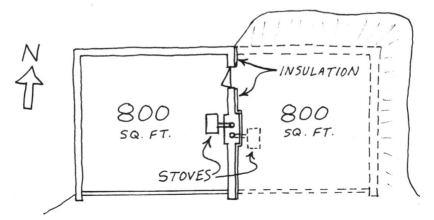

5-1. Add-on strategy for an earth-sheltered home.

new house. Our decision was influenced by other factors, especially a desire to greatly reduce our firewood requirements and my new interest in earth sheltering. We decided on the new house option. Not always one to learn from my first mistakes, I went and designed Log End Cave—also without expansion potential. In fact, the Cave was even more locked in to its size and shape than the Cottage! While it is true that the Cave's 910 square feet of useful living area is quite sufficient for a young family of three or four, it is a little disappointing to know that this size is pretty much what one is stuck with. Small is beautiful, yes, but have a care for the future.

If you're planning an earth-shelter, be aware that, unless expansion is specifically addressed at the design stage, it is very difficult to add on to an underground house.

A young couple with several small children visited us to discuss earth-sheltered housing. They insisted that they absolutely *had* to have 1,600 square feet of living area, minimum. The trouble was that they could only afford 800 square feet. I advised them—I always give better advice than I take—to build the 800 square feet that they could afford, leaving the east wall of concrete block externally insulated, but not backfilled. Since they were both making good money as truck drivers, they could afford to complete the other 800-square-foot module two or three years down the road. This could be accomplished by reusing the rigid foam insulation (possible if it is protected from the sun's ultraviolet rays) and utilizing the internal masonry wall as a thermal flywheel and effective noise buffer between one side of the house and the other. The result: an energy-efficient, debt-free home. The trade-off: two or three years of less than the desired living space.

I have heard of people using the add-on strategy to get around building permit problems. In New York, for example, any house over 1,500 square feet requires an architect or engineer to stamp the plans that are a part of the permit application. Here, building the house in increments can save a lot of money in professional fees. I've also heard of municipalities that have come up with creative ways to discourage or even prohibit the add-on strategy, so be wary. Sometimes zoning regulations will stipulate a minimum house size, maybe 2,000 square feet or more in posh neighborhoods, in order to "protect the property values in the neighborhood." The reader will have a pretty good idea by now of how I feel about such regulations. Taxes are based on valuations, and valuations are based on square footage first and foremost. So such regulations could be seen as rather self-serving on the part of the municipality.

Keep It Simple

This second planning guideline for sound and economical construction should not be confused with the first, "Keep it Small." A small house can be hopelessly complex, and a large house can be wonderfully simple. The next few pages deal with some of the considerations pertinent to simplicity of construction.

Keep to one style. There is a style of house, or a building technique, which suits your personality and pocketbook better than others; once you have found it, stick with it. If two house shapes are to be joined in some way, either by design or by an addition later on, let there be some unifying force to the architecture, for example, a consistency in choice of roof or wall materials. A hodge-podge house always looks like a hodge-podge house.

Avoid difficult lines. If you think they are tough to draw, wait until you try to build 'em! Sticking to simple lines is of particular importance if you're inexperienced. Gambrel, hip, and valley roofs (and dormer additions) should be avoided on the roof line, for example (see figure 5-2). Sunken living rooms, complex stairways, and split levels can all cause grief in the interior.

Geodesic domes, polygonal houses, and yurts may each have a strong appeal, but undertake these projects with the understanding that (1) the finish work is long and tedious; (2) furniture is designed on the premise that gravity runs perpendicular to the horizon; and (3) it's unlikely that there will be local people experienced in these techniques

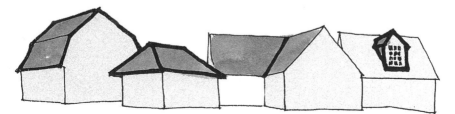

5-2. Some examples of complex structures to be avoided.

to offer advice when you get in trouble. You can't ask a local carpenter how to waterproof a dome for an earth roof. If in doubt, build a model of the intended structure. If you can't build the model, don't even think about building the house.

The round house. A cylindrical house of masonry, by the way, is not difficult to build. At first, this might seem contradictory to the previous comments on domes and yurts, but it is not. The walls of domes and yurts are not perpendicular to the horizon, whereas the walls of a cylinder are, aiding construction (including window and door installation) and providing better use of space in the upward direction (see figure 5-3). So-called "primitive" builders, such as ancient European stone masons, the Hopi Indians of the American Southwest, and present-day African tribes, all chose cylindrical buildings for the ease of their construction and their functionality. That the buildings are also beautiful is no coincidence, if, indeed, form follows function.

The efficient use of materials in cylindrical houses is demonstrated in figure 5-4. It is an indisputable function of plane geometry that a circle will enclose 27.3 percent more area than the most efficient recti-

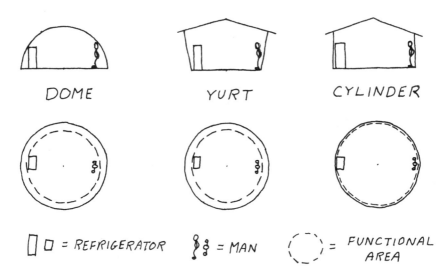

5-3. *A cylindrical house makes better use of floor space than does a dome or a yurt. Because of* πr^2 *(pi r squared), a great deal of space is lost when the radius or diameter is lessened by even a little.*

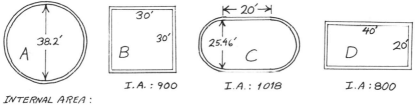

5-4. The perimeter of each of these houses is the same: 120 feet. However, the curved-wall shapes are a much more efficient use of masonry.

linear shape (a square) of the same perimeter. When compared to the more common rectilinear shapes that Western builders use for their shelter, the gain of round building is more like 40 percent. With masonry construction, the time savings are just as favorable as the materials cost, since labor is a function of handling a certain amount of masonry units: bricks, blocks, stone, cordwood, even straw bales. Note that the non-human building species—birds, bees, beavers, etc.—seem to know this instinctively, without benefit of geometrical formulas. They have the benefit of millions of years of building experience behind them.

I've been repeating this rap on the efficiency of round buildings in print and at my lectures for about twenty years, and it is absolutely true as far as it goes. But one very perceptive student, Isaac Smit of Ontario, was troubled by the math, went home, conducted a more detailed study of the problem, and came out with a lesser advantage for the round house. His astute observations have reminded me once again that nothing is as simple as it seems. See the sidebar, "Comparing the Efficiency of Circle and Square," from a letter by Isaac Smit.

Similarly, a round house is easier to heat than a square or rectilinear house with the same floor area. The economy of wall area is part of the reason, of course, but the lesser wind resistance offered by a curved wall is also important. And if a radiant heat source, such as a wood stove, is placed at the center of the structure, there will be no cold corners, because all points on the circumference will be equidistant from the heat source.

Building a round masonry house is easier than building a rectilinear structure of the same materials (see figure 5-5). First, a pipe is set

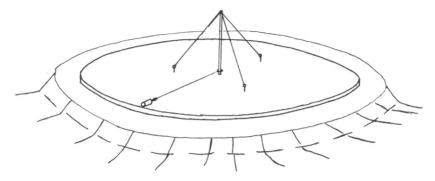

5-5. With the center pipe plumb, laying up masonry to the line assembly is a breeze.

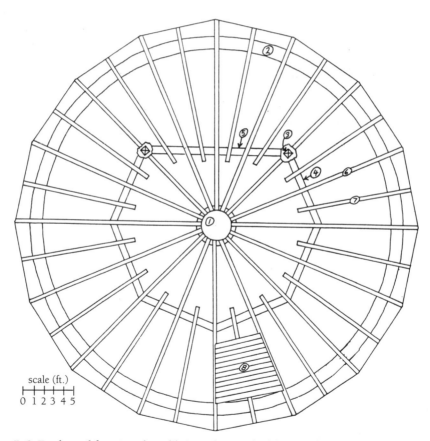

5-6. Earthwood framing plan: (1) Stone heat sink; (2) 16-inch masonry wall; (3) Post locations, seven in all; (4) Girders; (5) Special girder for greater span, 10-by-12-inch oak or equal; (6) Primary rafter; (7) Secondary rafter; (8) 2-by-6 tongue-and-groove planking.

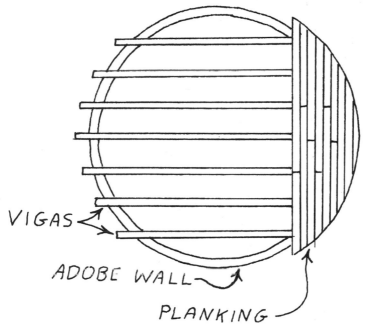

VIGAS

ADOBE WALL

PLANKING

5-7. *A parallel rafter system for a flat-roofed round structure, a common method with adobe construction.*

plumb at the center of a round floating slab. An assembly consisting of a bull's ring, a nonstretch line or wire, and a plumb bob or heavy spike establishes uniform distance from the pipe. If the stones, bricks, blocks, or log-ends are always set to the extended plumb bob assembly, the wall will be plumb, round, and smooth, without constant use of a level. As the walls go up, it is necessary to raise the bull's ring on the pipe accordingly or the wall will begin to slope inward like a dome.

The most difficult part of round house construction is the roof, but this is only slightly more awkward than a rectilinear roof, if it is planned with a view to efficient use of materials. The radial rafter system shown in figure 5-6 is probably the easiest where a roof pitch is required, but builders of adobe structures in areas of low rainfall successfully use almost flat roofs and parallel rafters called "vigas," as shown in figure 5-7. The *Complete Book of Cordwood Masonry Houses* (Sterling, 1992) goes into detail on round house construction and much of the commentary is equally applicable for stone, block, brick, or adobe houses.

Comparing the Efficiency of Circle and Square

As part of the tenth grade math course I teach, I ask my students the following: *Question.* I have a roll of chain-link fence 24 meters long and wish to construct a chicken run. A chicken requires 0.5 square meters of space. How many chickens could I keep if I build a square chicken run? What if it's round? *Answer.* The square is 6m x 6m = 36m², and can hold 72 chickens. A circle with a diameter of 7.64m can be made from the fence. ($24 \div \pi = 7.6394$). The radius of the circle is half of the diameter, or 3.8197 meters. The area is found by the formula $A=\pi r^2$, in this case 45.8367 square meters, which will hold 91.67 chickens. As we do not wish to keep two-thirds of a chicken in with the others, we'll call it 91. The circular run can store over 25 percent more chickens than the square run.

If, however, we build a round house, we not only get a greater living space per unit of wall perimeter, but, consequently, the area of floor and roof (cost of material, construction, heat loss, etc.) is greater too! Let's examine a 2,000-square-foot house on a slab foundation, two stories of 1,000 SF each. Like the slab, we'll make the roof flat for convenience of calculation, each 1,000 SF. Assuming a building height of 18 feet, the walls in a round house have a total area of 2,018 SF. Adding the floor and roof, 1,000 SF each, gives a total skin area of 4,018 SF for the house. The square house has 2,277 SF of walls, or a total of 4,277 SF of skin area. The total

Avoid basements. It is surprising how many people in the North continue to view a basement as a necessity, despite the fact that in a low-cost owner-built home, a basement can eat up almost half the building budget or half the person-hours or some combination of these, while providing low-quality space that will be used less than 10 percent of the time. We made this mistake at Log End Cottage. More than a third of the total cost of the house and considerable labor went into the basement. It was only useful for storing garden produce, which could have fit into a small root cellar under a floating slab and connected to the pantry by a trap door, at a combined cost (slab and root cellar) of less than half that of a full basement. We also stored junk in the basement, but that hardly qualifies as a useful purpose, and really surface area of a square house is about 6.5 percent greater than the round house of equal floor area. This is far less significant a difference than with the chicken run problem, because the chicken run requires neither roof nor floor. However, the round house has 8.6 percent less skin area exposed to the air, if no berming is used, and is, therefore, that much easier to heat (Isaac Smit, Mt. Hope, Ontario).

Author's reply: I was shocked when I received and analyzed Isaac's analysis, which begins with the reasonable assumption that we wish to build a home with a certain square footage, in this case, two thousand. Even when I factored in wall thickness and roof overhang, I could do little better than a 7.5 percent improvement in materials efficiency with the round house compared with a square one. Clearly, there is more to this discussion than meets the eye. How these figures actually affect the cost of a home will depend on a comparison between the unit cost of wall square footage and the unit cost for first floor and roof square footage. By the way, I took Isaac's example a little further and compared both round and square designs with a "ranch" design of 20 feet by 50 feet, also 1,000 SF. The round design was about 12.5 percent more economic by gross skin square footage than the ranch, and much better with regard to heat loss. Finally, and perhaps most importantly, masonry wall construction is labor intensive. About 11.4 percent less work is required to build walls with the round shape.

good stuff will deteriorate quickly in a dark, damp, dingy basement.

Perhaps it will help the hard-core basement junkie if we examine its history. As a foundation method in areas with deep frost penetration, the basement was, and still is, a great success. However, less expensive methods can accomplish the same thing: the floating slab, the rubble trench foundation (see Ki Light's case study, chapter 7), and pillar construction are just a few examples.

Before the advent of insulation, it could be argued that the basement was the best-insulated part of the house. This is no longer true, of course, and the two or three courses of block exposed above grade, so typical of basement construction since World War II, is the single greatest energy sieve in postwar houses.

Basements made some sense on the farm, where upwards of 70 percent of food was produced at home, and potatoes and other vegetables were best stored in dark, humid spaces and at temperatures just above the freezing mark. A closed-in part of the basement, the root cellar, served the purpose perfectly. A designated root cellar can serve the purpose just as well at a fraction of the cost.

Heating the rural home in the days before insulation and vapor barriers used to be a full-time chore. Three or four woodstoves fairly gobbled wood and had to be stoked every four hours or so. The development of wood and coal furnaces helped a great deal, and, as they worked on the principle that hot air rises, they were most conveniently installed in the basement. Coal could be stored there—remember the coal cellar?—although wood storage in the basement was not ideal because of damp conditions. Duct work could run all over the cellar, just below the floor, with registers strategically placed to deliver the hot air as required. Later, oil and gas furnaces replaced most solid-fuel models, and, again, the cellar or basement seemed the logical place to put these monstrous heating plants and fuel tanks. Nowadays, we have furnaces so small, so clean, and so safe, that they can be installed in an upstairs space as small as a closet. Area heating is on the way back (as opposed to "central heating"), thanks to the advent of more efficient space heating devices, such as wood stoves and gas-fired direct-vent wall heaters. Remember the sidebar, "On Central Heating," page 11 of chapter 1.

In short, most functions, including heating, are best enclosed in the house proper, not in a basement. Pure and simple, basements are not cost-economic, require familiarity with an additional structural system (which is why most owner-builders contract their basement out, usually at a high cost relative to the house), and provide low-quality habitat for almost anything except mushroom propagation.

Some readers may be wondering how an earth-sheltering advocate can be so critical of basements. After all, what's the difference? Writer Mike Oehler, in the first chapter of *The $50 and Up Underground House Book* (Mole Publishing Company, 1978 & 1992) says: "An underground house has no more in common with a basement than a penthouse apartment has in common with a hot, dark, dusty attic." Further, he says:

A basement is not designed for human habitat. It is a place to put the furnace and store junk. It is constructed to reach below the frost line so that the frost heaves don't crumple the fragile conventional structure above. It is a place where workmen can walk around checking for termites under the flooring, where they may work on pipes and wiring. Its design, function and often even the material from which it is built is different from an underground house. A basement is usually a dark, damp, dirty place and even when it is not, even when it is a recreation room, say, it is usually an airless place with few windows, artificially lighted and having an artificial feel. An underground house is not this at all (p. 9).

Our own experience bears out Oehler's commentary. The basement at Log End Cottage was dark, damp, dingy, and of little practical value. Log End Cave, on the other hand, was bright, dry, cheerful, and practical, just like the 40 percent of the space at Earthwood that is earth-sheltered.

If you still feel that a basement is a requirement in your owner-built home, let me make one final pitch. Instead of a "dark, damp, dirty place," go the extra mile and do the things necessary to upgrade the space into warm, dry, bright, earth-sheltered space. How? Include waterproofing and drainage systems, rigid foam insulation on the exterior of the fabric of the building, and design it to promote natural light and ventilation. Yes, all this will cost you more money, but you'll have high-quality space instead of almost useless space. Read books by Malcolm Wells and Mike Oehler, and my own *The Complete Book of Underground Houses: How to Build a Low-Cost Home*, all listed in appendix 3.

The capped basement. A common strategy in northern New York and elsewhere is for owner-builders to build a "capped basement" and move into it as a temporary shelter until they can afford to build a house on top. The primary advantages of this strategy are that these structures, if properly built, are easy to heat and carry a low property tax valuation. The main disadvantages are that they are often short of light, are humid, leaky, and singularly unattractive to look at. Again, think of earth-sheltered space instead of a basement. Even with the capped basement strategy, go the extra mile and include proper glazing, waterproofing, and insulating techniques. I've been accused of squeezing a shilling until the Queen screams, but money spent now to avoid the downside of basements (no pun denied) is money well spent in both the short- and long-terms.

Appropriate Floor Plans

The third planning guideline is to tailor the floor plan to the structural considerations and the available materials, not the other way around. I can best illustrate this rule by example. I have already told of the great expense that might be encountered in earth-sheltered houses where the structural plan is made subsidiary to an unrealistic floor plan, but the error of this line of thinking is not limited to earth-shelters. Economy of construction is largely predicated upon economy of building materials. We have said that a circular structure makes the most economical use of masonry materials. This might not be true with regard to standard frame construction, utilizing studs, plywood, sheathing, and the like. A square house may be more practical in this case. Long narrow houses, projections, and courtyards are all inefficient uses of material if it is the builder's desire to keep the square-foot unit cost down.

House A or House B? Look at figure 5-8. Both houses have exterior dimensions of 24 feet by 36 feet, a common and quite sensible size chosen by first-time owner-builders. House A has 864 square feet on the ground floor. The designer of House B took the same basic dimensions, but decided that he wanted a floor plan that puts the master bedroom and the children's bedroom in separate "wings," with a courtyard in front of the house. Moreover, he likes the look of the structure better than House A. Fine, these are all valid value judgments and, after all—music, please—everybody's different. But you should know what these value judgments will cost, in terms of time, money, ease of construction, and energy efficiency.

House B, with its 12-by-12-foot courtyard, loses 144 square feet of interior living space and adds 24 feet to the house perimeter. Each perimeter foot of wall encloses 5 square feet of interior floor area, whereas in House A, 7.2 square feet of floor area are enclosed by each perimeter foot. House B is only about 70 percent as cost-efficient in terms of external walls. The energy-saving characteristics of the respective walls have a similar relationship, too, because heat loss is proportional to skin area, other factors being equal.

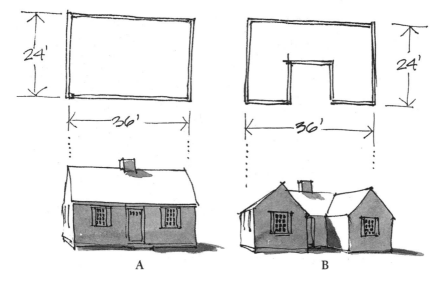

5-8. *Design considerations must be weighed against cost and energy factors.*

There's more. Roof B, though slightly smaller than Roof A, is much more difficult to build and wastes materials due to the varying sizes of rafters and the unusual shapes of the decking and roofing material. The foundation is the least inefficient part of House B's construction, but even here the features desired in the house must be paid for with other trade-offs. If a concrete floating slab is poured, there will be a very slight decrease in the amount of concrete used in Slab B—don't forget the extra perimeter, where the footings are 8 inches thick—but this minor gain is more than offset by more difficult, time-consuming, and expensive forming. And Slab B will not be quite as strong in terms of frost and settling resistance because of its shape.

Finally, House A is much more conducive to using upstairs space than House B. Sleeping lofts and attic storage space would both be more useful. If 2 to 4 feet is added to the wall height of House A, considerable expansion potential exists. A family might live on one floor for a year, finishing bedrooms on the second floor as time and money allow. The same extra wall height in House B will not yield anywhere near the same gain because of the size and shape of the attic space.

If, after weighing up the extra time, dollar cost, energy cost, and the building nuisance factor of Design B, you decide that you can indeed

5-9. House C, the compromise candidate, is an economical and easy-to-build structure.

build the house, that you can afford to build it, and that the desired features justify the cost, then you should carry on and build it. You have made an educated decision, you'll probably succeed in the endeavor, and you'll have built the house you truly want. Best of luck.

House C. I've deliberately stacked the deck against House B to illustrate certain design considerations. I do not mean to suggest that everyone should run out and build House A. A design like House B often results from fitting a structure to a desired floor plan or location of spaces. Perhaps the same goals could have been achieved in another way, by fitting the floor plan to an economical and easy-to-build structural plan. Figure 5-9 introduces House C, a compromise plan in which the desired design goals of House B can be achieved at a great saving of time and materials. A south-facing solarium replaces the courtyard, rendering it more useful throughout the year. The house still has separate bedroom areas, but the main frame and roof structure is greatly simplified. This plan may not satisfy the yearning for a sprawling ranch-style house, but it might make the pill a little easier to swallow.

Use common sizes. Floor plans should always take into consideration the availability of materials. If standard framing is to be employed, wall and floor dimensions must take standard building material dimensions into consideration.

Plywood is 4 feet by 8 feet, for example. If plywood is to be used in the construction, on either walls or floors, a house that is 25 feet by 35 feet with a wall height of 9 feet is not a good plan. A design that is 24 feet by 36 feet by 8 feet fits in extremely well with the use of plywood.

Dimensional timbers come in 2-foot increments. You can't buy a 13-foot floor joist off the store shelf, so you would have to buy a 14-footer and waste a foot. (And sometimes 14s are hard to find, too.) It is generally more cost-effective to keep to 12 feet, if possible. Beyond 12 feet, the larger dimensions, such as 2-by-10s, become increasingly expensive per foot because larger trees are needed to yield the extra length. Only the small end of a forest log is of interest to the sawyer. The greater the length and taper, the more the waste.

Integrating the floor plan with heavy timber construction. Jaki and I like to leave beautiful heavy timbers exposed wherever we can, particularly floor joists and rafters. We tend to use plank and beam frames with rough-cut floor joists and rafters at least 4 inches wide, and, often, 5 inches, 6 inches, or 8 inches wide, as at Earthwood. The wooden floor of the second story is the ceiling of the first story. The roof decking material is the exposed ceiling of the second story. The spruce V-joint tongue-and-groove planking is in harmony with the exposed heavy timber framework. Our aesthetic sense in this may have something to do with our British background. And, frankly, I find exposed heavy timber framing to be easier, quicker, and cheaper to do than sheetrock ceilings over stick framing, the more common approach in North America.

Out of thousands of people who have visited our various homes, only one or two have expressed that they don't like to see the exposed timbers. Too rustic for them, I guess. Most people find the heavy frame to be a positive architectural feature. The very wealthy pay top dollar to see big beautiful beams overhead in their expensive hand-crafted heavy log and timber-frame houses. I have a feeling that, subconsciously, rich and poor folks alike feel a sense of security that the house isn't in any danger of falling down. Even though modular homes are properly engineered to carry the roofloads, I wonder how confident the inhabitants would feel if they saw the relatively light-weight support structure hidden behind the thin ceiling. It's mildly humorous that some of these modular homes feature false plastic "rustic" beams overhead for effect.

Exposed beams in the ceiling present two practical problems. The first is, where do you put the insulation? We have taken two different approaches. At Log End Cottage, we installed one-inch planking (planed on one side) and a six-mil plastic vapor barrier over the beautiful rough-cut three-by-tens that framed the roof. Then we installed a second roof over the first, placing a two-by-six directly over every three-by-ten. Fiberglass insulation (not enough, I know; this was 1975) went between the secondary rafters, and a second layer of one-by planking was nailed on top of the two-by-sixes. It is important to leave a two-inch venting space above this insulation, open to a ridge vent along the peak, something we didn't know about at the time. It didn't cause us a problem, but you might as well know the right way to do it. Modern insulation standards would necessitate the use of two-by-tens for this secondary rafter system, which starts to get costly, but you get the exposed beam effect and you don't have to sheetrock the ceiling, tape, spackle, and paint two coats.

The other way we've insulated over exposed heavy timber ceilings is by applying a waterproofing membrane right on the wooden deck, which, in turn, is covered with four inches of extruded polystyrene, a crushed stone drainage layer, and seven inches of earth. This method is quick and easy (except for hauling the crushed stone and earth) and, when done properly, provides the longest-lasting roof of all, because the waterproofing membrane is protected from the two conditions that eventually break down every other roof: freeze/thaw cycling and the sun's ultraviolet rays.

The second practical problem with the exposed heavy timber frame is subdividing such a ceiling with respect to the room layout. It's a carpenter's bad dream to just miss a heavy overhead timber with an internal wall. It just plain doesn't look good, and cobs love to make their webs there. If a wall runs perpendicular to the run of the rafters, the bad dream becomes a nightmare. The internal wall has to be fitted around the rough-cut heavy timber frame on its way to the planking. In a house having a radial rafter system, like Earthwood, cutting across the exposed rafters with an internal wall is a full-blown hallucinatory screaming jeebies nightmare. As I hate bad dreams, never mind nightmares, I allow the structural plan to influence the floor plan. I like to think of the two as integrated, or having a *symbiotic* relationship. (Sometimes a fancy terminology is all that's needed to make a compromise easier to swallow.) At Earthwood, for example, many of our rooms are trapezoidal in shape, because the walls rise up and meet the underside of the heavy timbers. This not only looks great and is easy to do, but the internal walls actually help to carry the roof load.

Recycled materials. All this talk about heavy timbers leads nicely into a discussion on the use of salvaged building materials. When you are able to score a real bargain on some major structural component, don't throw the opportunity away because, say, the salvaged joists are only 11 feet long and you want a 24-foot-wide building. If there's enough bargain beams to do the job, change the plans to a 22-foot width. At Log End Cave, I virtually designed the basic house shell around three old 30-foot-long 10-by-10-inch barn beams that I bought for $90. Buying equivalent beams new would have cost several times as much, would have required cutting three spectacular live trees better left in the forest, and wouldn't have had the same character.

Another example: a local manufacturer of insulated glass panels is sometimes left with units that have been made the wrong size for a job or were not collected by the customer for some reason. The manufacturer's options are to dismantle the units and use the glass again on smaller orders, or to sell the units at a discount, often 60 percent and more. We used double-pane windows throughout Log End Cottage and Log End Cave. The total cost for all eleven windows at the Cottage, including one made to order, was only $161 in 1975. At the Cave, we spent twice as much, but the house was twice as bright.

The greenhouse attached to our shed was constructed of rough-cut two-by-fours, silo planking for the roof, and twenty units of one-inch thick insulated glass ($1/4$-inch plate glass, $1/2$-inch air space, $1/4$-inch glass), each measuring $15 1/2$ inches by 42 inches. This glass had been cut $1/2$-inch undersize for another job. I bought the lot for $96, less than 20 percent of their value at the time, and a couple of other useful units were thrown in for nothing. These window units have now been recycled yet again at Earthwood.

If you're stuck into a rigid plan, you won't be able to take advantage of this kind of bargain, even though a savings of $2,000 or more might be in the offing. That's why the correct strategy is to design around the available materials, be they indigenous to the site, salvaged from an old building, or obtained at an auction or a going-out-of-business sale.

Whole Living Systems

Planning guideline number four: Consider all the living systems at the design stage, not just Shelter. While we're going to all this trouble to put a roof over our heads, why not address the next most expensive "necessaries" of life, Food and Fuel? And what about recreation? And home industry? Take an integrated design approach right from the start. It's never easier than when you have a beginner's mind, a clean sheet of paper, and the most valuable tool you'll ever own: a rubber eraser.

We did not take a whole systems approach to either of our first two owner-built homes, Log End Cottage and Log End Cave. The concept was only just beginning to gain a wider audience by the late 1970s, although Scott and Helen Nearing's classic *Living the Good Life* (Schocken, 1954) had been in print for most of a quarter-century. Trouble was, Jaki and I didn't read it before designing Log End Homestead. Earthwood, I resolved, would pay more attention to integrated design, and the results of this effort are reported in chapter 6.

Fuel (Energy). Thoreau spoke of Fuel, and, for the most part, this meant fossil fuel (coal) or wood heat. In either case, the energy stored by this fuel was originally provided by the sun. Let's go straight to the source, solar energy. Likewise, stored energy, by way of thermal mass, was not an idea with great currency in 1847. It's not even all that well known or understood by the "masses of men" 150 years later. Nowadays, we should think in terms of Energy rather than Fuel. The word *fuel*, to me, smacks of the consumer economy, whereas civilization—if we wish to be worthy of the name—must now think in terms of a conserver economy. If we consider the word *energy* instead, particularly when used in such phrases as *energy efficiency*, *energy conservation*, and *solar energy*, we can begin to slow our wasteful consumption of the planetary capital.

THERMAL MASS. What is it? How does it work? And why don't we hear more about it? Thermal mass refers to the ability of a material to store heat. Water, for example, stores more heat by weight or by volume than any other common material, at 62.5 Btus per cubic foot per degree Fahrenheit. Stone (at 36 Btu/CF/°F) and concrete (at 32) are also excellent as thermal mass. Soapstone happens to have a particu-

Thermal mass.

larly high specific heat, which is why several brands of woodstoves are either clad in or actually built of soapstone. Going down through a list of common building materials would take us through adobe at 22, sheetrock at 13, and wood, which varies from 9 to 12 depending on species and density. All of these figures, except for water which is the defining benchmark for specific heat, are approximate. At the bottom end of such a scale, we'd find materials like extruded polystyrene, a wonderful insulation with virtually no thermal mass at all. In general, a material's value as thermal mass is almost inversely proportional to its value as insulation.

More and more architects, designers, and owner-builders are catching on to the idea of incorporating thermal mass into their designs for its ability to store heat. But thermal mass is equally good at storing "coolth," which is simply heat at a different temperature. So a house with mass can be both warm in winter and cool in summer. Notice the caveat in the last sentence: "can be." For thermal mass to work properly, we must be able to use the stored heat or coolth where we want it. To do that, to exercise control over the mass, we must place insulation correctly between the mass and the outside enivronment. If this is done, thermal mass will take the rapid fluctuations out of the temperature curve, fluctuations like the drop common in a well-insulated, low-mass house a few hours after the fire goes out, or, conversely, the rapid heat build-up experienced when the lowering sun blazes in through west-facing windows. In the former case, heat stored in the mass replaces air temperature heat loss as it departs the house through windows, doors, cracks, and up the chimney. In the latter case, a (relatively) cool mass can help absorb some of the excess heat build-up. Think of thermal mass as a giant battery, a battery that stores heat instead of electricity. This heat battery is extremely effective at keeping everything at a steady temperature. To draw an analogy, let's liken the rising and falling of the mercury in a thermometer to a small boat being tossed up and down helplessly in 20-foot seas. The boat represents a small thermal mass. Not far away, the QE2, representing great thermal mass, steams on steadfastly with hardly a drop of Chateau Rothschild spilled in the first-class lounge.

Thermal mass is wonderful, magical, the nearest thing we have to a free lunch. My theory on why we don't see more of it in contractor-built houses is that there are no manufacturers pushing thermal mass. How do you charge someone for a gallon of water or a pound of stone? There is no profit in it.

Usually, materials with high thermal mass also have high conductivity. Without the intermediary insulation layer, they will transfer the heat right out of the house. To illustrate this, I'm going to bring another energy-saving concept into the discussion.

EARTH SHELTERING. Many people still think that underground houses use less fuel because the earth is a good insulator. This is flat-out wrong. Earth is a poor insulator. However, earth is a very good capacitor, a very good thermal mass. Look at figure 5-10. An above-ground structure is situated in ambient (surrounding) air, which commonly reaches minus 20° Fahrenheit in our part of the world. If 70° is the desired comfort level in the house, it is necessary to heat to 90° above the ambient temperature. In an earth-sheltered house, the ambient is the earth itself, which reaches a low of about 40° at six feet of depth during

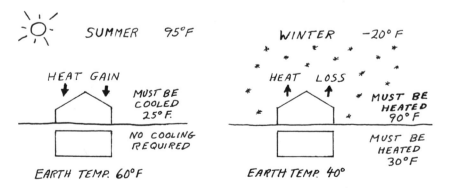

5-10. *Heating and cooling advantages of an earth-sheltered home.*

a North Country winter, so it is necessary to exceed the ambient temperature by only 30°. The left side of the diagram shows how a similar advantage is realized in summer cooling.

Now, while 40° Fahrenheit is a whole lot better starting temperature than minus 20°, it's not the comfort level we are looking for. We have to introduce some heat: wood, solar, six kids, whatever. Remember, though, that thermal mass is normally highly conductive. If our walls are concrete, stone, or concrete block, we will wick the heat out of the home almost as rapidly as we put it in. We're in a losing battle trying to heat up our little corner of Planet Earth. Here is where insulation enters the equation. If the mass fabric of the building is isolated from the earth's thermal mass with good insulation (such as extruded polystyrene), we can then exercise control over the temperature of that fabric. The thermal mass of the house, in other words, is now separated from the earth's mass by a "thermal break." We can exercise control over the mass temperature of the fabric, gently nudging it as required, and it, in turn, keeps the air temperature curve from oscillating wildly.

This commentary on thermal mass and earth-sheltering is only intended to introduce sensible and low-cost design considerations that are not in common use. In the South, where cooling is the more important energy consideration, builders of earth-sheltered housing will want to pursue a different insulation strategy, allowing the earth to draw unwanted heat out of the home. If interest is tweaked, the reader should research further. Appendix 3 is a good place to start.

SOLAR HEATING AND THERMAL MASS. Earth shelters don't corner the market on thermal mass. Passive solar heating has been around since classical times and its concepts and techniques have never been more refined than they are today. It is possible to use the sun's heat to charge a thermal mass during the day, and have that mass keep the house cozy at night. This is a huge topic, but a good concise book on solar heating and cooling is James Kachadorian's *The Passive Solar House: Using Solar Design to Heat and Cool Your Home* (Chelsea Green, 1997).

One of Kachadorian's main design breakthroughs (a formerly patented idea now available for all to use) is the solar slab, a concept that is adaptable to virtually any house design. In brief, a 4-inch concrete slab is poured over concrete blocks laid on edge so that the hollow cores line up with each other, creating a large number of concrete-walled tunnels under the slab. Air heated by the sun is passed through these tunnels, which charge the thermal mass of the slab, where the heat is stored until needed. Kachadorian's book describes the technique in detail, including the correct placement of insulation to prevent what Malcolm Wells calls "energy nosebleed." Worksheets are included that enable readers to design a solar slab for their location and for their particular house design.

Ecologists might legitimately criticize the large amount of energy-intensive concrete and concrete blocks used in the solar slab, and this is a valid concern with many underground designs too. But indigenous materials with mass, such as stone, adobe, and rammed earth can be substituted for concrete in many applications. If we are going to use concrete, we ought, at the very least, to use its wonderful thermal mass characteristics to save energy in the long run, instead of just burying it in the ground for structural purposes only, as is the case with perhaps 90 percent of homes being built in North America today. Many wonderful and workable passive solar designs have been built using such indigenous materials as earth, adobe, straw bales, cob (a mixture of clay and straw), stone, and cordwood. Water as thermal mass storage, while tricky, can be incorporated into the design, and,

A cordwood masonary home combines insulation with thermal mass, and is fun to build. Photo provided by Ted Holdt and Sara Mapelli.

for the hedonists among you, I know of several hot tubs and swimming pools that have also doubled as thermal mass.

The incorporation of passive solar design principles into the plan requires research—work!—but it's easier to do the work at the design stage than to try to retrofit passive solar into a house later on.

THE MASONRY STOVE. Eastern Europeans say that Americans don't know how to burn wood, and I'm inclined to agree with them. Most Americans know that fireplaces are hopelessly inefficient, and will actually empty the heat out of a house in the wee hours when the fire goes out, thanks to the draft established in the chimney flue. Modern wood stoves are a tremendous improvement, of course, but they still have problems. In an effort to keep the fire alive overnight, the airtight dampers are closed and combustion slows down greatly. Unfortunately, the firebox temperature drops below that required for complete combustion, causing unburned volatile gases to start their way up the chimney where, even more unfortunately, they either condense in the flue in the form of creosote or enter the atmosphere in the form of pollution. Dangerous and dirty. Enter the masonry stove, with its matrix of horizontal flues running back and forth throughout the stone or brick masonry.

It works like this. The stove is fired up once a day—the right time will be determined by experimentation—and an armload of wood is allowed to burn extra hot; that is, with plenty of air coming through the loading door or damper control. While the wood is being burned at high temperature, all the volatiles are combusted and no creosote is formed. In sixteen years of burning wood in our masonry stove at Earthwood, we've never had to clean the chimney because there has never been any creosote formation.

When all the colored flames are gone, and only clear flames are coming off the hot coals, the blast gate (an almost airtight damper) is closed and the fire continues to transfer its heat to the stone mass in its own good time. At Earthwood, we typically shut the stove down within an hour of firing. The long horizontal flues, criss-crossing throughout the masonry, provide lots of surface area for the transfer of the exhaust heat to the thermal mass. If properly designed and built, the exhaust into the atmosphere is cool enough that you can hold your hand comfortably over the chimney top—and almost no pollutants are put into the atmosphere.

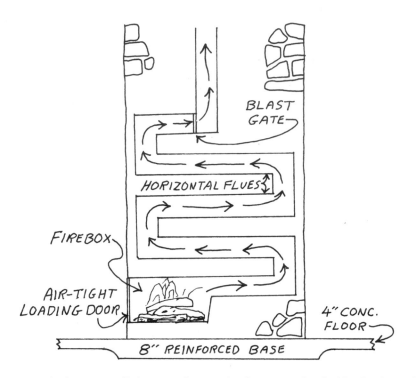

BLAST
GATE

HORIZONTAL FLUES

FIREBOX

AIR-TIGHT
LOADING DOOR

4" CONC.
FLOOR

8" REINFORCED BASE

5-11. The heat normally lost out of a straight chimney is absorbed by the thermal mass in a masonry stove, due to the increased contact time between hot flue gases and the masonry mass. When only hot coals are left, the blast gate is closed.

The tremendous mass of the stove stores the heat, giving it off slowly to the house interior. Twenty-four hours later, the mass is recharged with a new fire. With masonry stoves, less fuel is used, the fire burns cleaner (little ash is left), and the temperature is steady. The only drawback is that more kindling wood must be stocked. However, this is offset by the advantage of having to fire the stove and clean the firebox much less frequently.

WINDOW PLACEMENT. Windows should be concentrated on the south side of a house to promote winter heat gain and minimized on the north side to reduce heat loss. A generous roof overhang should protect the house from too much heat gain in summer, while permitting entrance of the low winter rays. A solar greenhouse on the south side can actually help heat the house—for free—on sunny winter days, while providing a place to start garden plants in the springtime. Our solar room at Earthwood even provides salad greens through the winter. Consult *The Passive Solar House* at the design stage.

I live, build, and write in the extreme north of the forty-eight contiguous states, and it's easy to forget that many, if not most, of my readers do not. Those of you in the American South have a different sort of energy consideration, and must be careful with window placement to prevent overheating of the home. Many energy-conscious builders in southern states use a northern exposure in their design to prevent overheating. An added bonus is that north light is less harsh. In fact, many artists prefer it for their work. Those in the extreme South, and here I mean south of the equator like my friends in Chile, should change all the norths in this book to souths, and vice-versa. But you're probably used to that.

Although skylights are not particularly energy-efficient, modern ones are a lot better than those of 20 years ago, and much less likely to leak. And they are extremely light-efficient, admitting about five times the light of a comparably sized wall window. Use them to illuminate otherwise dark areas. A dark house is a poor trade-off for, say, another quarter-cord of firewood saved. Owner-built and recycled skylights have not proven to be a great success: there is a high chance they will leak. In fact, sloping glass on a greenhouse, particularly when installed by non-professionals, also tends to leak. Keep glass vertical, the exception being modern manufactured skylights with their well-engineered flashing systems. Be warned, though, that these are expensive.

Other energy. Commercially supplied electricity should not be considered an absolute requirement in a home. Most of the people in our hill community—indeed, most of the people in the world—live quite happily without it. On remote sites, which I define as being $5,000 away from the nearest commercial power (in extended line charges), alternative energy sources, such as solar, wind, and hydro, should be *strongly* considered.

If you know that you will be hooking into commercial power, the economical (and environmental) strategy is to consume less of the stuff. Electric heating should be dismissed out of hand, as should electric water heating, clothes drying, and cooking. There are cheaper and less wasteful methods of accomplishing all of these jobs. Follow local insulation codes and standards, or *better* them. Plan your lighting system to take advantage of modern energy-efficient bulbs. Dimmers, if you use them, can save on electric bills. Later, when you purchase appliances, consider their electrical draw as a primary factor in decision-making.

Nowhere in this book do I mean to imply that your reasons for doing things should be based solely on dollar economy. Empiric economy has a place for dollars, but only insofar as they can be traded for something of more intrinsic value: time, freedom, less work, less energy, higher quality of life, better environment. What the heck, let's make a law out of it (my editor loves 'em). Roy's Fifth Law of Empiric Economics, then, might be stated thus: Money is neither good nor evil; it's what you trade for it—or trade it for—that counts.

> **Money is neither good nor evil; it's what you trade for it—or trade it for—that counts.**

Especially with regard to energy, then, you might find lots of other good empiric reasons to remain unplugged from power lines, even if "plugging in" is cheaper by the dollar. I have friends who have had an electrical service entrance standing on a pole just 20 feet from their kitchen door these past twenty years, and they have not plugged in. They use photovoltaic cells for their modest electrical needs. Like many of the wise before them, including the founders of most of the world's great religions, they find that their spiritual well-being is inversely proportional to their material consumption. You may have your own philosophical or environmental reasons to journey through life unplugged. I welcome your company.

Food. Consider including food production and preservation as a part of your construction design. A solar greenhouse can help supply food, heat the home, and provide a pleasant space to get away to for some quiet time. The garden should be in close proximity to the house and greenhouse, and sheltered from the prevailing winds by the nearby buildings, if possible. At Log End, the garden shed and greenhouse was a hundred feet from the house and the garden itself another hundred feet beyond that. It's hard to keep track of the garden's needs from that distance, things like watering, and protection from insects and the local rodent population. How we corrected the Log End deficiencies at Earthwood is discussed in chapter 6.

North Americans, at least the 99 percent of them still plugged into the consumer economy, have come to rely on huge refrigerators and freezers for food storage. This is expensive both in dollars and in energy. Europeans seem to eat well with far less expensive means of food storage, as Americans did, too, in our grandparents' generation. Dehydration, canning, dry storage of bulk goods, and cold storage of root crops are all viable methods of food storage, but the space for these kinds of storage must be incorporated into the plan. *The Pantry of Terre Vivante: Old World Techniques and Recipes for Preserving the Four-Season Harvest* (Chelsea Green, 1998) offers traditional, energy-efficient methods for storing food that preserve nutrition and taste.

In Ireland, Guinness Stout is probably included in the list of major food groups. Ditto wine in France. If beer- and wine-making is of interest to you, plan for a place to rack the fruits of your labor. But a kitchen usually suffices as a production venue, unless you're thinking in micro-brewery terms.

Recreation. Here's where I blow my "cover," showing that even the most practical designer will yield to temptation. Besides beer, one of my other vices—I'm not going to tell you *all* of them—is pocket billiards. This explains about 250 square feet of Earthwood's 2,000-square-foot total. Hopefully, your recreational interests will require less than 250 square feet of living space. And sometimes, "recreational" space can double as something else. Recreation, for you, might mean a hot tub, or exercise equipment. Maybe the solar room or greenhouse is a good place for things like that and the thermal mass of the tub can help keep the temperature curve a little more steady in a room with a lot of glass.

People's ideas of home recreation vary widely, but don't forget to include your own at the design stage. And outdoor space must be planned for just like the indoor space, so take note all you horseshoe pitchers and volleyball spikers.

Home Industry. Ah, back to practicality! Back to work! Well, maybe not. Many people who build their own homes want to become free of the rat-race in other ways, too. Writers, artists, potters, private machinists, beekeepers, mail-order, sewing, computer-based—the list of home businesses is virtually open-ended. Jaki and I run our Earthwood Building School and mail-order book sales out of our home. That 250 square feet devoted to punching plastic balls into the holes of a green table doubles as the classroom for our workshops, and the pool table is very handy for the slide projector, books, and other useful materials.

Space for your home occupation should be planned very carefully. Some occupations can be conducted in a relatively small office within the main structure. Others may require an attached or unattached outbuilding. Plan a home office at least 50 percent bigger than you think you need. I only say this because I never seem to make them big enough.

W**ork to *save* money, not to pay someone else to do what you can do yourself.**

Home industry does not necessarily mean income-earning industry. Don't forget such homesteading activities as food drying, canning, sewing, and workshop projects. Plan for them at the design stage too, even if only in the form of a nonspecifically designated work area. Roy's Sixth Law of Empiric Economics: Work to *save* money, not to pay someone else to do what you can do yourself.

THE ECONOMY OF TWO STORIES

The economy of building a two-story design comes from the fact that the second story can be added without additional roofing or foundation costs, each of which are expensive and time-consuming parts of the overall house. Floor space is almost doubled with the addition of the second story. (Remember that space is lost on each floor because of the stairs.) There are materials and labor costs associated with the second story, of course, but they are much less by the square foot than the cost of the first story. External wall costs are exactly doubled, but, often, this is not nearly as expensive as foundation and roofing costs, which have already been incurred. An extra floor and floor support system is required, and extra wiring and internal finishing. The stairway itself, which can be difficult for the inexperienced owner-builder or expensive if subbed out to a carpenter, must be factored in. Ancillary systems, such as well, septic, driveway, and alternative energy generation are required in either case. When you add it all up, the second story is inexpensive compared to the first.

Another potential drawback of the two-story design is the health, safety, and convenience problems associated with stairs. Jaki and I are firmly into middle age, and we know what life's next stage is, having recently seen our parents go through it. Stairs can be a real inconvenience for the elderly, not to mention risky. We tell each other that if we ever build a small retirement home, it won't have stairs.

While on the subject of stairs, we have been quite happy with circular stairs, aesthetically and as a means of saving space in the home. We bought our first set from The Iron Shop, Box 547, 400 Reed Road, Broomall, PA 19008. Both their prices and quality are good and they'll send you a catalog and price list if you call 1-800-523-7427. At Mushwood, our summer cottage, we made our own circular stairs, but we already had the experience of assembling the fine set we'd bought from The Iron Shop.

I don't recommend circular stairs of less than five feet in diameter, and the six-foot diameter stairs are a lot easier to negotiate than the five-footers. People not used to circular stairs can slip and fall on them, and I advise avoiding them where elderly or infirm people would need to use them regularly. Make sure *any* stairway is well lit, but especially circular stairs. And remember that you can't move furniture up or down a circular stair, so there needs to be an alternative route, probably from the exterior. This second route will double as a fire escape.

There is another economy inherent in the two-story design: energy efficiency. Given the same foundation and roof size, you can add a second story without increasing the total skin area of the home by all that much.

PLAN WITH THE SITE

Most people plan their houses assuming that the site will be flat. To be sure, flat sites are the easiest to build on. In some cases, however, the best site on a lot—best in terms of the visual impact, solar and wind orientation, or access—might *not* be flat. The two options are to change the plans or to change the site. It is easier, and kinder to the planet, to change the plans. By the same token, split-level homes, which might make perfect sense on sites with a particular slope, could be grossly out of place on a flat or very steep site.

On a steep building site, two options are 1) build a two-story earth-sheltered home, or 2) build a house on pillars. Get professional engineering advice when building any kind of house on a steep slope. Tremendous environmental pressures work unrelentingly to make everything flat. A builder's job is not to beat these forces, just to hold

HEAT LOSS COMPARISON OF ONE- AND TWO-STORY DESIGN

For the sake of easy figuring, we'll compare a simple 32-foot-square one-story design with a 32-foot-square two-story design, each built on a floating slab. Each story has 9-foot-high walls, and the stairwell space eats up 48 square feet on each floor, so 96 SF of useful floor area is lost to the need of accessing the second story.

Skin area, single-story home			*Skin area, two-story home*		
Slab	32' × 32' = 1,024 SF		Slab	32' × 32' = 1,024 SF	
Walls	128 PF × 9' = 1,152 SF		1st story walls	128 PF × 9' = 1,152 SF	
Roof	32' × 32' = 1,024 SF		2nd story walls	128 PF × 9' = 1,152 SF	
			Roof	32' × 32' = 1,024 SF	
Total skin area	3,200 SF		Total skin area	4,352 SF	

Floor area, single-story home			*Floor area, two-story home*		
Floor area	32' × 32' = 1,024 SF		1st floor area	32' × 32' = 1,024 SF	
			2nd floor area	32' × 32' = 1,024 SF	
			Less 96 SF lost in stairwell	-96 SF	
				1,952 SF	

Gain in skin area with two-story house: 4,352 SF – 3,200 SF = 1,152 SF
Percentage gain in skin area: 1,152 SF ÷ 3,200 SF = 36 percent
Gain in useful floor area with two stories: 1,952 SF – 1,024 SF = 928 SF
Percentage gain in floor area: 928 SF ÷ 1,024 SF = 91 percent

Bottom line: Adding the second story increases usable floor space by 91 percent with only 36 percent more skin area. And that's not all. Warm air rises. We may as well use it twice before it leaves us. If the primary heat source warms the air in the lower story, we can use the heat again upstairs. Strategic placement and use of floor registers, internal doors, and the stairwell itself will allow passive delivery of this heat, and the effect can be controlled further with a simple fan in the ceiling of the first story.

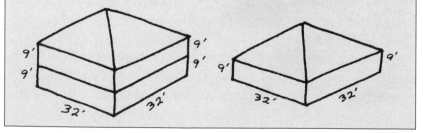

them off for some desired period of time. Even the Great Pyramids, even Mount Everest, will eventually succumb to gravity and erosion. But let's not go looking for trouble with shoddy structural engineering. If in doubt, don't.

I meet lots of people who think that an earth-sheltered house must be built on a south-facing slope. Well, that's a nice situation, to be sure, but it is not the only siting option. By shallow excavation and berming, an earth-sheltered house can be built on a flat site. This may sound like changing the site to suit the plans, but the end result will alter the beauty and ecology of the property less than most of the excuses for architecture that dot the landscape. Earth-sheltered houses do require excavation. Low-lying sites with drainage problems, such as bogs and river flood plains, are no good for underground houses and questionable, in fact, for homes of any kind. Also, avoid north-facing slopes, unless heat dissipation is desired, such as in the extreme South. Stu Campbell, author of *The Underground House Book* (Garden Way Publishing, 1980) says, "The perfect exposure for a window meant to collect solar radiation is 15 degrees west of true South, but 20 degrees to either side of this point is still excellent" (p. 21).

The more beautiful the site, the simpler the structure should be. When it comes to aesthetics, we will not improve on Mother Nature. The house should not take the eye away from the setting, but harmonize with it. This is why it is so difficult to design a house before the site is chosen.

BUILDING STRATEGIES

I've devoted a lot of space to planning strategies, because this is where you can reap the greatest savings with the least trouble. Pencils and scrap paper are cheaper than rafters and sheathing. Without getting into specific styles of construction, certain general building strategies have proven themselves to be valuable to owner-builders over and over again, as will be seen in the next two chapters.

Labor Barter

Compared with a single person's production, two people can get more than twice the work done. Except for individuals of rare tenacity and self-discipline, solitary workers are easily discouraged, prone to loneliness and goofing off, and have been known to throw their hands up in the air during black fly season and walk off the site, never to return. There's no one there to encourage, to inspire, to nag. The advantage of numbers is not limited to couples. If two individuals or two families are building at the same time, as often happened during the early years of our Hill community, it makes a lot of sense to trade workdays on each other's projects. More work will get done, and both parties will learn by the experience. Jim Schley's chapter 7 case study about the advantages of the intentional community drives the point home extremely well.

And there's a psychological benefit, too. If you've asked someone over to help peel logs, for example, you'll be sure to get some logs peeled. The job isn't so enchanting that you can afford to waste an opportunity for help. Also, certain jobs simply go faster with two or three helpers because of the mechanics involved, such as frame raising.

Sometimes you can barter materials with a neighbor who's building; sometimes you can barter materials for labor. These deals are particularly economical if no money changes hands. They're always more satisfying spiritually, and less likely to backfire into bad feeling. We're fairly racking up the laws over the last few pages, but this one can't be left out. Roy's

Help each other, but let no money change hands.

Seventh Law of Empiric Economics is simple, and saves all sorts of added costs: Help each other, but let no money change hands. (Remember to declare all benefits of barter on your income tax return, as required by law. And never, under any circumstances, exceed posted speed limits.)

Work Parties

Sometimes it's advantageous to organize a work party, particularly when it's time for the floor and footing pours, the wall raisings, and rafter and roof work. On the other hand, I have seen owner-builders arrange for several friends—sometimes too many—to come over to help, and end up playing hosts, serving up a couple of cases of beer while the crew stands around talking. This lack of organization is the fault of the owner-builder. You must be sure that all the required materials are ready by the end of the previous day (it's too late on the morning of work), that jobs are properly organized, that the workers will bring the right tools for the job, and that there are no pesky little details that have to be attended to before the day's work can begin. You can get a week's worth of work done in a day with organization. People come expecting and wanting to work. If they don't have a job waiting to be done, sure, they'll start in on the beer. "Might as well make a party of it. I've blown this day coming over for nothing anyway."

Don't let this happen. Plan ahead, involve everyone, and keep the beer out of sight until the end of the workday. Successful work parties are a constant thread that runs through the case studies of chapter 7.

Part-Time Building

Many owner-builders build in their "spare" time, maintaining a regular job simultaneously, which provides the needed financial support to the project.

Beam-raising work party at Log End Cave. The crew takes a well-earned rest after installing the third 30-foot 10-by-10 girder.

Our next-door neighbors adapted this strategy very well to their mortgage-free home. Frank kept his full-time job, working on the house as a second job, while Elizabeth worked on the house almost full time. Sometimes, a couple will take three or four years to build their house in this way, patiently staying in their present mortgaged or rented residence until the new place is completely finished. Others stay in cramped quarters in their temporary shelter during the long building process. A freshly married couple might survive this sort of thing okay—or not, if it turns out that they are really pursuing the "dream" of only one partner. And once the ice cream melts, adverse living conditions will diminish the chances of success for both the construction project and the relationship.

A young couple of our acquaintance live in a lovely little cordwood cabin, a 16-by-20-foot temporary shelter. The place is particularly charming, neat, and tidy, and the massive walls keep it from getting too cold in the winter while they are at their jobs. They travel to work together each day, and build their 24-by-40-foot main house in their spare time. The project will be a success because they have a goal and

Our next-door neighbors, great fans of the Nearings, built what I call "The Quintessential Homestead" in their spare time.

a good plan to achieve it, they pull together, they pay attention to detail, and they know that neatness counts. Life in the TS is not oppressive, so they're in no hurry. When they finally make the move, they plan on using the TS as a workshop. And it will be a neat and tidy one; that much I can guarantee.

Full-Time Building

This strategy means giving up your job, if you've got one. It requires a substantial grubstake or a high degree of skill and courage, or both. The point is that the house gets built fast. This usually happens, but not always! Some people find that after eight hours at a desk, they are capable of putting in eight hours more at the end of a hammer, whereas they might not be capable of putting in sixteen straight hours on the house. Physical and mental work can complement each other quite nicely, whereas either, by itself, can be exhausting.

In general, if you are not relocating, part-time building is the safer strategy. When you are making a major move, perhaps for a change of lifestyle or to take advantage of more favorable land values, the full-time building approach is probably more viable. Get the house up as quickly as possible, and the savings on shelter costs will make up for the temporary loss of income. Make sure you have a sufficient grubstake to see the project through, or you could join those who have had to stop house construction and return to regular jobs to renew funds. While this scenario is by no means the end of the world, it's frustrating to have to put the dream on the back burner. Valuable momentum is lost.

Renovation

I am not eager to recommend old-house renovation as an economic strategy today. Having both renovated and built new, I feel fairly strongly that building new is a lot easier, and probably cheaper, than renovating an old structure in need of a lot of work. There are bargains out there, particularly in small towns and rural areas, but definitely not in popular tourist areas, such as the mountains of Vermont. Sometimes you can find small houses in fair to good condition. They can provide a place to live while you renovate the place, if you are willing to move from room to room. Big, fancy period houses have become popular with the rich and with professional restorers, pushing up their real estate values. Even if you find an eleven-room Victorian for what seems to be a low price, be wary. Restoration is slow, painstaking, and expensive. A few years ago, a comedy starring Tom Hanks and Shelley Long was making the rounds. Called *The Money Pit*, the title referred to the inordinate amount of cash that the hapless couple kept pouring into their big "bargain" house. It wouldn't have been so funny if it wasn't so true.

Old houses probably need work that you can't even see. Bringing insulation up to modern standards, for example, can be extremely expensive. I've known of some old homes that deteriorated rapidly as soon as a new owner pumped insulation into the ancient walls. Wood that had breathed happily for 150 years was suddenly choked. Without a proper vapor barrier, house moisture would penetrate the inner fabric, enter the insulation, and rot the house out from within, like a particularly virulent cancer.

There are always complications with renovation: missing floorboards that are impossible to match, a major girder to replace, a window or door frame that needs to be relocated. Even more than with new construction, "little" jobs take infinitely longer than you ever thought possible. Don't enter into a major renovation project without a lot of experience, a lot of time, and/or a lot of money. There are good books on the subject. Read them. Restoration, which refers to bringing the old building back to its original condition, is extremely expensive, like antique car restoration. Exterior siding and the trim work will have to be matched, antique or antique reproduction fixtures will have to be purchased, a lot of custom millwork will likely be necessary. Love, patience, enthusiasm, time, and money are all prerequisites, and in good measure. An authentic restoration is not the way to a mortgage-free home.

Sometimes, you can find a small country cabin or house that you can whip into livable condition quite quickly and that won't add much to the cost of a parcel of land. Maybe the place just needs a good cleaning and fumigation. A situation like this could be quite valuable, as long as you don't spend too much time or money on it. Use the cabin as a temporary shelter; later it might prove useful as a barn, storage area, or workshop. Someday, when you've got lots of time and you're looking for a hobby, you might want to give it a complete renovation, or even restoration.

Conversions

Another strategy that has worked well for a lot of creative home-owners is to convert a non-house to a house. Some of the results have been spectacular, some cheap, and some expensive. Examples of buildings converted to homes include barns, silos, train stations, one-room schoolhouses, and churches. Quite a few cabooses have been made into homes, but I get the sense that this can be a fairly expensive option nowadays.

In cities, people have converted old breweries, warehouses, and other commercial buildings into housing, but these are generally found under the classification of development projects, not individuals seeking a mortgage-free home.

Underground housing enthusiasts have been particularly creative. One family near us lives in a converted Atlas missile silo, and artist friends in England are transforming a 90-year-old town water tank into a beautiful, spacious, low-cost underground home.

Conversion houses.

Jonathan and Shannon Rodney-Jones are converting this 32-by-64-foot water tank into a spacious underground home.

Jonathan made a doorway through four feet of concrete by drilling overlapping core holes until he could slide out the massive chunk.

Kit Houses

Jonathan Erickson, author of *Build Your Own Kit House* (Tab, 1988) tells us that out of 1.7 million houses built in 1985, about 34 percent were kit houses of one kind or another. The varieties of kit homes are almost endless. While most kit houses feature "traditional" stick-frame construction, all sorts of house options are available: geodesic domes, log homes, post-and-beam, pole buildings, even steel frame kits. What you get varies greatly with the type of kit purchased. Many lumberyards will supply pre-cut kit packages, which amount to a pile of lumber, windows, doors, sheathing, fasteners, and other components. The owner-builder doesn't need to measure and cut the lumber, but simply assembles all the components according to the plans supplied. There may be a slight savings in cost over buying the individual components from a variety of sources. Or not. The real benefit of this type of a pre-cut kit is in convenience and time saved.

Some kits have a little more value added to the materials, such as dome kits with special pre-made triangles or hub systems, and log home kits where the home has been cut, fitted, and assembled once already on the manufacturer's lot, then numbered and delivered to the client's property for reassembly. The important thing to know with any kind of kit is what is *not* included. Some kit prices seem very attractive until you total up all the missing stuff, perhaps wiring, plumbing, cabinets, flooring, etc. And don't forget the foundation. The cost of the kit itself usually turns out to be about half (or less) of the final cost of the home. Price all systems carefully or you may find yourself in for a very rude awakening.

The next step up in kit houses are panelized kits, where whole pre-manufactured wall panels are delivered to the site and assembled by the builder. I worked on one such home while working for a contractor. The panelized wall sections arrived on a big flatbed truck. The basement foundation had been built a few days earlier. With the help of a crane, the basic house was assembled on the foundation by about six men in one day. Roofing was another day. These houses will not present much of a savings over a contractor-built home, unless the owner acts as the contractor himself (see appendix 3, category 5: Self-Contracting). Again, the big savings is in time.

Modular Homes

Modular homes are not to be confused with "double-wide" mobile homes. A modular is delivered on a frame carrier and is either rolled onto the foundation or lifted into place with a crane. The double-wide (and single-wide) mobile home has its own metal frame and wheels. Modulars are built according to state-approved engineering specifications. Double-wides are less expensive, but built to a lower standard, known in the industry as the HUD standard. A typical difference is that the modular might have 2-by-10-inch floor joists, while double-wides use 2-by- 6s. Roof pitches and roof overhangs are generally greater on the modulars.

Modular homes come in an almost infinite variety of styles, shapes, and finishes. They can be large or small, one story or two. In general, they are more affordable than new contractor-built homes, but more expensive than owner-built homes. High-end luxury modular homes are becoming more and more common. In our area in 1997, a 26-by-52-foot modular costs around $64,000 (the same size double-wide will cost about $48,000). The modular is almost always put on a basement foundation, typically $8,000 in our area in 1997. Modular homes can appreciate in value, while mobile homes almost always depreciate. This admitted generalization is affected by location, initial quality of the homes, and how well the homes are looked after.

Even though modular homes are subject to strict standards, price, features, and—yes—quality will vary with the manufacturer. While this is one area where the adage "You get what you pay for" is generally true, there is also the opportunity for bargains if you bide your time. Dealers might need space on the lot, or have a home that was ordered for a customer and, for some reason, the contract never completed. Sales promotions are common and bargaining is imperative.

The modular home option might be affordable to some without a mortgage. And it is certainly quick. While they may not appeal to people interested in alternative building styles such as straw bale, cordwood, or underground, the reverse is probably equally true.

Mobile Homes and Double-Wides

In many parts of the United States, mobile homes are perceived as the only affordable housing option. This is sad. When I was administering

HUD and state housing improvement grants, we worked on many mobile homes that were literally falling apart Some of these were only ten years old. It wasn't worth putting money into rehabilitation. In many cases, we simply replaced the home with—you guessed it—a later model or even new mobile home. The grant programs were no more imaginative than that. Self-help was very difficult to administer, and, frankly, not many clients were interested in self-help options. Mobile homes are a money trap, a fire trap, and a lifestyle trap. They will not function on alternative energy, and they are expensive to heat and difficult to keep cool. Like a car, they depreciate the moment they leave the display lot, and their value goes down steadily after that. Reread Michael Potts's commentary on mobile homes (sidebar, page 123). I like it because my own experience and observations ratify every word. Mobile home manufacturers will not like it.

Organization

Lack of understanding of the order of events in house construction and the priorities that result from this order is a common reason for problems and even failure among owner-builders . Even when the plans are fairly complete, sensible, and well adapted to the site and the materials, it is still all too common that no thought has been given to implementing the plans. The basic order for virtually any kind of house is:

1. Site preparation
2. Foundation
3. Framing (or masonry walls and roof framing)
4. Roof
5. Plumbing and electric
6. Wall and floor finishing
7. Finish work

Every stage must be planned in advance to ensure that the necessary materials, tools, and/or labor are not missing. A few specific examples follow.

Heavy equipment contractors: If building in the North, bear in mind that these contractors are in great demand as soon as the weather breaks in the spring. A logjam of house planners and contractors wait all winter to break loose. Your whole project is stalled until the site work is

FANCY FINISHED, RUSTIC FINISHED, UNFINISHED

Avoid "fancy finishing," expensive trims, expensive floor coverings, bathroom tiles (unless you get a deal on recycled ones), gold door-knobs, and the like. These add greatly to the house cost with little practical gain. Choose structural materials that have pleasing surface qualities. Many rustic or alternative house styles, such as adobe, log, cordwood, and stone, are "ready finished."

Space that is to be used for storage or as a work area, such as a laundry, does not need its walls, floor, and ceiling expensively covered. Likewise, light fixtures can be simple, functional, and cheap. Finished space adds a lot more to your valuation than unfinished space—and, therefore, to your property tax bill—so take advantage of unfinished space wherever you can. You'll save when you build, and every year thereafter on your tax assessment.

Painting and staining wood serves little purpose outside of changing the color, and rarely is the change an improvement. Stain always darkens wood. Paint must be repainted, *ad infinitum*. Wood left on its own will start out pleasing, and get more pleasing with age. On the floor, consider the use of a natural penetrating oil that actually hardens the wood itself instead of creating a thin hard surface that chips away, as with varnishes and urethanes.

Interior wood does not need to be "preserved," and neither does most above-grade vertically applied exterior siding, the exception being in certain constantly damp coastal climates and inland rainforest areas. People pay fancy prices for weathered barn boards, but hesitate in putting new rough-cut lumber on their walls. Apart from dollar costs, consider the health cost of living in a home coated with toxic chemicals, even the exterior surface. What will a substance that "preserves" wood do to your body? The only places I will use pressure-treated material is for ground-contact pillar foundations and for horizontal exterior surfaces, such as decks. My son, who outflanks me on environmental issues, has no use for the stuff whatsoever.

done, so arrange for heavy equipment contracting as early as possible, preferably weeks ahead.

The pour. Have all forming, mesh, rebar, insulation, underfloor plumbing—in short, everything to do with your slab or footings pour—ready a full 24 hours ahead of time! This may seem unduly cautious. It isn't. When you think you're ready, you'll still work a few hours testing the plumbing, checking the forms for level and strength, gathering the right tools and crew, and so on. If you have a free hour to relax before the truck arrives, you'll have a more pleasant pour. Enjoy it. The next few hours are going to be the busiest time in the entire project!

Materials. Lay by as many of the materials as you can prior to the building season. Spring is also the busiest season for sawmills, and you will have to build with green wood if you delay to the last minute. Even a month or two of air-drying the lumber is a lot better than none at all. Do not predicate the whole project on a source of materials that is not absolutely reliable. Murphy's Law says you will be disappointed. I can personally vouch for this one.

Plumbing and electric. If you are going to do your own plumbing and electric work—and you can and should if you are building the rest of the place—one of the best strategies is to find an experienced tradesperson to get you started, even if you have to hire that person for a day to show you how to make the connections. Alternatively, hire yourself out to a tradesperson as an apprentice for the job. You might save a little money, and what you learn will certainly come in handy if you ever need to repair, remove, or extend systems. The apprenticeship idea is particularly valuable for those pursuing the Add-on House strategy. Do-it-yourselfers should work from a simple, easy-to-read plan and have one or two good reference books handy. With electrical installation, you could have an electrician check your work to make sure that it will pass inspection.

An old tip on plumbing, but worth repeating in case you haven't heard it, is that placing the bathroom and kitchen adjacent to each other makes for minimal plumbing. Similarly, an upstairs bathroom should be directly over downstairs plumbing, or nearly so.

Auctions and demolition sites are good places to look for recycled sinks, toilets, and bathtubs. This can save you a small fortune. Remember that new faucets are expensive and that an old sink with hardware is worth a lot more than one without fixtures. It is very difficult to find the right hardware for old sinks, toilets, and tubs.

Winter. Get the place closed in before winter (if you live in the North). This is the only absolutely imperative deadline you have to meet. Winter will begin in your area a full two weeks before the earliest date you think possible. Of course, you lucky Southerners can ignore this warning.

Interior finishing. Like everything else, but more so, finish work takes infinitely longer than you ever thought possible. Therefore, design for simple finishing. If you don't like hanging sheetrock, taping, spackling, and painting, avoid sheetrock, or plan for the joins to be covered with decorative wood stripping. I have no patience for sheetrocking, wall-papering, and window and door trimming, and will go out of my way at the design stage to eliminate these time-consuming features.

Time estimation. Owner-builders usually underestimate costs by 20 to 25 percent, which isn't bad when you think of all the components that go into building. But their time estimates are typically off by 100 percent. They see contractors putting up a house in five weeks and they say, "Well, then, surely I can build my house in five *months.*" It would seem so. Professionals cannot saw boards and hammer nails five times as fast as amateurs, but, because of their experience, they can think and make correct decisions five times as fast, and spend less time repairing bad decisions. In short, they know how to organize the job. Inaccurate time estimates often result in owner-builders moving into their structures long before they are finished. Ken Kern, in *The Owner-Builder and the Code* (Scribner's, 1976) observes:

> Besides cluttering the house with objects which must be moved or worked around, early occupation has the effect of altering the sequence of construction. . . . The importance of such things as running water, counter space, lighting, privacy, and heating increases greatly when the house is occupied. An understanding of the principles of sequence is critical here, since owner-builders are suddenly faced with the prospect of installing several of the most complicated systems in the house (p. 84).

Chapter 6 relates how Jaki and I have used the strategies of the first five chapters to build not one, but four mortgage-free homes.

6

Our Own Story

I should not talk so much about myself if there were anybody else whom I knew as well. Unfortunately, I am confined to this theme by the narrowness of my experience. Moreover, I, on my side, require of every writer, first or last, a simple and sincere account of his own life, and not merely what he has heard of other men's lives; some such account as he would send to his kindred from a distant land; for if he has lived sincerely, it must have been in a distant land to me.

—HENRY DAVID THOREAU, WALDEN

WORLD UNIVERSITY

Not wanting school to get in the way of my education, I decided to learn a little about work and commerce after graduation from high school, rather than to enter aimlessly into college. At age 16, and with capital borrowed from my father, I began to operate a water ski school in Massachusetts during the summer months. Upon completion of high school, I continued my little enterprise, and, during the off-season, worked as a department store sales clerk, and a molder at an industrial matchplate company, sometimes holding two jobs at once. During this time, I met Denis, a young man from New Zealand, on his two-year trek around the world. It seems that many (if not most) New Zealanders elect to "see the world" before they settle into a long, prosperous, and peaceful life in that idyllic island nation. Denis convinced me—or inspired me, it is so long ago—that I, too, should seek a more worldly outlook. With money saved from the ski school and my other jobs, I left home in October of 1966, age 19, and began my Journey to the East. The following May, twenty-six countries later, and having progressed continuously toward the East without ever quite getting there, I arrived back at my point of beginning, physically if not spiritually. I'd even visited Denis in Wellington. And he'd been right: the world, and my home, never looked quite the same again after the eight-month course of study at World U.

Living out of a backpack in places like the Middle East, India, Nepal, and Central America is a crash course in the Conserver Economy. A finite (and not very large) amount of money has to last throughout the journey. During some stretches, I lived on a dollar a day, more at other times. I taught water skiing in Australia for room and board, saving considerable expenditure in what otherwise would have been an expensive country to visit. I hitchhiked on petrol tankers through Afghanistan in the dead of night, and slept in a jail in Herat when 50¢ for the local hotel was beyond budget. I found that Hesse's Siddhartha was right: If one could think, wait, and fast, there was no problem that couldn't be either solved, circumvented, or ignored outright.

Because of the sheer number of events during such intense travel, formative input seems to manifest itself about four times as fast as during "normal" living at home, work, or school. The overworked cliché—"Travel is the best education"—remains good standard wisdom, not because of the sights seen, the varied landform and architecture, the museums, the different foods and languages, although these things are all important. The real education comes from the people met, their ideas encountered, their different cultures experienced. I found out that on a world scale, the American attitude toward consumption and waste is an aberration. When 5 percent of the world's people are consuming nearly 30 percent of the world's resources (leaving the other 95 percent of people to scramble over the remaining 70 percent), is it really any surprise that we are not the most popular people in the world? When I returned to the United States, I was appalled by the consumption, the waste, the attitude that we are automatically entitled to consume "more than our appointed share," because, after all, we are able to pay for it with good fresh American money printed just this morning in Philadelphia. "All perfectly legal," we say, as if legality equates with morality. I became depressed about my country's direction, and was, I am sure, a pain in the collective necks of my family.

October 1966, the idealistic young traveler surveys the heathlands of southwest England, part of the vast World U. campus.

After another summer at the ski school, my third, I left again on another eight-month journey, this time to Scotland, Spain, and across a fair chunk of the vast African continent. I stayed for a few weeks in an empty crofter's cottage in the Highlands, slept on beaches in the Canaries, and camped in another jail—the backpacker's motel—this time in Zimbabwe. I learned absolute basic living from a diminutive Swede, who kept all his possessions wrapped up in a towel: a spare shirt and shorts, his money, his pipe, and his passport. We traveled for days together, fourth class on a tramp steamer from the Canaries to Santa Isabel de Fernando Po, a tiny Spanish colony off the coast of what was then Biafra (in Nigeria). We hobnobbed with mercenaries traveling to Biafra to represent both sides in that bloody conflict, a German in search of the rare white gorilla in the Congo (he was successful; I later saw his pictures in *National Geographic*), and a supporting cast of colorful characters, every one of whom showed points of view that you're not likely to run into at the neighborhood bar. On the return journey, I stopped again in the Scottish Highlands, where I had made friends, and it was then that I decided that we are not necessarily born into the very place that best suits our temperament or personality.

I returned "home" again, not quite sure what this meant anymore, ran the ski school one final year, and took a job at a private school teaching algebra and geometry. After four months, I realized that I was not ready to settle down to being a math teacher for the rest of my life. Not at the age of 21 anyway. I moved—permanently, I thought—to Scotland.

I keep saying that everybody's different. It's the closest thing I know to a universal truth. But, outside of obvious genetic differences, what is it that makes everyone different? We are different because of the varied inputs on our lives: the books we read, the people we meet, the places we visit and live in, the ideas we encounter. The greater and more varied these inputs are, the greater the variety of differences. Although everybody's different, people who never go further than twenty miles from home, wherever that might be, and whose cultural exposure does not extend very far beyond range of the TV set, are not likely to vary as much as those with a less parochial outlook. I mention all this, and take a little of the reader's time, to give you a sense of some of the things that make *me* different, which have pushed me toward *my* outlook on economy, values, even housing. Be thankful that you have the short version; when I was 25, I wrote a 350-page autobiographical novel about this very subject.

It is good to know in what ways you are different. Through honest self-examination, you may glean insight into whether or not your current mode of existence suits you, whether or not a mortgage-free home will really grace your life. Perhaps it won't. Perhaps pursuit of that dream is not as important as pursuit of some other dream: full concentration on a promising career that you love, for example. If you learn that much from your introspection, it'll be worthwhile.

SCOTLAND

My first property search was in Scotland. A few of us used to ski on a loch called Achility near Dingwall in the Northwest Highlands. There was a stone house and barn falling to ruin on the edge of the loch, and I could see great potential in the place. The wooded, hilly, and sparsely populated setting was idyllic. Loch Achility would be my Walden Pond. And the property was for sale. An architect in Dingwall valued the property for me at £600, about $1,500 in those days, and I submitted an offer for that amount. It sold to an airline pilot for £1,500, about $3,600. I was disappointed, because I knew that I would have been willing to pay as much for it myself. The lesson learned: when a real bargain shows up, he who hesitates is lost. The architect, however, told me of another property for sale: two attached farm cottages in the middle of a 600-acre sheep and cattle farm, just 1½ miles from Dingwall, the county town. I visited the property with the owner, who also owned the surrounding farmland, and fell in love with the position. It had the isolation I was looking for at that time in my life, and a south-facing view of the tidal Cromarty Firth and the Black Isle beyond. The cottages were perched on the side of a hill about 500 feet above sea level, and the view was clear for many miles in three different compass directions. The farmer wanted £1,000, about $2,400, and I offered 800. He said, nope, £1,000 it was, not a penny less. I knew it was a bargain, and fresh from the Loch Achility experience, I agreed.

My grubstake was about $9,000, money that had been saved by my parents for my college education. As I was now over 21, and it became increasingly unlikely that I would be going to college, they gave me the money, to sink or swim with as I might. I think they knew by this time that I could get as much mileage out of it as anyone.

Mountrich Cottage, Dingwall, Scotland, before renovation.

Prime Minister Harold Wilson leveraged my grubstake in the form of a 50 percent matching grant for housing rehabilitation. In truth, it was the Labor government of the day that provided these grants, but I always think fondly of dear old Uncle Harold. My architect friend told me about the grant, and I protested that, despite my name, I was not Scottish, had not yet made any contribution to British society at all. I'll never forget his answer, which was this: "Och, mon, it's not yerself gettin' the grant, it's the hoose!" The socialist government had taken it upon itself to look after everyone in the United Kingdom from cradle to grave. A sheepfarmer friend said to me, "Rob, the folk in this country have lost their right to starve." Not such a bad right to give up, you might think, but think a little further. If you lose your right to starve, or fail, you also lose your right to succeed. How can anyone truly succeed without the chance of failure? A slave, too, has lost his right to starve. I digress, but only slightly.

The upshot, with regard to the housing grant, was that I would be helping Her Majesty's government to provide one additional dwelling unit. The government was building hundreds of county council houses in the Dingwall area for which they paid the entire cost. Well, the people did, really, through very high taxes. Here was a chance to save a building from going to ruin for a fraction of the cost of a new unit. The fact that the house would be occupied by a single American did not come into the equation. A dwelling unit would be saved. And, eventually, the home was occupied consecutively by three different young British couples, during times when Mrs. Thatcher, whatever else she might have done, returned to the citizenry their right to fail.

Here's how the housing grant worked. The grant application involved submitting the planned renovations to the powers-that-were (grantspeople, the local planning authority and the building inspector), as well as a detailed costing analysis for the project based upon bids from qualified tradesmen. I drew out the floorplan of how I wanted to use the building's shell, and the architect helped me by drawing plans suitable for submission and doing work write-ups for the tradesmen. We needed a carpenter, mason, electrician, and plumber, and had to get bids from at least two of each trade. The low bid was accepted, unless the owner wished to make up the difference out of pocket, which I did in one case, because the bids were close and I felt better about one plumber over the other. The total cost of the renovation was about £5,400, or $13,000. I paid half, Uncle Harold paid half. All told, I was the owner of a beautiful, fully renovated cottage in an idyllic location for the grand total of $8,900 out of pocket. The only string attached was that if I sold the home within three years, I would have to pay a portion of the grant monies back: 100 percent payback during the first year, 67 percent during the second year, 33 percent during the third year. After that, I was home free. Or would that be Scot free?

STRATEGIES USED TO KEEP MOUNTRICH COTTAGE MORTGAGE-FREE:

1. Land search in area of low property values.
2. Used college money for grubstake, a personal choice.
3. Use of housing rehabilitation grant.
4. Provided sweat equity to reduce interim housing costs (worked for carpenter in exchange for accommodation).

Rob and Jaki Roy at Mountrich Cottage after renovation.

"Good for you," says the cynic. "You lucked out. You found low property values, a place ripe for renovation, and a government grant." That's right. Go ye and do likewise. All three are good viable strategies. Property bargains can be found all over the country. You may have to relocate to get them. I relocated right off the continent, and returned to find another bargain a few years later in New York.

And government grants exist in North America, too. I know, because I administered them for over four years. For income-eligible families, housing rehab grants can be up to 100 percent. There are also 50 percent matching grants available, like the one I had in Scotland. You will have to inquire locally to see what's happening in your area. A good place to start is a local rural preservation company that administers such grants. Sometimes municipalities do the grant applications and administration themselves, and sometimes they retain not-for-profit companies to do all this for them. I worked for an NFP company. One word of caution, though. Often, one of the eligibility rules for a HUD-type grant is that you owned the property at the time the municipality was funded for the grant. The idea is to stop people from buying property just to take advantage of a newly funded grant. Therefore, in many cases, the strategy of using state or federal grant monies will only be available on a property that you already own.

And renovation is a viable strategy, too. I've already told of a friend who bought an old house on Murtagh Hill at very low cost. The purchase price was a function of all the work that needs to be done on the place, a new roof, for example. But with a quick patch on a couple of leaks, our friend will actually be able to live in the home, saving shelter costs, while fixing it up as he can afford to.

In fairness, I must tell the other side of the renovation coin. I have been involved in renovation (in Scotland) and in building new houses from scratch. It is easier to build new—everyone will tell you this—and you are less constricted in the floor plan when starting with a clean sheet of paper. But I would be equally remiss if I did not point out the satisfaction that comes from saving a beautiful old building, and the fact that there are some great potential bargains available by way of the renovation route. When you think about it, renovation is more in tune with the Conserver Economy than is building a new house. The basic fabric of the building is already there, saving the manufacture and transportation of tons of materials. Far fewer trees will need to be cut, much less environmentally disastrous cement will be needed, no new lifeless driveway needs to be created. Saving the house from falling to bits avoids a blight on the landscape for, perhaps, many years, as well as the energy and environmental costs associated with removing the blight, including dumping the remains in a landfill. That's another nice thing about building a home with indigenous materials: When the place finally gives up its ghost, it just recedes gracefully into the very landscape from whence it sprung.

I spent six wonderful years at Mountrich Cottage, but the best part was that I met Jaki there.

BACK TO AMERICA

My mother couldn't figure out why I moved to a seemingly remote part of Scotland. But, after my father died, she came to visit for a while at Mountrich and found it quite charming. I had taken a job with the masonry contractor who did all of the stone work at the cottage, and, by so doing, stumbled upon another strategy: getting building experience by working for a contractor, prior to building one's own home.

In 1974, Jaki and I came to America for an extended visit to family, none of whom had been able to attend our wedding in Scotland, and to travel around the States, partly just to tour, but also to look for homesteading land. We wanted to pursue a self-reliant lifestyle, something that was not easy to do in Britain. We owned our Shelter, no problem there. But we were not self-reliant in either Food or Fuel. We didn't know it at the time, but we probably could have been just as self-reliant in food in Scotland as we are in northern New York. We hadn't heard about bio-dynamic (or French intensive) raised bed gardening. We only had a quarter-acre of land, and the cottage sat on part of that and shaded another part, so we really had only about 2,000 square feet to grow vegetables. This would have been plenty, but we didn't know it.

Fuel was more of a problem. We heated with energy-inefficient fireplaces, backed up by electric off-peak (or *night storage*) radiators. The farmer allowed us to drag home dead branches from the trees lining the fields, and they burned well, but after five years we were dragging branches a considerable distance, and there was always the possibility of being cut off from this free fuel altogether.

Rightly or wrongly, our choices seemed to boil down to these: (1) Abandon the dream of a totally self-reliant lifestyle and stay in our idyllic cottage (by this time, I had attained permanent resident status in the United Kingdom); (2) Move to New Zealand, a beautiful country where self-reliant living was the norm (not surprising considering that it has the greatest ratio of resources to population of any country in the world); (3) Move to the United States, where I still had citizenship (Jaki would be allowed in as my wife). Well, we sent off to New Zealand for their immigration materials, but were totally put off by the nature and tone of the bumph that was sent to us. We got the impression that the political climate was somewhere between that of Victorian England and the early 1950s in the United States. And, of course, it was as far away from our families and friends as we could get. I knew that people like my friend Denis often traveled the world once in their youth, and then never left New Zealand again. Jaki had never been to America, and I'd seen very little of it myself, so we decided to travel around the United States and check out the land at the same time.

Using money saved while living in Scotland, we flew to the States in 1974, bought a used VW camper van for $2,600, and set out on a four-month belated honeymoon, traveling through some thirty-five states, but only getting to know a few. Quite early on in our search, we found the land on Murtagh Hill (our discovery is described in chapter 3). Although we'd put a deposit on the Hill property, we kept looking as we traveled, because, in the backs of our minds, we worried a bit about the long North Country winters. In fact, we found another piece of land in the western part of Virginia, adjacent to a beautiful protected recreational reservoir, and we even put down a $100 deposit on it. We stayed a few days in the area and inquired about the services and amenities available locally. During these researches, we developed a negative feeling about the people and political climate of the area. We met a lot of good people, too, but one fellow who we considered sincere let me know that it would be risky to leave my beautiful young wife on the remote property by herself. You have to realize that we were long-haired types and one of us had a beard, and in those days, such outer appearances were easy bait for bigotry, or so we perceived. After a couple of days, we were imagining rednecks behind each tree, and we went back to the real estate agent and asked if he would consider giving us our $100 deposit back. No problem. He was within his legal rights to keep the money, but he returned it, and cheerfully.

Our first stay on Murtagh Hill.

We looked at land in Tennessee and Arkansas, and felt some of the same kinds of negative vibrations that we'd picked up in Virginia. I must hasten to add that this is not intended to be a criticism of the South. Vibrations work both ways. And we only experienced two or three isolated—perhaps *too* isolated—areas. I was, am, and always will be a Northerner, just as Jaki is British, and we understand that it takes time to learn the ways and gain the trust of rural peoples anywhere.

Weedy Rough

I must tell of one pleasant stop that we made in northwestern Arkansas, as it influenced our building, homesteading, and community outlook in several important ways. Weedy Rough was—and perhaps still is—a community of people who had gone through high school and college together and bought a large parcel of land collectively. Their community contained artists, musicians, builders, and craftspeople of all kinds. With mutual assistance, each individual or family built a home. Geodesic domes and log cabins were in vogue when we visited in 1974. Half of the community wanted commercial electricity and the other half didn't, so power was extended along one side of the stream, but not the other.

Jaki and I were impressed by the good feeling in the air. We happened to be there at Easter and joined in with the potluck dinner celebration. Someone published a monthly newsletter, "The Weedy Reader." During the time we visited, a few of the menfolk had a job building a log cabin for a client nearby, and we were told that we could work on the project, too, if we liked. This came at a good time for us and it was nice to settle in one place for a while, even if only for ten days. We discovered two things on this project. First, we couldn't manhandle the 13-foot-long-by-8-inch-diameter pine logs. We'd considered building a log home ourselves until this valuable experience. Second, the owner introduced us to the *Mother Earth News*, then in its very early days. Here was a magazine that catered to the kind of lifestyle that we wanted to pursue. Its trademarked subtitle was, "more than a magazine . . . a way of life."

We left Weedy Rough knowing that we would like to be part of a community, wherever we finally settled. After Arkansas, we stopped looking for land, deciding that Murtagh Hill was the place for us. We traveled another month out west, and arrived back in northern New

York in late May to finish the final paperwork on the land purchase, and to record the deed and the bond and mortgage at the county clerk's office. The seller seemed to like dealing with us and he gave us a one-year option on an additional 180 acres that he owned, right across from the 64 acres we'd already bought. He probably figured that we would find buyers for him. And, for our part, we welcomed the chance to try, as we'd learned at Weedy Rough that we would really rather be part of a community than to try to go it alone as a couple of hermits.

We sold the camper van for $2,300, $300 less than we'd paid for it, although a $250 valve job in San Francisco needs to be factored into our true cost. Still, $550 plus gas was not too bad for 11,500 miles of transport. And, in over one hundred nights on the road, we only had to pay for a camping space once, at the Grand Canyon, so accommodation was practically free.

It was about this time that we happened to notice an article in the April, 1974, *National Geographic Magazine*, which showed a picture of a cordwood masonry home built by a lady and her son. Although there was no detailed information on construction, we knew as soon as we saw the pictures that the technique made sense, and that, unlike the heavy pine log cabin we'd worked on in Arkansas, this was a building method that we could do ourselves.

Organizing a Community

We arrived back in Scotland on June 1, 1974, having spent five months in the United States, visiting, travelling, and purchasing our land. Now we had to go through the process of getting a green card for Jaki and selling Mountrich Cottage so that we'd have a grubstake for our homesteading venture. During these last ten months in Scotland, we placed a letter in the "Positions and Situations" column of *Mother Earth News*, as follows:

> We're a young couple moving this spring to a secluded 244 acres near Plattsburgh, New York, to build a house and grow some food. We're looking for several peaceful folks—to come in with us on an individual ownership basis—who have respect for nature and are willing to help each other out as necessary. We own 64 acres and have an option on the rest, which could be bought at $125 to $175 per acre. Land rolls gently, has mature wood, good meadows, clean streams and no buildings. Access

by town road, plowed in winter. Details by return of post. Tell us about yourselves.

We gave our names and address in Scotland.

During the next few months, we received over ninety replies, mostly from people looking for land, but also a few from people in Clinton County, New York, who just wanted to say "hello" and invite us to stop in to visit when we got to America. This was an unexpected bonus; some of these people became good friends.

We replied to each inquiry, and exchanged several letters with many of the correspondents. A huge chart domimated our kitchen wall at Mountrich Cottage. After a while the list kind of pared itself down to a dozen seriously interested families, and we all agreed to meet on the land in April of 1975.

As a result of our efforts, eleven families ended up joining with us on the original parcels and four other families have since joined the community on riparian land. We now have over fifty people living on "The Hill," a loose-knit intentional community.

Each family obtained a warranty deed for their parcel, and, in most cases, five-year mortgages were arranged through the owner at 6 percent interest. Typical land payments were $500 to $1,000 per year, depending on acreage and ease of access (which affected the per acre land price). By dividing up a large parcel of land, at a relatively low cost per acre, we all benefited over what individual 20-acre parcels would have cost.

Before a group jumps in and buys such a property, you should make sure that you all understand any subdivision restrictions that might apply in your chosen town or county. Where we settled, for example, a property divided into more than four pieces came under the authority of rather stiff subdivision restrictions. Luckily, the land that the group bought was in three parcels and we were able to divide them into two lots, three lots, and four lots respectively, without hassle.

Each family on The Hill owns its own piece of land. I outlined options involving co-ownership in chapter 3, but such options must be entered into very carefully indeed, and legal assistance is a good idea. Co-ownership by a group drawn together as casually as ours has definite risks. The success of the Weedy Rough folks, in my view, was due to their long friendship all through high school and college. Personalities, by this time, were pretty well known to each other. Another great example of a successful community land purchase is detailed in Jim Schley's article in chapter 7.

Intentional communities proliferate all over the United States, and more are being started all the time. Some are based upon religion, some are not. Many of them will allow extended visits first, to kind of try out the lifestyle. A source book appears in appendix 3.

Selling Mountrich

My wife is an alien. She has to have what used to be called a green card to prove that she can legally reside in the United States. Things have changed in the 1990s; the card is now pink. In 1975, the U.S. government would give only a ninety-day window of opportunity between the time a green card was issued and the time you had to be physically present in the United States. We couldn't really risk selling Mountrich Cottage without the green card, so we only had three months to sell it after Jaki's papers came through. It's never good to have to sell something under pressure like that. Just before the time limit expired, just days before we had to be in the States, we sold the cottage for $26,000. The sale occurred so late that we were not able to bring the money to the States with us. Then it got lost for a while by being sent to the wrong bank, disconcerting to say the least. Finally, the check made its way into our bank account in Plattsburgh. It was "clean" money, no taxes to pay either in the U.K. or the U.S., and the terms of the home improvement grant had been completely satisfied. As our down payment on the land had already been made, we had a little over $26,000 of a grubstake to buy a vehicle, build a temporary shelter, build our house, and pay ordinary living expenses while doing all of that. Imagine our chagrin when, a month later, a young Frenchman's disability settlement came through and he offered us $35,000 for Mountrich. Toulait, Lautrec.

WE MOVE TO THE LAND

We'd sold most of our possessions back in Scotland, and arrived in North America with a minimum of baggage and Sabre, our German shepherd. One of our correspondents met us at Montreal Airport and we stayed the first two nights with him and his wife about twenty miles from the land. In a few weeks' time, this young couple would be one of the families to join us on Murtagh Hill.

Tom, the old gent who sold us the land, provided us with a small camping trailer for a couple of weeks while we built our TS. We arrived on The Hill on the last day of March 1975, and the land was clear, just the slightest trace of snow still left in the woods. It began to snow on April 2 and didn't stop until the fifth, 48 inches of snow later, with drifts to six feet. Tom was worried about the green young couple from Scotland and sent the State Police to try to find us. They were not able to make it through to us with either ordinary or widetrack snow machines, so they abandoned the effort. The town grader started up the road, but made it less than a mile before it could go no further. Meanwhile, Jaki and I were as warm as toast and enjoying the blizzard. On the fifth, we were scheduled to meet with several families from all over North America to look at the land, so we decided that we'd better try to make our way down off The Hill on foot. It was a tough slog through the drifting snow to the point where the grader had failed, and we pushed through onto the cleared road at about the same time that a station wagon with New Jersey plates arrived from the opposite direction. We knew who it must be. "Steve Dorresteyn, I presume," I said. "Rob Roy!" said Steve.

One of our correspondents happened to have a father who lived nearby, and eventually, all of the interested parties met together at his house, a meeting of high energy and good vibrations. It was a few days before we could actually view the land, or at least the snow that covered the land, but eventually six other parties joined in with us to take up the option on the remaining land.

Transportation

I am not mechanically inclined. Or, more accurately, I do not like automotive mechanics, which boils down to the same thing. I know all about the savings that can come from doing maintenance and repairs on one's own vehicles, and I try to keep up with the simplest things, like battery, tire, and oil changes. But to fix the brakes or even change a fan belt . . . forget it. I'll work longer at something else to earn money to pay a mechanic to do it. Knowing this, Jaki and I opted for a spanking new Toyota pickup truck. We figured the truck would be reliable, economical to run, and a valuable tool for building our house. It was all three, and we never regretted the $3,000 cost. It was the first new vehicle either of us had ever owned. We didn't know it at the time, but it would eventually serve us in the construction of four houses, while proving invaluable to our homesteading lifestyle: hauling firewood, hay, topsoil, manure, you name it.

Our Temporary Shelter

The storm set our building plans back a couple of weeks and Tom had to return the camper he'd rented for us. Luckily, the local people who owned the summer camp across the road from our property, the only habitable building on The Hill, offered to let us live there while we built our TS. We stayed there four weeks and moved into our 12-by-16-foot shed about May 15.

New friends asked if Sabre, who was a second place finisher, puppy class, at the Edinburgh dog show, would like to service their purebred shepherd bitch. Always an obliging sort of dog, Sabre performed his end of the bargain and our payment was "pick of the litter." Soon, our little family consisted of Jaki, Rob, Sabre, and puppy Strider. Cozy. At least the dogs couldn't climb the ladder into the loft.

LOG END COTTAGE

We'd researched cordwood masonry as far as we could, but, outside of the *National Geographic* article, we were only able to find one or two references about the method being used for barns in nineteenth-century Wisconsin and in Canada's Ottawa Valley. One day, while describing the technique to our local sawyer, he told us that, yes, he'd seen that sort of construction when he'd been up around Winchester, Ontario, a hundred miles or so from where we lived. Old Tom, the house builder, was curious to see this for himself, and offered to drive us up to Winchester to see what we could learn. By knocking on doors, we were able to learn about two or three old cordwood houses, which we visited. But the cordwood had been largely covered up, and the occupants of the houses couldn't tell us much about the technique. Then, on the way back home, late on a Sunday afternoon, we came across a farmer actually laying up a cordwood masonry barn. Incredible. The knowledge was still alive. The farmer had also built a vacation cabin for a client in Guelph, Ontario. He was happy to share what he knew about cordwood masonry, which was, in short, "Use dry wood and plenty of lime in your mortar." Words of wisdom to a couple of neophytes.

Design

Architecturally, we wanted a home that would combine both European and American elements. We have always enjoyed the atmosphere of a good olde English half-timbered pub, so we wanted plenty of big exposed beams in the place. The cordwood masonry infilling would give the cottage an American flavor, although there is anecdotal evidence that cordwood buildings may have been built in Europe a thousand years ago. The steep roof pitch and great overhangs around the edge of the building gave the design a little bit of the flavor of a Swiss mountain cottage.

Recycled Materials

The design was somewhat influenced by our good fortune in finding two different sources of 100-year-old, full-dimensioned, 3-by-10-inch rafters and floor joists. An old masonic hall in West Chazy was being torn down, as well as the Saranac Lake Inn, about sixty miles away. We bought thirty-six 12-footers and thirty-six 16-footers at an average cost of less than $3 apiece. The long ones served as rafters, and the shorter ones as floor joists. We secured posts and beams from a variety of sources, including several old barns, but the main floor support girder as well as the ridge pole, both 8 inches by 10 inches in section, came from the same masonic hall. They were already notched to receive the three-by-tens, saving us hours of meticulous and highly skilled work.

Log-ends are what we call the short ends, butts, or pieces of wood that are mortared up in the cordwood wall. About 40 percent of ours were cut from cedar growing on our property. Steve gave us some leftover short pieces from his cedar log house that he was building at the same time, perhaps another 20 percent of our requirement. The rest we bought locally. We hired a powered cross-cut saw for bucking long logs into the 9-inch log-ends (too short!) that would be laid up widthwise in the wall. Ever since building Log End Cottage, however, we have simply marked the logs with a crayon, and cut the log-ends with our chainsaw.

This is not intended to be a construction manual, so I'm not going to tell how to build a cordwood home. I've written three books about that already. But I do want to tell you about some mistakes we made, mistakes we corrected on our second house.

Mistakes

I wish we'd had access to the previous chapter of this book before we designed and built Log End Cottage. We could have saved a lot of mistakes. But, I suppose, it's good that we made them so that you don't have to repeat them. Go and find your own mistakes!

Basement. Almost half of the $6,000 cost of Log End Cottage went into a basement. Back in the early 1970s, conventional wisdom was still that a house should be built on a basement. Someone talked us into it and I guess we really didn't know much about the alternatives. Even today, people think they have to have them, and I was told recently that over 99 percent of modular homes in our area are installed on basement foundations. If you are still of that mind yourself, reread the section on avoiding basements in chapter 5, and get a good clear idea about the difference between a basement and an earth-sheltered space.

Loft. Our sleeping loft was cozy, but it was lacking about two feet of height for comfort. It was like living in a tent. I had to position my head next to the ridge pole in order to stand up. If a loft is in your plans, draw a section of the space to scale. This will tell you if you'll need to sit down to put your trousers on.

Shape. We like the appearance of Log End Cottage, but it's twice as long as it is wide, an inefficient use of labor and materials. And the oblong plan doesn't help when it comes time to heat the building, either.

Siting. We made not one, but two, serious siting mistakes. First, we didn't pay attention to solar gain. Bad enough that the house was relatively long and narrow. Having made that basic shape mistake, the least we could have done was to let the long side get the most solar gain in the winter. But, n-o-o-o-o, we oriented the house so that the short side, the gable end, faced south. The other siting mistake was to build below the crest of a hill, with the long side parallel to the contour lines. Water running down the hill would collect against the side of the house and put great hydrostatic pressure against the home. See next item.

Backfill. Although we installed what should have been a good French drain system next to the footings, we made the egregious mistake of backfilling with the same clay-like material that came out of the excavation hole. What good is a drain if the water can't get into it? The hydrostatic pressure built against the sidewalls, finally causing a ¹⁄₁₆-inch movement in the third course of concrete blocks. Our waterproofing layer on the outside of the blocks consisted of a coat or two of Thoroseal™, a cement-based crystalline waterproofing that is great until it cracks. We had a couple of inches of water on the basement floor in the springtime.

Wall thickness. Cordwood walls should be a minimum of 16 inches thick in northern climes, not 9 inches. The house took seven full cords of wood to heat each winter. That's a lot. Earthwood, three times the size, uses less than half the wood and stays at a much steadier and more comfortable temperature.

Lack of add-on potential. As designed, Log End Cottage was not conducive to additions. The importance of this design flaw did not become apparent until the arrival in the household of a six-pound baby boy, when the building suddenly seemed to shrink dramatically in size. This mistake (no, I don't mean Rohan) helped lead us toward construction of our second house at Log End, where we promptly repeated it.

If I make it sound like the Cottage was nothing but mistakes, then I give the wrong impression. It was a charming place to live, and we spent three very happy years there. Building it was one of the most positive experiences and accomplishments of our young lives, and prepared us for all the innovative building that we've done since.

Luck

Although some people seem to fall into good fortune at every turn, like Donald Duck's irritating cousin Gladstone, I really don't see luck as a viable building strategy. Prayer won't work for me, either, but it might for someone who believes in it. Because I place more credence in probability theory, I suspect that luck is actually a frame of mind,

Log End Cottage was built in 1975.

how people react to situations. Case in point: One day, while clearing around the cottage site, Jaki called my attention to a pile of rocks on the ground. "Do you think this could be a well?" she asked. "I doubt it," I—the eternal pessimist—said, "but let's take some rocks away and see what it is."

We did not stop taking rocks away until we were twenty feet down. Jaki had discovered a wonderful old stone-lined shallow well, probably dating to the nineteenth century when the Murtaghs, fresh from Ireland, settled this hill. The catchment area was a hole about fourteen feet in diameter, which had been carefully reduced with fieldstones until a shaft of less than three feet in diameter remained in the center. The rocks around the well opening were carefully laid in keystone fashion, so that stones wouldn't fall into the well. When the farm was abandoned, the well was filled with clean stones for safety reasons, preserving it until Jaki made her discovery. Lucky, yes. But Jaki actualized the luck by her observation, and then we had to take advantage of the luck with a lot of difficult stone removal. The snakes, not the poisonous kind, might have put some people off, but we kept at the task, driven by curiosity about the well's depth, apart from our hopes of realizing a good cheap water source. It was as exciting as an archaeological dig, and neighbors began to get caught up in the adventure as well. Our friend Steve, a man of muscle and extraordinary body control, manhandled one gigantic boulder up from 12 feet down. The upshot is that we wound up with a great well, requiring only a shock treatment with a gallon of bleach to purify the water. The well is still in use today, twenty-two years after we reopened it.

You may or may not discover a well on your site, although they're not all that rare on abandoned farmland. We actually found another one a little while later. But something lucky *will* happen to you. Probability rewards lots of events, and lots of events are going to happen along your quest for a mortgage-free home. You can help the process along. Look over the property with an open eye. Talk to neighbors. Let people know your needs. Luck, in the form of cultivated coincidences, will follow.

Time and Cost

We built the Cottage in seven months, while we lived in the shed. Moving in was not particularly exciting for us, because we didn't even know we were doing it. An unusually warm south wind moved into the area on December 15, temperatures in the 50s. Although we were heating the cottage by this time—warm enough to work, anyway—we didn't think we'd actually move in until springtime. It seemed that there was still so much to do and we were resigned to toughing it out in the shed for the winter. But, for fun, we spent the night in the Cottage, and really enjoyed it. The 16th was still unseasonably warm and we decided to make a priority list of what absolutely had to be done to move in. It wasn't all that much, really. We never spent another night in the shed, although we cooked our meals there for a few days until we moved the kitchen over to the Cottage.

Log End Cottage cost about $6,000 to build in 1975, $5,000 for materials and $1,000 for labor. We hired Steve to lay the blocks of our basement, and a heavy equipment contractor for the excavation and septic system. The home had a 500-square-foot basement (which saw very little use), 500 square feet on the main floor, and 250 square feet of loft space, as already described. It had an excellent indoor sauna, a small bathroom with gravity shower, and a bucket flush toilet. The main part of the house was a large open-plan kitchen/living/dining area, with a cathedral ceiling over the kitchen and a low-beamed ceiling over the living room. We achieved the English pub atmosphere we were after. Since we were the first people to complete our home, it became quite a gathering place for the community, as families moved to The Hill, one by one.

Homesteading

We found the life we'd dreamed about in Scotland. We discovered the benefits of raised-bed gardening and had an unlimited supply of fuel in the forest. We washed clothes in an old cedar hand-cranked washing machine that we found at an auction. The white porcelain kitchen sink unit with cabinets beneath cost $5 from the same place. Our furniture

either came from auctions, or was given to us. We bought an old barber's chair in Canada, which Jaki reupholstered with gold-colored felt. We were having a great time homesteading—but we had caught the building bug.

Work. During the first few years on The Hill, our cost of living was between $3,000 and $4,000 a year, most of it coming from our grub-stake, but some coming from odd jobs. Jaki, a registered nurse in Britain, passed her New York State exams in 1978 and began to work at the hospital. I decided to write a book about cordwood masonry, as there was nothing in print on the subject.

LOG END CAVE

Log End Cottage was cute, romantic, small, and energy inefficient. We'd originally considered an earth roof on the Cottage, and it was certainly built strong enough to take it, but the 45° roof pitch was much too steep, so we went with roll roofing instead, and, eventually, cedar shingles. But I couldn't let go of the earth roof and underground

---

STRATEGIES USED AT LOG END COTTAGE

1. Extensive land search.
2. Temporary shelter, three different variations, allowed us to be on-site during construction.
3. Made use of indigenous materials, cedar logs on property.
4. Made use of recycled materials: heavy timbers, low-cost insulated glass units from local glass manufacturer.
5. Reclaimed old well, taking advantage of "luck."
6. Work party for lifting heavy ridgepole into place.
7. Furnished home through auctions and passed-on furniture.
8. Worked steadily on home, possible because of sufficient grubstake.
9. Chose low-cost method of wall construction, cordwood masonry, just $112 total for all of the external wall infilling.
10. Hired a friend to do the blockwork, at reasonable rate. Cash money helped him, too.
11. Kept it small.

ideas, and figured we could make a warmer, roomier house for ourselves. Thus, while living in the Cottage, we designed and built our second home at Log End.

Still operating out of our original $26,000 grubstake, we broke ground at Log End Cave, just 125 feet from the Cottage, in July of 1977. We were determined to correct all the deficiencies of the first house, already described. And we very nearly did. The Cave was a 30-by-35-foot earth-shelter, bermed fully on the east and west sides, almost fully on the north side, and partially on the south side, as can be seen in figure 6-6. Below-ground walls were made of 12-inch-wide surface-bonded concrete blocks. Large windows dominated the south elevation. The roof was earth over 4 inches of rigid foam insulation, supported by a heavy plank-and-beam rafter system, itself supported by an even heavier post-and-girder frame. Construction of the home is detailed in *The Complete Book of Underground Houses.*

Some Details

The Cottage basement walls let water in for three reasons: (1) extreme hydrostatic pressure on the walls, caused by poor-quality backfill material and poor house siting on the hillside; (2) a mortared block wall with insufficient strength to resist lateral load caused by (1); and, (3)

Log End Cave, the author's earth-sheltered home, built in 1977.

the use of a waterproofing that lacked the ability to bridge a small crack. We knew that drainage and waterproofing were the highest priorities in an underground house, but we also wanted a better wall structure, and one we could afford. We considered poured reinforced 8-inch concrete walls very seriously, but felt this was not something we could do ourselves. (Note: I still feel this way and try to dissuade our earth-sheltered housing students from pouring their own walls unless they have lots of experience in this specialized trade. One nearby owner-builder saw his homemade forms blow out during the wall pour, spreading several cubic yards of concrete on the ground. This sort of thing can spoil your whole day.)

Surface bonding. We obtained bids from three contractors for the wall pour, but the low bid of $3,000 was more than we could budget. We decided on the surface bonded block method, in which a special fiberglass-reinforced cement is applied to both sides of blocks stacked without mortar. Such a wall has been found to resist lateral pressure twice as well as a conventionally mortared wall. With 12-inch-wide blocks, we were well within the parameters of strength required for the home, and we eliminated the pesky internal pilasters (also known as pillars or buttresses) every eight feet along the inner surface of the wall, required with 8-inch walls. By doing the work ourselves, we built all the earth-sheltered walls for a total of $900, just 30 percent of the lowest estimate for a poured foundation wall.

Framework. We stayed with the heavy timber support structure, something that owner-builders can do, as opposed to expensive and dangerous methods like pouring the roof in reinforced concrete or installing pre-stressed concrete planks with a crane.

Waterproofing and drainage. We waterproofed our walls and roof with 6-mil black polyethylene, bedded in hundreds of gallons of black plastic roofing cement. It was a lot of dirty, sticky, time-consuming work, and I now advise the use of one of the manufactured membranes made for the purpose, such as the W. R. Grace Bituthene™ 4000 System waterproofing membrane. Application is as simple as pulling off the Teflon™-coated backing paper and pressing the membrane onto the wall or roof substrate. Learning our lesson from the Cottage basement, we backfilled with 125 cubic yards of sand, obtained from another part of our property. Rain and surface water travels very quickly to the French drains, thanks to the good percolation quality of the backfill.

Common systems. Cost-wise, we benefited greatly at the Cave by making use of several systems shared in common with the Cottage, including a driveway, a well, a septic system, and a 200-watt Winco wind machine mounted on a tower located between the two houses. Later, when I went into the wind energy business, we upgraded the wind system to a Sencenbaugh 500-watt wind machine on a new 60-foot guyed tower. Photovoltaic panels were still expensive in those days.

Cost cuts. We kept the costs down further at Log End Cave by designing the house to fit the site and by designing it around some great bargains we found in materials. We planned the excavation to fit with the natural contours of the area, this time building at the top of the knoll, instead of along the side of it. We knew we'd have to bring backfilling material in, but we planned the depth of the house so that the excavated material could be used in the construction of the earth-berms on the east and west walls. No material was hauled away.

We found two great bargains in materials. The first was a consignment of three large double-pane fixed unit windows, each measuring 4 feet by 8 feet. They were $20 each from the back room of a local manufacturer of insulated glass. I think they were ordered by a customer and then never paid for. The other great find was a source of barn beams about thirty miles away, including three 30-foot 10-by-10 girders. The north-south dimension of the house became a function of the length of these wonderful girders. At a dollar a foot, they cost us the outrageous sum of $90. It's worth designing a house around bargains like that.

Following Thoreau's example, I offer a complete accounting of spending at Log End Cave, up until the time we moved in. During our three years of living there, we probably spent another $500 on improvements and finishing off. Keep in mind that these are 1977–1978 dollars, and would probably translate to nearly $20,000 today. But, as with Thoreau's accounting, it is interesting to see where the money went, and we did keep a very detailed accounting.

It took about 1,800 person-hours to build the Cave, including about 450 hours of outside help, some paid, most volunteered. I noted actual

Log End Cave Cost Analysis

Heavy equipment contracting	$892.00
Concrete	873.68
Surface-bonding cement	349.32
Concrete blocks	514.26
Cement	47.79
Hemlock for rafters and planking	345.00
Milling and planing	240.26
Barn beams	123.00
Other wood	167.56
Gypsum board	72.00
Particleboard	182.20
Nails	62.88
Sand and crushed stone	148.21
Topsoil	295.00
Hay, grass seed, fertilizer	43.50
Plumbing, pipe and connectors	124.95
Various drainpipes	166.23
Water pipe	61.59
Metalbestos' insulated stovepipe	184.45
Rigid foam insulation	254.93
Roofing cement	293.83
Six-mil black polyethylene	64.20
Flashing	27.56
Skylights	361.13
Insulated glass windows	322.50
Interior doors and hardware	162.80
Tools, tool rental, and tool repair	159.43
Miscellaneous	210.31
Total materials and contracting cost of house, landscaping, and drainage:	$6,750.57
Labor	660.00
Cost of basic house	$7,410.57
Floor coverings (carpets, vinyl)	309.89
Fixtures and appliances	507.00
Total spending at Log End Cave	$8,227.46

hours worked in my diary, especially when I needed to pay help, but only for about half of the days, so the time estimate may not be quite as accurate as the costing analysis. Son Rohan had his first birthday during construction, but despite serious mothering duties, Jaki still managed to devote a lot of hours to the project.

Performance

Log End Cave exceeded our expectations. It was much lighter and brighter than the Cottage and we were able to heat the Cave with just three cords of wood per year instead of seven. And the home maintained a steady comfortable temperature, summer and winter. The view was better than at the Cottage, thanks to more sensible siting. Oh, sure, there are things we would do differently. Here's a quick list:

- We'd have two entrances instead of one. This is an important safety issue and a code requirement. Even a chipmunk has a back door, in case a fox (or the code enforcement officer) comes to the front entrance.
- We'd have more opening windows. At the Cave, we used all fixed units with several large insulated wall vents that could be opened for fresh air.
- We wouldn't berm up the south side at all. In northern climes, every square foot of the south side converted to double-pane insulated glass can actually make the place easier to heat by taking advantage of solar gain, particularly in combination with insulated shutters to arrest nighttime heat loss. As it was, snow would begin to collect against the big south-facing windows and Jaki would have to go out with a snow shovel to remove it. Had the house been properly designed, that would not have been necessary.
- We still didn't think of incorporating add-on potential into the design. Although earth-sheltered houses are difficult to add on to, it's not impossible if considered at the design stage, as we saw in the previous chapter.

That's about it for "mistakes." Comfort-wise, the home was a quantum leap forward. But situations were conspiring to lead us to yet another, more ambitious, project: Earthwood.

Again, there was very little literature available on how to actually build an underground house, so I took a lot of pictures and wrote my second book, *Underground Houses: How to Build a Low-Cost Home* (Sterling, 1979) soon after we moved in. I totally rewrote and updated the book in 1994.

Another House?

Several circumstances converged in the late 1970s that eventually led to the construction of our Earthwood home, where we have lived since 1982.

Strategies Used at Log End Cave

1. Efficient shape, nearly square.
2. South-facing orientation for solar gain.
3. House is adapted to the landscape.
4. Sufficient grubstake for full-time building.
5. Used recycled materials such as huge barn timbers and large windows of insulated glass.
6. Used indigenous materials: sand for backfill, stone for retaining walls, earth for roof. Planking and rafters came from native trees, sawn at local sawmill.
7. Earth-sheltered design for energy efficiency.
8. Surface-bonded blocks for low-cost owner-built foundation.
9. Volunteer help from my nephew, Steve Roy, and his friend, Bruce Mayer, for a very productive three weeks.
10. Able to live on-site, comfortably, at Log End Cottage next door.
11. Made use of same driveway, well, septic system, and windplant as Log End Cottage.

Windfall. During the construction of Log End Cave, Jaki and I were beneficiaries of a windfall having to do with my brothers taking stock control of a family business started by my father, but with which I'd never been involved. Suddenly $18,000 came into our lives that wasn't there before. That was a lot of money for a young couple still living on about $5,000 a year. Later, this money provided a bridge between building Earthwood and selling the Log End Homestead.

Business partnership dissolution. In the late 1970s, a friend and I were partners in a business called Wood, Wind and Earth, Inc. We sold and installed woodstoves and wind electric systems. We also did general contracting, as it was pretty hard to support two families on the wood and wind parts alone. After a couple of years, we decided to dissolve our partnership, with Bob retaining our wind "division" and the contracting, while I kept the stove dealership. Prior to the dissolution, Bob and I had entered into an agreement to build a single-story round cordwood house for a young couple from Maryland. They'd even put a $500 down payment on the house, which we used to buy floor joists and other materials. The contract fell through when the couple decided to return to Maryland, and I wound up with the small quantity of materials for the round house, as a part of my dissolution agreement with Bob.

Land. When the 180 acres of additional land was subdivided a few years earlier, there were not enough families in our group to buy the whole thing. Jaki and I were the only ones who could afford to make the payments on the unclaimed land, so we actually wound up with two small parcels, one that sold very soon thereafter, and another 17 acres that we sold to our friend Pat (of Stump House fame) on a mortgage contract. After a few years, Pat was in arrears on payments and we mutually agreed that he would deed us back six acres in full satisfaction of all remaining payments.

The six acres was the eyesore of Murtagh Hill. About two acres had been completely denuded of all vegetation and topsoil when gravel had been quarried there. We could see from the cut at the edge of the pit that the gravel layer was only four to five feet deep, followed by either clay or sand, depending on the part of the pit. The upshot was that an average of about four feet of material had been removed from nearly two acres of land. We don't know if the original land was still farm pasture at the time of quarrying, or if it had already reverted to woodlot, like much of the land on The Hill. In any case, it was a mess, not a property that one would think of as an ideal building site.

But we remembered what underground architect, visionary, and now cartoonist Malcolm Wells said about the use of marginal land, and we decided to build Earthwood there, gradually reclaiming these two acres of moonscape and bringing it back into living, green, oxygenating, food-producing land. If we wanted a tennis court (and we did), well the site was already cleared. We have moral difficulty with removing vegetation to create a lifeless tennis court, but a clay court on this site would be much easier to justify. (As of 1997, we still haven't built the tennis court, but most of the gravel pit is now green again. One area of moonscape remains, though—just about the right size and shape for a tennis court!)

We needed a third house about as much as we needed another hole in our heads, and Jaki saw this more clearly than I did. But I wanted to try out important building techniques, like building round, and I was increasingly caught up with the idea that we should take an integrative approach to design, that a house is more than just shelter and should address all of the living systems: food production and storage, energy production and conservation, home industry, and even recreation. By 1980, Jaki and I were conducting workshops in cordwood masonry and underground housing and I saw our work evolving into a kind of constant research and development program in building, energy, and living systems.

I spent a lot of 1980 writing the forerunner to *Mortgage-Free!*, a smaller version called *Money-Saving Strategies for the Owner-Builder* (Sterling, 1981), a book in which I first discussed Earthwood and Integrative Design, although I didn't use the term back then. Many of these ideas, now backed by many years of testing, have been a great success.

TWO STORIES AT EARTHWOOD

Earthwood evolved from a variety of circumstances, one of which was the availability of materials already earmarked for a round house of 39 feet in diameter, about 1,000 square feet usable within the cordwood walls. In late 1980 I costed the materials for the original single-story design at $12,000, or $12 per square foot. Then I figured out what it

Pouring the footings at Earthwood, June 1981.

Earthwood, the author's home and the location of Earthwood Building School since 1982.

would cost to add a full second story to the design. Extra materials would include about five cords of wood, a few windows, an external door as well as two or three interior doors, seven extra posts, a floor joist system, 1,000 square feet of 2-by-6-inch tongue-and-groove planking, a stairway, and some extra internal wall framing and covering. At the time, the extra materials costed out at about $4,000, or just $4 per square foot for the additional floor area. A little space, about 100 square feet, would be lost to the stairwell. Nevertheless, the extra story seemed too inexpensive to turn down, and, in the actual event, my costing analysis came out to be very close to the truth. The great cost advantage of the second story, of course, comes from the constant ancillary systems, such as the septic tank, well, foundation, and heavy earth roof.

Energy

Energy consumption at Earthwood is low, as a result of its design, orientation, and various energy systems. The shape is cylindrical, which has many advantages (see discussion in chapter 5). The fact that it is a two-story house, however, also contributes to the ease of heating. If 2,000 square feet were spread over one floor, a mechanical system would be required to deliver the heat to all parts of the house. Inside Earthwood, no part of the house is more than 16 feet from the heat source, a 23-ton masonry stove. In rooms that do not need to be kept to 70° Fahrenheit, such as workrooms and bedrooms, which we prefer at about 65°, the internal wall construction and the opening and closing of internal doors adequately regulates the temperature.

The external walls at Earthwood are 40 percent earth-sheltered, virtually all of this occurring in the northern hemisphere of the building. Although the home is earth-roofed, it is not a true underground house, but earth berming is almost as energy efficient as a fully recessed building. Thanks to the earth temperature just outside of the underground portion of the walls—roughly 40° Fahrenheit in March, 60° in September—heating and cooling starts out, effectively, in a much more favorable climate. It's almost like building in Charleston, South Carolina instead of near Plattsburgh, New York.

The fabric of the building itself also contributes to a steady internal temperature. The walls, 16 inches thick, are of cordwood masonry above grade and 16-inch-thick surface-bonded concrete block construction below grade. The mortared portion of the cordwood wall consists of an inner and an outer 5-inch mortar joint, with six inches of sawdust as insulation (R-3 per inch) in the cavity. The blocks are all 16-inch corner blocks (flat ends, no recesses) laid transversely in the wall, much like the log-ends in cordwood masonry. All the hollow cores of the blocks are filled with sand for additional thermal mass. Surface-bonding cement is applied to both sides of the block wall, followed by the W. R. Grace Bituthene™ waterproofing membrane on the outside, and then two to three inches of extruded polystyrene insulation (Dow Blueboard™) between the membrane and the earth backfill.

The thick cordwood walls above grade have exceptional thermal characteristics. With thermal mass (the tons of mortar) on each side of the insulation, the walls stay warm in the winter and cool in the summer. The log-ends themselves have built-in characteristics of both insulation and thermal mass. I can't think of another above-ground building system with this perfect juxtaposition of insulation and thermal mass. Below grade, some ninety tons of wall store heat—or "coolth" in summer—to help keep the house comfortable. Likewise, the slate-covered 4-inch-thick concrete floor downstairs, another twenty-five tons of mass, has an inch of Dow Blueboard™ beneath it, as do the footings themselves. There are no "energy nosebleeds," to borrow a term from compatriot Mac Wells.

The earth roof weighs another sixty tons, but this is not very useful for winter heat storage because of its location above the Styrofoam™ insulation. But the earth roof does keep the snow better than any other kind, and fluffy snow is worth about R-1 per inch of thickness. The earth is also very useful for keeping the house cool in summer. Moisture evaporating from the earth causes a cooling effect. While an asphalt shingle roof could fry an egg in the summer, the earth is cool just an inch or two beneath the grass cover.

The combination of several factors allows us to heat the 2,000-square-foot Earthwood home with just 3¼ full cords of dry hardwood each winter: the round two-story shape, the earth-sheltering, the ther-

Part of the 23-ton masonry stove at Earthwood.

mal mass juxtaposed with external insulation, the thick cordwood walls, and the efficient fuel use in the masonry stove.

Like the homes at Log End, a half mile away, Earthwood is not connected to the national electric power grid and derives virtually all its electrical energy from renewable energy, particularly solar and wind power. The main difference is that we now get most of the power from solar energy, which has become much more cost-effective since 1980. We have ten 50-watt Siemens PV panels, an array built up gradually over the years; the modular nature of photovoltaic power is one of its attractive features. In addition, we still use wind power, particularly useful from November through January, when lighting needs are highest and available solar energy is lowest. For most of fifteen years, we used a 1,000-watt wind machine, but it had a series of problems over the last couple of years of its life and we replaced it in 1996 with a new Whisper 600. Although we do have a Honda gasoline generator available as a back-up source of power if needed, we have not had to use it for house power since putting the new Whisper on-line.

Food

Solar room. At Earthwood, the south-facing solar greenhouse is attached to the main building and adds to our living space as a pleasant place to have lunch or read a book. On sunny days in winter, we can open the sliding glass door into the downstairs and use the solar gain to help heat the house. But the solar room's main purpose is food production. It is here that Jaki starts the seedlings for the eight raised bed gardens in front of the home, and here that we grow garden greens over the winter.

Garden. The raised beds are watered by underground soaker hoses which spiral around each bed, about three inches below the surface. These porous hoses, made under several different brand names including Hydro Grow and Earth Quencher, allow water to drip slowly into the soil so that the plant's roots, rather than leafy tops, are watered. Much less water is lost through evaporation, and the possibility of "burning" the plants by top-watering is reduced. Rainwater is collected in two sixty-gallon oak barrels and, by opening a valve, delivered to the soaker hoses by gravity.

The solar room and raised-bed gardens at Earthwood.

Bike pump. Alternatively, we can water the garden directly from our rather unusual house water system. Water is pumped into the home by way of a bicycle frame married to an old Myers double-action piston pump. This system, designed by my good friend George Barber and described in more detail in *Complete Book of Cordwood Masonry Housebuilding*, has worked beautifully for us since 1982. Our regular family water needs are met by "riding the bike" for about four minutes, twice a day. (I figure that if I do this every day until I'm 100 years old, then I'll live to be 100!) Incidentally, our family of three (sometimes four) uses about 110 gallons of water per day for all purposes, about one-third of the American average. Our well is a "shallow" well, 24 feet deep, dug with a large tracked backhoe and lined with 3-foot diameter concrete culverts.

How do we get by on so "little" water? (A small sub-Saharan village might do as well!) We use toilets that require only two gallons per flush, instead of five, and we don't flush for every little piddling affair. We adjust our shower head for low pressure, and turn it off altogether for lathering up. We don't use a dishwasher, rarely wash the cars, and never water the lawn. When you physically deliver every gallon into the home with a bicycle pump, you get a whole new sense of the value of water, and don't waste a drop. The question I can't answer is how the average American home manages to use more than three hundred gallons every day. As a nation, it is imperative that we do better.

Food storage. We dry, can, and store vegetables, mostly in the "pump room," which has evolved into a kind of all-purpose "basement"-type area. In the pump room, besides the bicycle pump, we have the twelve deep-cycle batteries that store our electricity, shelves for food storage, and even a small wine cellar. With internal walls of concrete blocks, the room stays slightly cooler than other downstairs rooms.

Recreation

I have already mentioned that we devote 250 square feet to playing pool. There is also a British dart board set up nearby, with the toe line incorporated into the slate floor. The pool table actually doubles as a work table. For example, it provides a great place to spread all the chapters of this book, with associated notes, illustrations, captions, etc.

For a few years, we had a hot tub in the lower story, a kind of recreation, but it finally gave way to additional living space as the family grew from three to four. Our hot tubbing is limited now to about six months at Mushwood, our summer cottage. Now that Rohan has left home (for the most part), the downstairs living room has become a pub-like den, where we can enjoy an open fire in an efficient woodstove made by Vermont Castings. Another kind of recreation. And the room doubles as a changing room and relaxation area for the sauna, a separate round building just outside the solar room.

The sauna. Is sauna for health, cleanliness, relaxation, or recreation? All four, and more. We learned at Log End that it is preferable to have the sauna built outside of the home, but not *too* far away. The sense of escaping to another world is there, you can't hear the phone, and you don't overheat the house while bringing the stoveroom up to temperature. Since our sauna is only ten feet from the home, we do not need a separate changing/relaxation room attached to the stoveroom. We kind of like running that ten-foot gap, naked during a howling blizzard, with the womb-like reward at the other side. The construction of several different cordwood saunas is described in *The Sauna* (Chelsea Green, 1996), which also has chapters on sauna lore and customs.

Home Industry

Earthwood is more than a home. It is an ongoing experiment in living. It is also our place of work. We conduct classes here as part of Earthwood Building School, and we sell books, plans, and videos out of our mailbox. Never realizing how the business would grow, we now find that we did not allocate enough space in the office for storing books, for processing orders, and for writing. We wish that our office was three times as big as it is. Space problems have forced the copying machine into the downstairs den, my book chapters are spread all over the pool table, and books and videos are stored in two round outbuildings. We ask ourselves, how can we find more space for the business? It's tough, because, again, we built a house that is very difficult to add on to. I'm like the carpenter who said, "Dang, I've cut this board three times and it's still too short." So, please, friend reader, take my advice on this—after all, I'm not using it. If home business is in your tarot cards, give it as much forethought and planning as you do for the function of the home as Shelter.

Stop the press! The above paragraph was written in the spring. By the end of summer, the office situation had become critical. The entire Earthwood household seemed overcome by paper gridlock, originating in the tiny office, but spreading to the kitchen table, nearby counters, any square foot of horizontal surface. In September, we cleared out the twenty-foot diameter shed, just thirty feet from the front door, and converted it to the new Earthwood office with fully three times the previous space, so my wish is granted. It's great! Should've made the move years ago! And the office inside now serves as a home office and guestroom. Now I just need to figure out what to do with all the junk that was in the shed.

Home industry is not limited to earning money, a necessary part of the Consumer Economy. Home industry can be equally valuable as a means of saving money, the keystone of the Conserver Economy. Sewing, canning, beer making, furniture making, home workshop activities. The list goes on, and everybody's . . . different! We have a sewing nook, a workshop, and enough space in different parts of the house to set up activities as required.

Bottom Line

We were able to keep costs way down at Earthwood for several reasons. The land was almost "free," having got it back from Pat in return for presenting him with a Satisfaction of Mortgage on his remaining land. As marginal land, it had a low value anyway. About $500 in materials came back to us as the result of a reneged contract. Indigenous and recycled materials came into the equation again, of course, and this time we built the perfect shape for economy: round and two stories. We did not keep records as accurately at Earthwood as we did at the Cave, but I can provide ball-park figures, albeit from two different ballparks. Here's why:

Sponsorship. I approached three different major manufacturers and requested free materials in exchange for testing their products in new or unusual applications and writing reports on our experience. All three were willing to play ball in our ballpark. Dow Chemical Company agreed to supply all of the Blueboard™ insulation that we needed for the project: 1 inch under the floor, 1 inch under and around the footings, 2 inches on the outside of the sand-filled block walls (3 inches down to the local 4-foot frost level), and 4 inches on the roof. Earthwood was one of the first houses to use Blueboard™ under the footings, which stops an important energy nosebleed at that detail. Conproco supplied all of the Structural Skin™ surface-bonding cement for the below-grade block walls. We may have been the first to use corner blocks widthwise in the wall like cordwood and held fast with surface-bonding cement. And W. R. Grace and Company supplied enough of their Bituthene™ waterproofing membrane to cover the below-grade walls and the entire roof. Again, we were one of the first to use the membrane on a plank substrate. I estimate that the total value of all the materials donated to the project was about $6,000 in 1982, and would probably be close to double that amount today. I am pleased to report that all of the products equalled or exceeded performance requirements.

So what we actually spent was around $9,500 in materials on the house, well, and septic system. We also spent around $7,500 on hired help this time around. It was a big project and Jaki was working regularly as an RN, so we needed the help. One fellow, Dennis Lee, worked almost full-time for about six months, and we hired other help at different critical times: one guy for three weeks and another for five weeks.

The masonry stove, incidentally, cost $540 in labor and $500 in materials. This was an exceptional price. My friend Steve Engelhart, who had learned masonry stove construction from an old Lithuanian immigrant, built the stove in fifty-four hours with Dennis and me laboring, and most of the stones came right off of the surface of the old gravel pit where we built. I know of another couple who were building in Connecticut just a few years later, who spent $10,000 to have their masonry stove built for them.

So we actually spent about $17,000, including labor, but not including the wind and solar systems. Without the corporate sponsorship, it would have cost us an additional $6,000 or a total of $23,000, right around $11 per square foot. I'm sure that we have spent an additional $3,000 on extra wiring, outbuildings, and remodeling since 1982. The wind system was all done at cost, as I was in the business at the time of purchase, installation was almost free, and the federal and state

---

STRATEGIES USED AT EARTHWOOD

1. Built on marginal land, practically free.
2. Most efficient house shape: round and tall.
3. Low-cost building methods: cordwood masonry, surface-bonded block walls, post-and-beam and plank-and-beam construction.
4. Use of recycled materials: cheap insulated glass windows, barn timbers for posts.
5. Use of indigenous materials: sand for the floating slab pad, stone for the masonry stove, earth for the roof.
6. Use of materials remaining from cancelled contract.
7. Successful procurement of materials from sponsors.
8. Fit floorplan to structural plan, not the other way around.
9. Kept the design simple and symmetrical.
10. Use of add-on photovoltaic system.
11. Wholesale prices and energy tax credit advantages on wind system.
12. Hired help on an hourly cash basis. (Be sure to obey all applicable state and federal laws.)
13. Worked five days a week myself, sometimes five and a half.
14. Lived in another mortgage-free home nearby during construction, Log End Cave.

tax credits that existed at that time saved us a full 55 percent of the cost of the system over the next few years. The photovoltaics were added on an as-we-could-afford basis.

Knowing now what I didn't know then, I would probably not bother with the wind system if I was starting over. Windplants require a lot of maintenance and they are off-line a lot of the time, usually when you really need them. This comment is based on my experience with four different wind machines. We'd do quite nicely at Earthwood with just the ten 50-watt PV panels and our reliable Honda 3,500-watt generator as a back-up for prolonged cloudy periods, particularly from November to early February. If need be, we can run the generator to do a wash, and, at the same time, charge our battery bank with a strong and steady output from a large battery charger. Our PV system—panels, mounting brackets, safety equipment, inverter, and twelve small golf-cart batteries—would cost a total of about $6,000 today, with about half of that for the panels themselves. A good reliable long-lasting generator will cost between $1,500 and $2,500. A new wind system like ours would probably run another $6,000, an outlay not justified, in my view, for the very few times in the year that it's needed.

Adversity

Building Earthwood wasn't all hunky-dory. Despite having built two houses previously, we were unprepared for the massive scale of the Earthwood project. And we'd seen other marriages and personal relationships go sour during the—seemingly—never-ending construction process. I knew the wisdom of building small, but thought I could ignore it now that I was an "expert." Jaki knew better. She was not surprised when the pressures of house-building began to take their toll on my equanimity. But neither of us was prepared for the mysterious and highly discouraging problem that began to surface in June, and persisted for a month.

The original design of Earthwood called for dense hardwood log-ends below grade instead of the concrete blocks. I was confident that I could waterproof the exterior if I applied two coats of plaster parge to the cordwood wall prior to applying the waterproofing membrane. The choice of hardwood, as opposed to the light and fluffy cedar we'd used at Log End, was for extra thermal mass. We had four full cords of beautiful hardwood log-ends cut, split, and dried three years. In July, our below-grade walls began to break up. Cracks formed between all the log-ends and the wall began to tilt out of plumb. We had no idea what was happening and we were trying to conduct a cordwood masonry workshop at the same time. It was a maddening situation and I was not reacting real well. It took over two weeks of building walls and tearing them down again before we realized that the very dry hardwood was swelling with water that collected on the slab during rainstorms. We tried all sorts of "solutions": expansion joints, pre-swelling the logs, you name it. Finally, after another two-plus weeks of building walls and tearing them down, we gave up. We'd learned a lot about using dry hardwood in a cordwood wall, which can be summarized in a single word: Don't!

Then we fell back on the tried and true method of earth-sheltered house construction which we'd learned at the Cave, namely surface-bonded blocks. Fortunately, all of our above-grade cordwood walls were always intended to be dry, light cedar, like we'd used in the past, and there was no problem there. The hardwood expansion debacle had cost us five weeks of work, almost $2,000 in labor and materials, and a blot on my normally cheerful disposition. We made up some time with the much quicker block construction, but other more familiar problems returned: rushing to beat the winter (we had the coldest, wettest October in years), financial pressures, and just plain disenchantment with the long building process. Two things got us through the project with our marriage intact: Jaki's patience, and the fact that we had a comfortable home to return to each evening.

Even without "the Problem," as it came to be known, Earthwood was a huge undertaking. I would never recommend it to someone as a first building project. It's not that the techniques were difficult; they aren't. The place is simply too big.

We had the building closed in just in time for our annual Guy Fawkes Night Bonfire on the fifth of November, and we could begin to use the masonry stove. We were out of money—Log End still hadn't sold—and we worked at things that were materials-cheap and labor-intensive, such as sanding and oiling the floor, and sheetrocking and painting internal walls. We moved into Earthwood thirteen months after breaking ground.

We love the home, but it took us a couple of years before we could say honestly that we were glad we did it.

MUSHWOOD

We built our summer cottage over a period of several years, on a lake lot bargain that we happened to stumble onto. Of course, we'd been looking for just such a bargain for a long time, so it's a bit like the "overnight success" singer who'd been struggling in honky-tonks for 20 years before being discovered. We call the cottage Mushwood because it looks like a mushroom and the lower story is cordwood masonry. The cap of the mushroom is a geodesic dome covered with cedar shingles.

I will not enter into quite the detail about Mushwood as I have with the other houses. But it is mortgage-free, and came in at a materials cost of $10 per square foot, about the same as Earthwood. The construction was rather unusual. First we poured a 22-foot-diameter floating slab. Then we erected the 29-foot-diameter dome for the first time at ground level and clad it in plastic, effectively covering the building site with a huge umbrella. We conducted cordwood workshops for two years under that cover—using nothing but cedar log-ends! With the dome still in place, we cut holes in the plastic to allow the second-floor joists to poke through, and floored the upper story with two-by-

Mushwood.

Strategies Used at Mushwood

1. Bided time buying land. Waited for bargain.
2. Built round.
3. Built in spare time, as we could afford it. Took time to enjoy the lake, too.
4. Built cordwood walls under cover, over a two-year period.
5. Geodesic dome is an economy of materials, although it takes a long time to finish off.
6. Built cordwood walls at workshops.

One of our students said that he never believed the story of Tom Sawyer and the whitewashed fence until he paid us to help build our cordwood walls!

---

six tongue-and-groove planking. Then we dismantled the dome (this took about six hours) and re-erected it in its permanent location on the second-story floor (this took twelve hours). Then the dome was covered with plywood triangles and black felt paper.

Over the next few years we gradually finished the place off, as we could afford the time and money. The cedar shingle roofing, for example, took Jaki and me a full five weeks, although it was pleasant work, and the place has never leaked. The "camp" is now valued at $43,000, more than twice what we've put into it, land and all. I grieved the valuation to no avail, and I suppose we could get $43,000 for it if we put it on the market. Sweat equity, like it or not, adds to valuation, and, therefore, taxes. Ironically, our tax burden at the lake is greater than at Earthwood.

Now let's see how others have managed, one way or another, to secure mortgage-free homes of all kinds, and all over North America.

7

Mortgage-Free People

At length, in the beginning of May, with the help of some of my acquaintances . . . I set up the frame of my house. No man was ever more honored in the character of his raisers than I. They are destined, I trust, to assist at the raising of loftier structures one day.

—HENRY DAVID THOREAU, WALDEN

On a world scale, only a small percentage of people live in mortgaged homes, but in North America, particularly middle-class North America, the problem is endemic. Still, there are millions of mainstream people in the United States and Canada who have managed to avoid the death pledge. In this chapter, we'll look at six such case studies, and see how homeowners used many of the strategies described in earlier chapters, as well as a few others, to achieve mortgage freedom.

All of the studies except the first were actually written by the homeowners themselves, which, I think, provides a variety of perspectives on the subject of mortgage freedom. I wrote the first study about a young couple here on The Hill, based on several interviews with Ki Light in early 1997.

<hr/>

Mortgage-Free:
The Next Generation

When you get to that fork in the road, take it.

—YOGI BERRA

Ki and Judith Light were coming to the end of a two-month visit with Judith's parents in the Dominican Republic. They were in the second year of their marriage and had a one-year-old baby boy, Makima. Their lives were free to go in any direction they cared to push them. They had reached Yogi's fork in the road.

One possibility was to build a house on Murtagh Hill, not far from Earthwood, where Ki grew up. His parents, Ron and Debbie Light, had built their own mortgage-free home there a generation earlier, and their case study appeared in the earlier incarnation of this book, published in 1981. It was natural that one of Ki and Judith's options was to build their own home.

Their next move was to New York's Columbia County, a few hours south of Murtagh Hill, where they stayed rent-free, sometimes with Judith's grandmother and sometimes with Ki's aunt. They each found jobs, and were able to save a grubstake in less than a year and a half, about $11,000 in savings plus about $4,500 worth of tools, materials, windows, a generator, and the like. It was short of the $20,000 that they'd hoped to start with, but Ki knew that his parents had started on The Hill with only $400 a generation earlier, so he figured they'd make it.

A fortuitous event occurred about the same time that Ki and Judith were wrestling with that fork in the road. Ki's mother and stepfather had been negotiating to buy the 20 acres adjacent to their own homestead, and the property was secured not long before Ki and Judith were ready to build. Thus, the land, the one absolute requirement for building, manifested itself in the form of what Ki thinks of as "an early inheritance" from his mother. Although the land where they finally built their home is not yet in their name, they have absolute confidence that it will be someday. Building on land that belongs to someone else is not a new strategy, having been popularized by Henry David Thoreau 150 years earlier. And it would not be an advisable strategy if there was any bad blood between the principals, certainly not a problem with the Lights. Ki and Judith did not build their home with a view to resale. Each only twenty-five years old when they moved into their home—Makima was three and a half—their young lives may take them all over the world, but the substantial mortgage-free dwelling they have built for themselves will always be there to await their return.

Makima Light, three, is cozy in his parents' house of straw. The internal walls are now plastered.

Growing up, Ki had seen all kinds of owner-built homes on Murtagh Hill: several log homes (including the one he was brought up in), cordwood homes, framed houses, even an underground house or two. It was his aunt, though, who suggested that the young couple have a look at *The Straw Bale House* by Steen, Steen, and Bainbridge (Chelsea Green, 1994). Ki made a thorough study of this low-cost, highly energy-efficient technique, and then another coincidence occurred. Jaki and I had already arranged to host a straw bale workshop at Earthwood Building School when we heard of Ki's plans. Ki and Judith moved back to The Hill on June 5, 1996, staying with Ki's folks, and the hands-on workshop, conducted by Scott Carrino, was held on June 8–10. We built a small straw bale guest house during the workshop and Ki got to learn and practice the straw bale construction techniques that he would use on his own home.

During a visit the previous year, Ki and Judith had cleared a house site in the forest and had the shallow well installed by the same fellow who'd dug ours fifteen years earlier at Earthwood. The first eighteen-foot hole yielded only a little wet clay at the bottom, so the operator moved his traxcavator to a more favorable location downgrade, a little further from the house site. The second hole had wet clay at six feet, and trickling water at nine feet. Fortunately, the hole was dug at a very dry time and it was possible to go eighteen feet down and still get the concrete culverts and crushed stone in before the hole filled with water. Today, the well water is very close to the surface! While the traxcavator was on-site, Ki had the operator remove lots of stumps from the house site and level the ground somewhat.

The "first hurdle" after the workshop was getting a building permit. Our town requires any home over 1,500 square feet to be backed by architect- or engineer-stamped plans. The Light's house plan would be 1,836 square feet based upon gross outside dimensions, although only 1,360 square feet would be actual livable space. Almost 500 square feet would be lost in the thickness of the 19-inch straw bale walls. Unfortunately, building inspectors—and assessors—figure square footage by outside dimensions, which seems just a little unfair to builders of rammed earth, straw bale, and cordwood houses.

Ki figured that the stamped plans could cost between one and two thousand dollars, if they could find an engineer or architect to verify straw bale construction at all. "At this point, Judith took charge," according to Ki. "She called every architect and engineer in the phone book, and we wound up meeting with this older eastern European engineer who agreed to look at the plans I'd drafted." Ki calls his plans "rough," but they were neatly drawn with drafting equipment. "We showed him what we had, and he says, 'What would you like to know?' We talked with him for a couple of hours, all about rafter spans and frequency. It took a while to explain straw bale construction to him, but, as we'd be laying up the straw bales within a heavy post-and-beam frame, he was okay with it." The meeting cost the Lights $100. The engineer stamped their plans and in a day or two they had their permit.

Once the plans were stamped, the young couple launched into their project at full steam. They hired a backhoe to dig the trenches for their rubble trench foundation, and, while the equipment was there, Ki installed his septic system. The Lights had seriously considered a composting toilet, but found out that they'd still be required by the county health department to have a septic system. Ki considers this a real deterrent for composters. As it was, the materials for the approved septic system cost only $400.

The rubble trench foundation was a great cost saver for the Lights, and a system that I'd only heard of, but never seen actually used. Ki showed me a great article in a compendium entitled *Fine Homebuilding on Foundations and Masonry* (Taunton, 1990) about this low-cost, frost-proof foundation method. The article, entitled "Rubble-Trench Foundations," by Elias Velonis, first appeared in the December 1983 issue of *Fine Homebuilding* magazine. Velonis, incidentally, founded the excellent Heartwood Owner-Builder School in Washington, Massachusetts (see appendix 2). In the article, Velonis tells us:

> The two functions of load-bearing and drainage are solved separately with a solid foundation, but a rubble-trench system unites these two functions in a single solution: the house is built on top of a drainage trench of compacted stone that is capped with a poured-concrete grade beam. The grade beam is above the frost line, but the rubble trench extends below it, and the building's weight is carried to the earth by the stones that fill the trench. The small air spaces around each stone allow groundwater to find its way easily to the perforated drainage pipe at the bottom of the trench.

The perforated drain pipe then carries the water out above grade. Velonis explains that the rubble (or *ballast*) trench was one of Frank Lloyd Wright's favorite foundation techniques. The *floating slab* was another. Although his "dry wall footings" were successful, Wright admitted that he occasionally had trouble getting the system authorized by building commissions. Any disapproval by a building inspector, according to Velonis, shows a lack of familiarity with the technique, since the Uniform Building Code states that any system is acceptable as long as it can "support safely the loads imposed." Velonis tells of one building inspector who studied the rubble trench plans, "ahemmed in good New England fashion, and said, 'Yep, that looks as if it oughta work.' "

While this book is not intended to be a construction manual, I cannot help mentioning the rubble or ballast trench as an effective low-cost foundation method. Using it was one of the strategies that helped the Lights achieve mortgage freedom, and it can do the same for others. Ki says, "It's cheap and I could do it myself." He brought in the ready-mix truck for the grade beam pour, and figured his volume pretty well: there were only two wheelbarrow loads of concrete left over.

The Lights wanted a crawl space under the house to run electric and plumbing and to provide space for a root cellar, so he laid up four courses of blocks on the grade beam, being careful later to insulate the outside of the block wall with 2 inches of extruded polystyrene. Eventually, most of the insulation will be backfilled with earth and any part exposed above-grade covered with a protective cement coating.

The other major cost-saving method at the Light's house, of course, is the straw bale construction, a building style that has gained a great deal of popularity in the past few years, and with good reason. Ki enthuses, "I like the aesthetics of the straw bale walls: the curves, the texture of the cement parge, the thickness of the walls. I chose a heavy post-and-beam frame for our house, because it is two stories and I was concerned about settling of free-standing straw bale walls, but now I really like seeing the exposed barn beams every ten or twelve feet around the house, inside and out. Of course, the high insulation value of the straw bales themselves is a big draw. It's about R-40!"

The Lights and Jaki and I bought our straw bales together from a source downstate recommended by instructor Scott Carrino. The bales were not cheap at about $4 each (including haulage two hours from the source). But they are high-quality, tightly strung, wire-bound, dry, rye straw, about the best you can get. The 260 bales for the Lights' house cost about $900. By comparison, the fiberglass in the roof (12-inch, R-38) cost about $600.

Because they started the house project with less of a grubstake than they figured they'd need, it was important to save money at every turn. Ki found a number of excellent barn beams which he incorporated into the main external frame of the home. The great thickness of the walls meant that he had to set two heavy posts side by side along the walls, if he wanted to see them both inside and out. This technique also meant less difficult shaping and fitting of the straw bales themselves. Ki recommends watching the classifieds for building materials. He got a large multi-paneled casement window unit in excellent condition for just $150 that way, about $1,000 less than a similar unit bought new. Ki bought discounted items at our local building supply center, including a window and patio doors. His front entrance features a beautiful pair of oak church doors salvaged from a job years ago by his father.

Like Jaki and me, and so many of the other case study people in this book, Ki and Judith scored a great deal on "leftover" insulated glass units. Unfortunately, Ki did not store them as carefully as he might have, and several of the units lost their seal and became cloudy. As the frames were already installed within the straw bale walls, Ki used them. Someday he will either try to clean and reseal them, a very difficult job, or order new ones. Ki strongly advises everyone who pursues this strategy to store the units carefully after purchase. "Store them inside and never lying down. The base of the windows should be supported by a pair of two-by-four stickers, so you can get your gloves under to move them, and they should lean almost vertically against a wooden wall or a pair of upright planks. You can always tack a piece of wood at the top to prevent them from getting knocked over."

Ki worked full time on the home for six months. Judith had a part-time job during the construction time, and, of course, a three-year-old needs a lot of attention, too, although Makima is a pretty independent and self-reliant type. Runs in the family. Friends, neighbors, and relatives—and some qualify as all three—helped the Lights on their project. Stepfather John Schulz, a high school teacher, helped Ki for more than a month over the summer. Ron Light (father) and John Light (uncle) also helped. A plastering party in the fall got the first outside coat of cement parge on the straw bales.

The house is sensibly shaped, with its two stories and almost square outside dimensions of 27 feet by 34 feet. The downstairs is mostly open-plan kitchen, dining, and living area, with a woodstove right in the center. A bathroom occupies one corner downstairs. Upstairs is also open-plan for the time being, until Ki can get around to subdividing the separate bedrooms.

Judith and Ki moved into their new straw bale home on December 15, 1996, twenty-one years to the day after Jaki and I moved into Log End Cottage. Ki was the first of the "next generation" of pioneers to build a home on Murtagh Hill.

As they'd feared, the grubstake was too small, and the couple had to borrow $8,000 from Judith's parents to get the home to its present state. There is still a lot to do: interior plastering, floor insulation, finished floor downstairs, more plumbing and electric, and interior bed-

The Lights' straw bale house. For a play on words—a straw bale lighthouse—see Mac's cartoon frontispiece for this chapter.

room walls. Ki is working on getting his PV electric system and his bicycle pump working properly.

Despite minor hardships, the Lights, at twenty-five, have created a home of great power. With the strong foundation, post-and-beam frame, metal roof, good roof overhang, and timely outside parge coat for protection, the straw bale walls should last forever or one hundred years, whichever comes first. Now, both Ki and Judith are working at full-time jobs, and, living in their own home, they're in the rapid saving mode of life again. By next winter, the home should be finished off and paid for. After that, who knows? One thing is certain, though: when they get to the next fork in the road, they'll be free to take it, knowing that their labor of love will always be there for them.

Ki stopped by one day after he and Judith had read their case study for accuracy. Ki felt that there was something missing, a feeling that I hadn't captured. He handed me a hand-written paragraph, which said:

> We never considered a traditional bank mortgage as an option. When we were planning our house, our future seemed wide open. We wanted to own our own place, but did not want to be tied to it financially. Now we're becoming attached to it for much better reasons: it's beautiful, cozy, and has been ours from the start. Granted, there's a whole lot different price to pay, as any owner-builder will tell you. There are rare moments—once a day or so—when the pain, frustration, and seeming endlessness of the whole undertaking kind of gets to you, but the pride and joy of being surrounded and sheltered by your own accomplishments more than makes up for all the grief.

Strategies and Circumstances

1. Built on parent's land.
2. Lived next door at parent's home during construction.
3. Intense eighteen-month savings period to raise grubstake.
4. Ki grew up in a community of mortgage-free owner-builders.
5. Chose low-cost rubble trench foundation.
6. Chose straw bale construction for economy, aesthetics, and energy efficiency.
7. Researched chosen building methods thoroughly.

8. Attended a three-day straw bale workshop.
9. Made good use of heavy equipment while on site: combined well digging with stump clearing, combined septic system with digging footing trenches.
10. Chose efficient two-story, nearly square shape.
11. Judith worked hard to find just the right engineer to get their plan and permit approved.
12. Used lots of recycled materials, especially windows and beams.
13. Ki worked full-time on home for six months.
14. Made good use of work parties.
15. Lots of help from family, friends, and neighbors. In true Yogi-like understatement, Ki says, "Plenty of help really helped."

From the Ground Up: The Art of Home

by Ted Holdt and Sara Mapelli, Washington

Locust wood lasts two years longer than stone.

—FOLK WISDOM

Inspiration carried us on her shoulders throughout our project. What we learned by building our own alternative (cordwood masonry) home will keep us going for a long time, mentally, physically, and spiritually. We found inspiration in the great architectural feats that came before us. And now, by building with our own hands, we have taken part in creating shelter, an act that can connect people to Mother Earth. That we owe no money on the house seems to make that connection stronger.

The need for shelter is an ever-evolving, changing, and creative experience. We have chosen to go against the norm, and, as artists, have adopted an alternative palate. This palate influences every aspect of our lives: the way we live, the way we work, the way we create our Shelter. As Humankind has evolved slowly from our "natural environment" to "space-age technologies," many new and interesting materials have been invented, and ways of using them. We chose to look to the past for our inspiration.

We both admire the Spanish master architect Antonio Gaudi, who played with both mosaics and the laws of gravity to create astounding structures. Our travels through India and Asia were also inspirational, not only for the exposure to the long history of different architectures, but also because of the realization that the incredible works we witnessed were all hand-built. What more does anyone need to realize that anything is possible in the creation of personal shelter?

We started building our home when we were each twenty-five. It is as much of a sculpture as it is a home, and it took us a year and a half to complete, although we actually lived in it part of the time during construction. Now, at twenty-seven, we are ready to start our studio. When we began, we weren't really sure where we were going, what we were doing, and how we were going to reach our final goal, whatever that would turn out to be. It seemed that the project simply created itself.

We had hired someone to regrade the old overgrown 600-foot-long logging road that led through winding turns to our "year-and-a-half full-time project." Now our mortgage-free cordwood house lies at the end of that road. Without getting into cordwood masonry, which Rob covers in another book (we called it "the cordwood bible"), we'd like to share some of the philosophies or strategies that we used to keep the bank out of the project.

When our drawing was approved by the local building department, we sent invitations to all our friends from Minneapolis to Germany to come with their tents and help us build. We got two responses; our friends Kay and Heike came from Germany for a month, and our good friend Laura from Minneapolis helped for two weeks.

As if on wings, we floated through day after day, creating a beautiful, functional monster. Half of the days were on the phone, half in the car, and the other half (it seemed) trying to remember the directions on how to do some particular task. We had lists everywhere directing us and pushing us ahead. Each day, upon rising, we would look at our lists and set a daily goal. This "ritual action" prepared us for the day's work and gave us confidence and direction to keep going.

Money can be a barrier to the processes that allow one to mature into a being truly in tune with oneself. It doesn't have to be that way, but it can. We didn't start without means. Sara's mother, Liz, gifted us two acres of land and water access in Washington State. Without such a jump start, we might never have built anything, or, at the least, our experience would have been entirely different. Liz also invited *her* mother and aunt to move out here from Denver, so there was always a place to go for a warm meal or the occasional shower. Sara's grandma and aunt helped us out with appliances, propane, and a warm woodstove. Liz was an incredible typhoon, helping us when she could and supporting us all the way. She was also a great coordinator and worker. In fact, when she came out to help, we sometimes couldn't keep up with her. We couldn't make the mortar for the cordwood walls fast enough. She was excited to see, upon return to the site after a few weeks away, that the roof was on or that the stone floor was well on its way.

We would not have been able to afford building if we had to pay rent, so we moved into an Army tent. Near to our construction site, we built a small temporary framed structure where we kept an old refrigerator, a rice steamer, and griddle. Since we were within 150 feet of a major transformer, the power company gave us a temporary construction supply without cost. We had no water until we had almost finished

Sara Mapelli and Ted Holdt's temporary shelter.

the house. So, for cooking and for mixing cement, we hauled water in three 55-gallon maple extract barrels. At first, everything tasted like maple syrup, a very nice treat.

We lived in the Army tent until we could move into the upstairs of the mostly open house. And there we stayed until it started to snow. Up to that point, our only heat was an electric blanket which we turned on an hour or so before we finished work for the night. We normally worked from early morning until 10 p.m. When it started to snow on us, we took refuge in a nearby cabin on Liz's property that nobody was using. In the springtime, we went back to "homesteading," our term for living upstairs. Now, thinking back on the experience, it would have been better, probably, to have built a quick temporary straw bale structure to live in. It would have been easier, more comfortable, and drier than the tent.

Outside of the help alluded to, we did almost all the work on our house ourselves. The exceptions were: grading the road, grading the site level (although we did dig all the footing tracks by hand), installation of the septic tank and digging the drain field, and the propane gas installation. We did all the electrical and plumbing. A good electrician cost too much for us, and a bad electrician would have cost more in the end, so we decided to do the work ourselves. We learned how from books and from talking with others.

We also scheduled two work parties. Both the preparation and the work parties themselves gave us much-needed pushes and inspiration to continue. The major one was the timber frame raising. At the end of that day, we were so impressed with ourselves and our community of friends and neighbors that we took a couple of days off.

One of the greatest savings in our house design is the use of cordwood masonry construction for the walls. How else can you get your structure, insulation, thermal mass, and an artistic interior and exterior finish for so little money?

We like to think that another reason we were able to keep bankers at bay was our approach to materials procurement. We started stockpiling materials the winter before we built. Here is an itemized accounting of some of our finds and methods. Some may be obvious, but, hopefully, some will inspire others to discover useful materials in all sorts of unlikely places.

1. Tommy Tucker is a friend and logger with a portable sawmill. Seek out this kind of friend! In our woods, we found a 108-foot standing dead white fir. The tree eventually would have fallen on the railroad tracks or close to a nearby cabin. For a fair fee, Tommy milled this indigenous resource into posts and beams.

2. Tommy also wanted to get rid of a grove of locust trees so he could make his yard more open. He gave the trees to us for the removal and we wound up stripping and stacking nine full cords of excellent log-ends.

3. For months we gathered stones from an old rock quarry, stones that eventually became our downstairs floor.

4. We bought lots of 5-gallon buckets at a fruit company. These buckets can also be bought cheaply from fast food restaurants, where they are used, once, to deliver pickles, donut fillings, and the like.

5. We took our buckets from Item 4 and brought them to a tile manufacturer, where we'd received permission to gather all the tile we could from their dumpster. We used the tile to create the mosaics on our floors and walls in our kitchen and bathroom.

6. We gathered bottles from our neighbors and the local bars, to use as "bottle-ends" in our cordwood walls. In some areas, recycling centers or county landfills are good source of bottles.

7. We needed aluminum cans to build our bathtub, but we had a hard time finding them because of their market value as recycled aluminum. We asked our neighbors to switch from drinking out of bottles to cans, and even got desperate enough to buy some from a grocery store at twenty cents a pound. An aluminum-can bathtub? Yes, we built it after the fashion of some of the interior walls in the Earthship houses (with walls of earth rammed into recycled tires). The cans are mortared up like log-ends, then a plaster parge or "scratch coat" is applied to both wall surfaces. Tiles are set in a coat of mastic applied to the original parge.

8. In exchange for the materials, we tore down a wood structure that covered a double-wide mobile home. This project yielded our floor joists and lots of plywood and two-by-fours.

9. We bought most of our windows from a business that sells perfectly good window units that were misordered for size.

10. Labor exchange or barter is a good deal for both parties. We made and traded some flower planters with hand-painted fused glass tiles on them for the special stainless steel flashing for our skylights. As skylight flashing needs to be done right, this was quite a useful deal.
11. For our roof substrate, we bought new roof rafters and sheathed with recycled plywood. The roofing surface consists of "end batches" of asphalt three-tab roofing shingles, all approximately the same color.
12. Most of the materials that we couldn't scrounge up were purchased at the local Home Depot or specialty stores.
13. We rarely passed a dumpster without sticking our noses in it. We once found a large construction dumpster full of great trim and conduit, all in good condition. If we felt as if we were breaking the law, we would go and ask if we could take stuff out of the bin. Most people will just look the other way. Demolition sites are great finds. The only problem is that a lot of the people working in demolition are also scavengers and don't want to share. It is getting harder to use recycled materials because it has become so popular, so fashionable, so smart.

Gathering your wits can be every bit as arduous as gathering building materials. And then you have to keep what you have gathered. Some simple philosophies and strategies helped us to stay sane, or reasonably so, throughout the eighteen-month building process. Others might find them equally useful.

First, we learned to trust ourselves. This sounds simple, but it is a quantum leap forward from the alternative.

Second, we kept our sense of humor. Rob tells us that this is reflected in the house itself.

Third, and this was big for us, we built our whole house listening to books on tape, about ninety-five in all, checked out of the library. Hallelujah for talking books! Even now, we can't look at the roof without thinking of *The Phantom of the Opera*. The northwest cordwood wall, appropriately, brings back *One Flew Over the Cuckoo's Nest*.

If someone were to ask for our advice, based on our building experience, we could boil it down to a few hard-earned words: Plan ahead. Know what you want, and what you need. Give yourself lots of time,

Sara and Ted's cordwood home is a work of art, and of love.

because everything seems to take longer than you thought it would. And, most of all, be as creative as you were when you were eight years old.

The role of the artist is to create art. Many people look at art and try to define and categorize it. Some disagree about what's art and what's not. The word *art* comes from a Greek root meaning *skill*. We, Ted and Sara, paint, sculpt, write poetry, and make music. We make an effort to interact with people in the community and at work, as well as with family and friends, with different levels of artfulness or skill. The skill in bringing to others the meaning and the story of one's own experience contributes to a whole and healthy life; ours, certainly, and yours, hopefully. We believe that in building our own house and using all the skills we had—most of them having little to do with conventional housebuilding—we have built a house that is a work of art. We hope . . . we believe . . . that the house reflects skills that have to do with living, our love of nature, and our trust in ourselves. We own our own home and are stewards of the land. There is no mortgage, no Big Bad Wolf, and we owe this to our friends and family. When people take part in our experience by feasting and visiting with us, we feel fulfilled and inspired, because they are part of our creation.

Rob Roy's Thoughts

As the reader will have gathered by now, Ted and Sara are expert scroungers, as well as skilled artists. They take found and recycled materials, and sculpt them into delightful architectural features. Here is a list of tips they would like to share:

- Trade a skill or materials that you have for something of near-equal value from someone else. What can you provide for something you need?
- Get to know people who can help you. Specialty stores can usually give you names of people who can accomplish specific tasks. That's how we found someone to mill the wood for our future steps, counter tops, and dining table.
- Use what's on your land, either natural indigenous materials like sand, stone, and wood, or even old dilapidated buildings. You can clean up the site and maybe recycle something useful.
- Find out what buildings can be torn down in your community in exchange for materials. Check the local papers and Pennysaver-type advertising sheets for information on these opportunities. Make sure that you have an agreement with the owner for your protection and your helpers'.
- Put ads in the same papers specifying what you want or need. Somebody's been storing it just for you down in the basement or out in the shed for these last twenty years.
- Recycle with fever! Call your local recycling office. They probably have enough connections to give your procurement process a flying start.
- Check dumpsters everywhere, especially those near business buildings. We've found incredible solid core doors there. And dumps can be as good as dumpsters.
- Ask for end batches, such as tile, carpet, and floor vinyl. "End batches" is what manufacturers call the end of a production run. There is not enough material left in the end batch to fill a box or bundle, or to make a large enough piece of floor covering, so they sell it cheaply.
- Check out construction sites. Leftover flooring from the American Legion Hall is now our beautiful upstairs floor.

Strategies and Circumstances:

1. Inspired by architecture in foreign countries visited.
2. Saved up $15,000 grubstake before building.
3. Borrowed $3,000 from Sara's mother, later worked off.
4. Walls built of cordwood masonry, a low-cost technique. Log-ends obtained free for clearing a friend's yard.
5. Invited friends and relatives to help.
6. Built on gifted land.
7. Lived in a tent, on site, for eight months.
8. Did most of work ourselves, including electric.
9. Scheduled two successful work parties.
10. Stockpiled materials the winter before we built.
11. Had our own timber milled into posts and beams.
12. Scrounged lots of recycled materials.
13. Extensive use of barter and labor exchange.
14. Planned ahead.
15. Kept our sense of humor.

❧

The House,
A Work in Progress

by Don Osby, North Carolina

Man who finish house, die.

—Old Chinese proverb

Our house is not completely finished. I could explain that there are over 140 heavy oak timbers in the house, representing 6,482 board feet of hand-planing. I could tell you that I had to cut (with saw and chisel) 850 perfect joints on the first try. I could even let you know that I did all this in the evenings and on weekends, and mostly by myself until it came time to raise the frame . . . but it might sound like either bragging or excuses. I'm not worried about justifying my schedule. I just keep the old Chinese proverb in mind; I'm not ready to die.

Despite its larger-than-life scale, timber framing is an incredibly exacting craft. The standards of workmanship that have evolved over many hundreds of years represent the essence of carpentry, visible today only in fine cabinet work. This refinement of skills occured not by accident, but by necessity. Also, with better tools came better joints. And as good timbers became more scarce, each generation of joiners became more creative in working with what they had. Colonists of early America combined the techniques of the Old World guilds with a practical approach that blended traditions and welcomed cooperation. In that spirit, the belief in the common man as home builder was fostered.

I didn't choose timber framing to try to revive a disappearing craft. Rather, I adapted it to my needs as a would-be homeowner unwilling to tie my life up to a thirty-year mortgage.

My situation was probably a lot like that of many people. I'd relocated for my job (as technical illustrator for *Mother Earth News*) and felt pretty comfortable with the North Carolina mountains after a couple of years. The experience of three rental houses had worn thin, and all of us—myself, my wife Mary Ann, and two small daughters—were ready to settle into something of our own.

At that time (1982) interest rates were slowly recovering from a near-catastrophic peak of two years earlier. When I thought about the uncertainty of financing, then figured out that a $55,000 mortgage loan would actually cost over $234,000 when it was finally paid off, I decided that my modest nest egg of a savings account was ready to take on some real responsibility. It would become our grubstake.

I developed a strategy to build as I could afford to, and, by careful planning, to avoid the pitfalls of long-term, absentee construction. The first step was to purchase the land, which turned out to be a double stroke of fortune. The two acres I was most interested in were owner-financed, and located within five minutes of the house we were renting. The seller also happened to be part of a family-run sawmill operation specializing in hardwoods.

With the land deal settled, I began to search in earnest for a building style that would fit my plan. I was lucky that, through my job, research materials of all kinds were right at my fingertips. Not a week went by that I wasn't rendering someone's solar home or studying a construction technique for low-cost building. On top of that, our editorial library was overflowing with books on alternative architecture, owner-building, traditional construction, and everything in between.

I contemplated earth-sheltered housing, geodesic domes, yurts, and all types of energy-efficient structures. But it wasn't until I found a book by post-and-beam builder Tedd Benson entitled *Building the Timber Frame House* (Scribner's, 1980) that I could comfortably begin to flesh out my plan.

The more I read about timber framing, the more I liked its integral strength and utilitarian simplicity. I felt particularly attached to a modified saltbox design with a two-foot overhang and a shed extension to the rear.

A real attraction was the fact that even a superb framing job required just a minimum of tools. Although there are a couple of motorized tools I consider essential (a 1/2-inch variable-speed reversible drill and a heavy-duty circular saw), the tool investment for the whole project was less than $400.

Don Osby's framework takes shape. See also the cover of this book.

People are always amazed by the paucity of implements needed to work such massive timbers. My favorite is the slick, two-handed bruiser of a chisel—as wide as my fist—whose paradox lies in its delicate shaving and slicing functions. The framing chisel, 1½-inches in breadth, has a socket handle and a steel butt ring. It's extremely stout, and has to be, because it's beaten with a two-pound hickory mallet to carve the mortises. A beetle—one full stone weight (14 pounds) of handmade wooden mallet—comes in handy when fitting joints.

A combination-blade handsaw is an absolute necessity, as are framing and combination squares, a sharpening stone, and a measuring tape. A drawknife and a jack plane are certainly useful for finishing work, but I broke down and bought a Makita power planer, more out of convenience than absolute need. Later, I picked up a couple of come-alongs, clamps, and rope loops in preparation for pulling the bents together during assembly. A *bent* is an assemblage of timber-frame components that can be put together on the floor, and then tilted up into position.

I felt that timber framing could accommodate my time frame and cash flow. Publishing is an unpredictable business at best, and periods of perpetual deadlines interspersed with spells of bad weather didn't do a whole lot for my progress. During times like these, I took the opportunity to figure load calculations and create—and recreate—my house on paper. I even built a ¹/₁₂ scale model of carefully cut pine to aid me in planning the finished frame. Sometimes it is easier to work out a difficult jointing detail in three dimensions than with paper and pencil. If you can't do it in the model, the chances are that you can't do it in the house.

My plan became a blend of old and new; beautiful in its traditional style, but practical in its application of modern techniques. To remain true to the joiner's craft, I stayed with time-tested designs where practicable—like shouldered mortise and tenon, housed dovetail, and tusk tenon—and added embellishments such as curved-bottom knee braces, and carved pendants for the exterior framed overhang. If this all sounds a little Greek, don't worry; it did to me at first. Whatever building style you choose, be prepared to learn a whole new set of technical terms. After a while, you'll even know what you're talking about.

Determined to make use of solar gain, I planned an 8-by-10-foot concrete block storage chamber in the basement, to be filled later with coarse filtered gravel and capped with a layer of brick, which would also serve as the entry floor. The rock bed's mass, I figured, would absorb heat from warm air directed through the chamber by a fan connected to a peak-high central duct, and release it into the house by way of a grille in the entryway. Insulated glass on the south face would give the interior plenty of access to the sun's heat when needed. Four skylights, aided by open ceilings in the kitchen, dining area, and one bedroom, would lend the interior an airy feeling. In actuality, the mass helps to keep the space at a comfortable steady temperature even without a fan.

Once I'd settled on the dimensions of the house, I was able to itemize my timber order (specifying straight white oak) and give it directly to my neighbor at the sawmill. Knowing that it would take a while to locate and cut the trees, I prepaid the $1,620 bill, and began surveying my site and staking out the foundation.

The first of the rough-cut timbers would be ready eventually, and the thought of hauling 400-pound beams to a work shed away from the building site, then all the way back again, didn't appeal. What did make sense, though, was to get the footers poured and to lay up the basement block walls as soon as I could. Then it wouldn't take much to nail floor joists in place, cover them with subfloor, and drape the wooden surface with builder's felt and reinforced polyethylene tarps. The 27-by-35-foot space would then be effectively dried in and could serve as a warm, secure and—best of all—on-site workshop.

Closing in the basement didn't happen as quickly as I thought it would, but what does? Considering that I had to supervise the excavation; hand-pour a good deal of concrete; learn masonry skills; waterproof, insulate, and backfill the perimeter walls; install a garage door; and take care of temporary electrical service—well, I was just ecstatic when it was finished.

The next thirty months was a period of endless measuring, cutting, paring, planing, and trial fitting. As the various posts, girts, and braces were finished, I'd stack them to the side on spacers and haul in a fresh load. Sure, I made a few mistakes and replaced a few pieces, but, joint by joint, there was clear progress.

By the time of the final fit, I had to make a major decision. Should I tough out another winter and plan on an early spring house raising? Or should I scramble to piece together the four bents, or main arches, that define the structure and count on a pleasant early-winter week-end to host a framing party? My decision was aided by the abysmal condition of the plastic sheet that no longer adequately protected my subfloor and floor joists. I had to get the frame up as quickly as pos-sible. I fell in tune with the timeless strategy that is imposed upon us all: Things get done when they *have* to get done.

The assembly of each bent was made easier because I could use the broad subfloor as a work area. I constructed each section and stacked them where they'd be needed. Then, with the dreary days of Novem-ber just over the horizon, we hosted our frame-raising.

What an event! Co-workers, friends, relatives, and neighbors showed up in force on the Saturday morning I'd carefully chosen: the first cold, wet day we'd had in weeks. No matter. With the help of a crane to lift the 1,700-pound bents into position, the whole crew—probably only five of whom had any carpentry experience whatsoever—got busy fitting the posts into their deck sockets and nailing braces in place to keep everything aloft. Two or three of us used our beetles to fit the joints of plates, girts, knee braces, and summer beams. Then we locked them in with oak pegs.

At noon, my mom and grandmother arrived with a carload of hot lunch, coffee, pies, and desserts. After a short break, we returned to the deck to fit the front overhang and erect the remaining bents. By day's end, most of the structure was up, except the shed sections and roof parts. A week later the frame was complete and I could see, for the first time, the house shape silhouetted against the sky.

On and off through the winter and spring, I enlisted the help of a friend with experience in heavy construction. Together, we fitted two-by-sixes over the horizontal purlins and installed roof sheathing and four inches of expanded polystyrene. Later, an additional 3½ inches of fiberglass would bring the roof insulation up to the required R-30 for our area. We also installed four insulated glass skylight panels and the shingles, a "high anxiety" job that I had trouble contracting out because the roof pitch was so steep!

When the watertight cap over the frame was completed, I turned my attention to exterior walls. My original plan was to use stress-skin panels, a prefabricated combination of drywall, insulation, and exte-rior sheathing. This plan was modified when I seriously considered the difficulty of wrestling the heavy 4-by-8-foot and 8-by-8-foot units

Don and Mary Ann Osby's lovely (and mortgage-free!) timber-frame house.

into place—by myself—on the second and third stories. Instead, I built up lightweight, conventional, nonstructural wall sections and hoisted them into place with a block and tackle. Circumstance—call it *reality*—will dictate such changes in plan. The trick is walking the fine line between "Think it through" and "Go with the flow." They don't have to be mutually exclusive.

When the entire wall frame was enclosed by a skeleton of two-by-fours (24-inch on center), the backer board was applied and the doors and windows were hung, including seven large first-floor windows on the south side made from inexpensive sliding glass window replacement units. From this point on, working inside the house was a real pleasure. Even on cold days, the sun would keep the interior at a comfortable working temperature. And when we installed the fiberglass insulation, things got even better. It seemed like there was light and warmth at the end of a very long tunnel.

A stroke of good fortune came the morning I was going to buy the Texture 1-11 siding. This was a purchase I'd been putting off, partly to let my cash flow improve, and partly because plywood, even fancy textured plywood, was not exactly what I wanted for the exterior of my frame. As I skimmed through the paper, coffee in hand, I spotted an ad for cedar siding at a local salvage supply company. Some quick calculations put the 6-inch beveled cedar at about the same price as the T1-11 siding. A few days later, a large truck arrived with enough material to keep me busy for quite a while.

Installation of interior partitions went without a hitch until it came time to fill them with electrical wiring and plumbing. It's always tempting at times like this to call in a pro, but my bank account balance always seemed to have just enough for labor or for materials, but never both. So, as with so many portions of this project, I realized it was time to drag out the books and develop a few more skills. Another choice made simple by fiscal reality.

Having gained a sincere respect for people who can wire a three-way switch without looking at a diagram, I turned my attention to the tedious task of fitting drywall between posts, beams, and curved knee braces. Even though it was time-consuming, the end result of smooth white walls against the oak frame is visually striking.

It was at this point in the evolution of "The House" that things got a little crazy. The magazine where I worked for 11 years was sold and the new owners decided to move the entire operation to Manhattan. The North Carolina staff was let go, no golden parachute, not even a safety net. And, in the middle of the late-1980s recession, jobs were scarce. Fortunately, Mary Ann was still employed in the public school system. But it was obvious that a single paycheck wasn't going to complete the house any time soon. Enter Plan B.

I called the local building inspectors, and, with the addition of a few items like handrails and a temporary kitchen sink, we were given a "Certificate of Occupancy." With the C.O. in hand, our next call was to the credit union. A representative came out to inspect the house and, after reviewing our old material bills, they approved us for a line of credit that allowed us to finish enough of the house so that we could move in. This ended our cycle of monthly rent.

That was six years ago. Since then, I've started my own graphic arts business, based out of the house. Mary Ann is looking at a career change.

My oldest daughter has made us grandparents. And my "little girl" has gone off to college. The old magazine staff has even started its own employee-owned magazine. It's amazing what financial freedom allows you to do.

Of course, I still have a basement full of salvaged hard rock maple flooring to install on the second and third floor and around the windows and doors. I know this should have been done years ago, but, then, it is a work in progress!

Rob Roy's Thoughts

Complete plans for Don's 1,700-square foot timber-frame saltbox are available for $30 postpaid. Send check or money order to Don Osby, P.O. Box 1276, Mountain Home, NC 28758.

The employee-owned magazine where Don works is BackHome, listed in appendix 3 as an excellent source for all sorts of homesteading information. A few years ago, I visited Don and Mary Ann's home, and was impressed with both its power and beauty. Despite Don's closing words, I did not get the sense that this was an unfinished house. Living on a subfloor can be considered a form of life insurance, if the old Chinese proverb is to be trusted.

Strategies and Circumstances

1. Built as could be afforded, the pay-as-you-go strategy.
2. Financed the land purchase through previous owner.
3. Researched many building styles, settled on timber framing.
4. Pre-purchased heavy timbers from local sawmill.
5. Closed in basement first for an on-site workshop.
6. Sensible three-story 27-by-35-foot shape.
7. Solar orientation and mass heat storage for energy savings.
8. Bought inexpensive sliding glass door replacement windows for solar gain.
9. Successful frame-raising party.
10. Pre-built own wall sections and hoisted them into place.
11. Learned plumbing and electrical skills to save money.
12. With C.O. in hand, secured line of credit to finish home and move in. Payback of loan is offset by savings on rent.

≈

A Small House
in Wisconsin

by Gregg and Janet Butz

Ah, yet, e'er I descend to the grave,
May I a small house, and large garden have!
                    —ABRAHAM COWLEY, "THE WISH"

In today's world, the emphasis tends to be on what you have, not on what you give back. Janet and I were tired of being marketed to and pigeon-holed. After much soul-searching, we decided that the status quo was not for us. We wanted and needed to find those values that so many have lost, particularly a sense of connectedness and personal responsibility. We decided to follow the lead of Thoreau, the Nearings, and many others in going back to the basics, back to the land.

Knowing what we wanted was the first step, and knowing what we were willing to sacrifice to get there was the second—maybe even electricity and running water for a while. We made a list of what we needed to do to accomplish our goal and started to work on it.

Reading books and articles on buying land and what to look for in a good building site is the best way to start the search. Living and building in northern Wisconsin, we wanted a place with a good southern exposure for solar gain, as well as a slope for good drainage. With a grasp of what to look for, we then drew a thirty-mile radius around a small city where we could find employment.

Armed with maps and realtor listings, we spent three months driving the country roads looking at land. We cared less about the quantity of acres and more about the quality of good building and gardening sites. When we found a property we liked, we'd return several times to observe the potential homestead at different times of the day, and walk around it to gain familiarity with the subtle features of the landscape. One piece we considered was about thirty miles from town, which did not seem like much until we drove it a few times.

We found a fifteen-acre parcel located eight miles from town, off of the appropriately named Hillview Road. Our south-facing slope is in an open field of seven and a half acres, and the remainder of the land is wooded with oak, spruce, apple trees, sumac, and mushrooms galore! There is a spring that runs into a small marshy area. We like the biodiversity of the land and the wildlife it supports. The asking price was reasonable because the owners were eager to sell.

Finding the land was easy compared to trying to get traditional financing. Most banks do not want to loan money on undeveloped land. We also found that interest rates varied in our area by 3 percent, a huge difference. We offered to buy on a land contract, letting the sellers finance the transaction. They were not interested at first. At our third meeting, we paid our earnest money, and, after we told them about the current bank rates, they offered to sell on land contract. Their lawyer drew up a contract and we split the cost of the paperwork. It was a big win for both of us. We were able to get the land for only $300 down and payments of less than $200 per month for seven years.

Cutting out the bank's profit is only one of the advantages of a land contract. The seller actually gets more for the property while the buyer pays less. Win, win. The down payment, payment schedule, and terms are negotiated with the actual seller and not with a suit at the bank. Since both buyer and seller have a personal stake in the transaction, there is more positive energy to make it work.

However, there are risks in buying land this way. You do not actually own the land until the end of the contract. Missing a payment, illegal activity, ruinous land practices, and other situations enumerated in the land contract can lead to loss of the land. Any investment made in, on, over, or under the land is forfeited. Draft the land contract together so that both parties have their concerns protected as much as possible. Having your own lawyer look at the contract is a good idea if you do not understand all of the terms. Having the contract notarized and recorded in the county clerk's office gives valuable protection to both parties. We've been paying on our land for just over two years with no problems.

With the land contract and legal documents in order, we now had a place to call our own. Well, almost. We won't actually have the deed until we finish our payments. However, we could start to plan a home and figure out how to finance our dream. The decision to buy on a land contract precluded us from getting a standard mortgage from a bank. A bank will not loan money for a home if you do not have clear title to the land. The other condition most banks have on mortgages is that an experienced general contractor must build the home. On the average, about 90 percent of the money used to build the home is the bank's. In essence, it is the bank's house and the bank wants to be sure that it is saleable if you default. We decided to opt out of the thirty-year mortgage, as well as the bank's influence on how to build our home.

We have a good credit rating and were able to secure a $5,000 signature loan. A signature loan, or personal note, carries a higher interest rate than a mortgage, since you are borrowing the money on the strength of your good name alone. We set ours up as a ninety-day note

---

Before You Build
by John and Edith Rylander

Building your own home should start with self-appraisal. A few questions now may save anguish later. Here's what you need to know before you start:

1. Can you motivate yourself? Building a home takes a long steady effort. Will you keep at it, good weather or bad, 'in the mood' or not?
2. Have you the physical stamina to see the job through? Weight-lifter strength isn't necessary, but some strength, balance, and general good health is.
3. Can you get professional help when needed? We hired pros for some of the block laying, plumbing, wiring, and carpet installation, doing the rest ourselves. We wanted to finish in one summer and were willing to trade money for time.
4. Can you organize other people? We hired two recent high-school graduates for much of the summer, and had to plan each day's activities, making sure the right tools and materials were on hand—and do our own work at the same time.
5. Are your finances adequate? Be sure you'll wind up with a building fit to live in, if not entirely finished, before you begin. Discuss your cost estimates with people who have experience in building and building costs. Don't start unless you're sure that you have at least the bare minimum. Lenders are skeptical about owner-builders using unconventional techniques.

with a lump sum payment at the end of the term, anticipating that we would have a place to live in by then. Building a small home takes more time than we thought and we had to get another ninety-day note to pay back the first one. Buying ninety more days allowed us to finish the project and get out of the rent trap. Now we could set up a monthly payment schedule to repay the loan with the money formerly put toward rent. In reality, we borrowed $5,000 three times, paid it back twice, and are in the process of paying it back for the third time.

If you do not have a credit history, build one as soon as possible. Borrow some money from a bank on a ninety-day note. Deposit the

6. Have you checked local building codes and regulations? Which permits are needed? Which inspections are required, and when? Codes are written for the standard, not the unconventional. Better to cross every 'T' and dot every 'I' than be forced into expensive changes.
7. Can you tolerate frustration? Things don't always go smoothly. A job you thought would take five hours may take five days. Tools break, materials run out or aren't available, or the weather doesn't cooperate. Have a Plan B, even a Plan C.
8. If you have a domestic partner, are you sure he/she really wants to get into this? Not every pair that lives together can work together. Mothers-in-law sometimes regard house building as a form of spouse abuse. Building isn't a task with which all women will be happy, nor will all men.
9. If you're working with a partner who has fewer building skills than you do, can you transmit instruction and criticism in a way that doesn't leave your partner loathing both you and the project? Can you take instruction and criticism without too much ego-bruising?
10. Can you put up with each other's work habits? Domestic tensions don't improve with the addition of hammers and saws.

This sage advice is reprinted from *The Complete Book of Underground Houses* (Sterling, 1994), with permission from the publisher. You can read the Rylanders' story of building their own mortgage-free underground home on pages 122 to 126 of that book. See appendix 3.

money in a savings account but do not spend it! At the end of the term, repay the loan with interest, thereby establishing a good credit history. A bank is a business, so don't be afraid to shop around for a good interest rate, or to negotiate a lower rate on your loan. The bank likes to loan money to people who always pay it back. Because a modest signature loan is small to them, they charge a higher interest rate to make it worth their while. We had established our credit history while in college and now we had the land and a little money to build a small house.

Our plan to build a small shelter was inspired by Janet's sister and her spouse in Alaska, who lived in a very much smaller cabin for eight years while they paid off their land and saved to build a bigger home. I hate to tell you how small it was. Suffice it to say that you had to step outside to change your mind. It was warm and cozy, perhaps *too* cozy. They finally accomplished their goal and their long-term temporary shelter is now their daughter's playhouse. We decided that we needed a little more room for our starter home. The idea of building something small on the second-best location is a great way to get onto the land and to stop paying rent. We designed our 480-square-foot home so it could be converted into a work/pottery/produce shop someday. Others have turned their first home into a guest house or built it on skids so it could be sold when not needed.

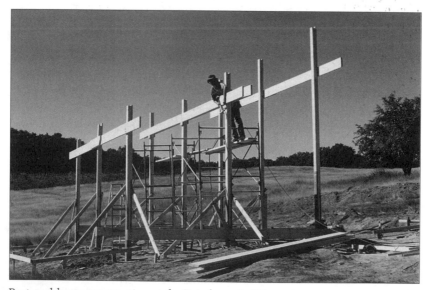

Post-and-beam construction at the Butz home in Wisconsin.

We looked at straw bale construction, cordwood masonry, rammed tire (Earthships), and rammed earth. I am interested in these environmentally friendly building techniques and will use one—or a combination of more than one—for our final home. In the meantime, we needed something that the building inspector would understand and that would easily pass code, so that we could start living in our own place. We put in a call to the building inspector about using straw bales as insulation, but he was not interested in any "experimental" homes. The reality is that the building inspectors have a tough job and a heavy workload. They don't want to take the time to learn about alternative building techniques. I applaud all the people out there who are working along with building inspectors and helping to ease the way toward more sustainable building practices.

We decided on post-and-beam construction, based on the ease of building, minimal impact on the land, acceptance by building inspectors, and the availability of several good books on the subject. Some of the books give basic step-by-step procedures for putting up a building, as well as building plans and tables showing maximum spans for various dimensions of lumber. We were required to submit a set of working drawings before we could get a building permit. Aided by a book, as well as materials on the Uniform Building Code from the library, I was able to draw a decent set of plans. The application for a building permit also required a sanitary permit, a soil erosion plan, and heat loss calculations. Much to my surprise, the application was approved. This was a proud moment for me, kind of like passing a test, one that really counted.

While working on the drawings, we felt a need to gain some real-world experience in building. The first project was to build a deck at the edge of the woods. We had salvaged some decking from another project I'd worked on, so the cost was minimal. The deck provided a dry, level platform for a large tent. This worked out great. We were getting some building experience and were able to spend all our time on the land. We spent the summer in the tent, overlooking the sumac grove that sparkled with fireflies every evening. By taking small steps, we were gaining the knowledge and confidence to build our own home.

The sumacs' red tops foretold the coming of fall, so we decided to build something with a roof on it, a garden/tool shed. We would use the same skills for the shed that we would need for the house. Only

Gregg and Janet are already adding onto their small but mortgage-free home, built in 1996–1997.

the scale was different. Besides valuable practical experience, we gained a place to store our tools and live in while building the home. Originally I thought we could rough it through the winter in the tool shed if necessary. Four cats and a large dog made it a little cramped, and Janet was a might nervous sleeping with the pitchfork over our bed.

The deck and garden shed were invaluable practice runs and gave us the opportunity to make mistakes, the best teachers. Although we could have lived on the land at this time, we continued to rent a place in town. We were both working full-time jobs and needed a place to shower and store our stuff.

We stapled our building permit to the shed, took the post hole digger out of it, and began the foundation for our 16-by-24-foot cottage on Labor Day weekend. In no time we had nine holes dug to frost level. We set our pressure-treated pillars as square and plumb as we could, and, using post-and-beam framing techniques learned from books and our practice projects, we soon had a roof overhead. Getting the roof on early is an advantage of a pillar foundation and post-and-beam framing, allowing us to work even when it was raining.

Projects followed logically, one right after the other. We installed a wood floor, preferring it over concrete because it is much more comfortable to stand on. Next, we enlisted some friends to help with the framing and window installation. (Most of our windows face south for solar gain.) We installed the siding and insulation ourselves. The final inspection for our certificate of occupancy was done on a cold, clear day in December. Another proud moment occurred when the inspector commented on how toasty it was inside, even without a heater!

We spent the next month and a half sheetrocking, painting, and building a loft. Our kitchen is supplied with a propane stove and refrigerator that were rescued from a garbage heap and old tavern, respectively. As I write, February of 1997, we have just celebrated our first anniversary in our home, and hope to install a PV electric system this summer. We won't refuse donations!

What we have done is by no means extraordinary, although we now feel personally responsible for and connected to our home and our future. We have learned that our contribution is in what we do with our lives, not what we have.

Rob Roy's Thoughts

In November of 1997, I phoned Gregg to find out how he and Janet were getting on. The news is all positive. They did install two Siemens M-55 photovoltaic panels that supply basic lights and radio. Also, Gregg has painted the house and finished an attached garage, built on a pay-as-you-go basis. He is in the process of converting a portion of the garage space into a bathroom.

Their last loan payment will occur in March of 1998; then, they will continue the $230 per month payments, except into their own interest-bearing savings account. In this way, they'll lay by the money for a house addition. Short-term small-scale borrowing can be an effective bridge to ease passage over troubled waters, and, as Gregg and Janet have shown, can even instill an ability to save.

Strategies and Circumstances

1. Bought land on land contract.
2. Borrowed money on signature loan, having established a good credit rating.
3. Practiced building techniques on small projects.
4. Researched building method and worked out design details on paper.
5. Built small, just 440 square feet.
6. Used pole building foundation.
7. Built roof first, allowing work to proceed under cover.

On Building Your Own

by Rob and Bonnie Watt, British Columbia

You can't always get what you want,
But if you try real hard,
Sometimes, you can get what you need.

—M. JAGGER AND K. RICHARDS

Not knowing any better, we presumed we could build a house. After all, we could read, and we had always maintained that if you can read, you can learn to do anything. Well, we did it, and along the way we learned a few things about construction, a few things about reducing costs, and a lot about life. Thoreau was right about the Zen involved in making your own shelter. "What does architecture amount to in the experience of the mass of men?" asks the hermit rhetorically, answering himself, "I never in all my walks came across a man engaged in so simple and natural an occupation as building his house." Building a house has its own intrinsic worth, apart from function.

Here are our Top Ten Tips:

1. Nothing in life is free.

You can pay in dollars, time, or tears, but pay you must. The bargains you make will reflect your willingness to make those particular, and peculiar, sacrifices. Our own personal craziness was to construct a daylight basement first, which we ended up living in for nine years as we saved money to complete the structure. Looking back on it, it seems unbelievable. On the other hand, we owned a completed home twelve years after we started it, instead of holding a mortgage for thirty-five years.

2. When things look darkest, relief may be closer than you think.

In a particularly virulent spasm of Sixties angst, our neighbors had obtained a milking goat and, along with a few chickens and pigs, felt themselves well on the way to self-sufficient rural living. One afternoon, we were called away from a discouraging battle with pink fiber-

Rob Watt gets ready to brace the gable truss on his home in British Columbia.

glass by the panic-stricken cries of "The goat is in the rhubarb!" Apparently, this would result in a terminally negative experience for the goat, so hurried calls were made to the vet for remedies. Advised to purge the animal, we struggled to hold the definitely unenthusiastic nanny whilst castor oil was administered with a gravy baster. A single application sufficed, to everyone's relief, and we went home to our pink insulation woes, having learned from the goat a valuable lesson: this, too, shall pass.

3. Two heads are better than one, and a head that's not involved is even better.

If you have a problem (and you will have problems), try a different approach, ask a friend, write to Dear Abby, or tell your mother about it, but, when you do, listen without judgment. Often the solution is not in what they say, but rather in how it jolts you out of the rut your thinking is in. Our land is level, so our sewage and drain water has to be pumped up out of the basement to a lagoon. It is collected in a holding tank under the basement floor until there is a sufficient level to activate a float valve that starts the pump. Since the lagoon's surface is above the holding tank, it seemed prudent to install a check valve between them to prevent backflow into the house. This system, a paragon of design, just didn't work. The check valve was continually clogging up, which required pulling the pump, dismantling the pipes and valves and couplings, then cleaning and reassembling the whole mess. (Did I mention that this was a sewage pump?) We did it so many times that I eventually installed flexible couplings instead of solid pipe.

We were focused on the stuff getting caught in the check valve, certain that the problem was the type of paper or other material going through. After months of this, a whine to Rob's mother prompted her to ask if it was like a stove and could it have a burnt-out fuse? We almost dismissed the remark, but, luckily, caught the essence of it: this was a system, and some one thing was not right. Going back to the system design and examining the physics of the thing, it was fairly simple to isolate each element and look at it anew. Then, late one night, when no one was around to see, we furtively removed the check valve and put it back in the other way around. It has functioned flawlessly for thirteen years.

4. Don't give up. Keep asking.

There are a lot of free or very inexpensive things out there. One year we built a sauna for just under $100 (Canadian dollars, yet!). This came about when a neighbor mentioned that he was going to burn an old shed down. We offered to dismantle and remove it. Soon, we found folks who were glad to be rid of old windows, a stove, old timbers . . . and, for many years, we enjoyed our "free" sauna.

Another time, when we couldn't afford to hire a backhoe to fill in a waterline ditch, we contacted the local youth detention center, which obliged us by bringing over a crew of strong young people with shovels. We had our ditch filled before winter, and the kids made some pocket money and had an afternoon out of the hoosegow.

5. Use a smaller bucket.

To paraphrase the old Chinese proverb, the moving of a thousand rocks begins with but a single pebble. If it's a big job, reduce it to manageable components and get started. When people ask us how on earth we built our own house, we usually say we just ordered a truckload of sticks and a bucket of nails and began.

6. Measure twice, cut once.

We framed our walls in manageable sections that allowed the two of us to lift them into place. On the last one, though, we got a bit rammy and framed the whole forty-two feet at once. To erect it, we called on friends and neighbors (great resources, by the way). Standing every four feet or so, we bent over, grabbed the wall, and heaved it upright into position, at which point it became evident that we had framed it upside down. The door was on the ceiling and the cat could look out the windows. We must confess that we call our place the "thrice-built house," since everything in it was constructed three times: the first time, the next try, and then the right way.

7. There is a special place in Hell for the individual who mixes nails.

Be organized. It will save you time, money, and frustration. Put your tools away. Tidy up at the end of the day. Keep pencil and paper handy and make lists. Set aside a time each day for a little conference to consider what you accomplished that day and what your goal is for the next. Keep a scrapbook of ideas, costs, estimates, timelines, bills, and budgets. We regret now that we didn't keep a daily journal. Take pictures as you go along. You will look back and laugh one day.

8. Make it legal.

If you do borrow money, we would advise you to formalize the agreement on paper, and have it notarized. We can hear you saying, "Well, of course we would!" But what about an agreement among family members? Sometimes things are taken for granted among people who love each other. Trust us, bad stuff happens even in families, and no one can predict how the world will change ten years down the road. You may end up making the lawyers rich. Urge your children to attend law school.

9. Know when to flex in order to reach your goals in a way you hadn't anticipated.

Our dream was to pay cash for this house as we went along, and that worked fine, as far as it went. The problem was that we were living in the basement nine years later, still saving for the rest of the house.

Rob and Bonnie Watt's well-earned home.

(This might be a good time to reread Rob Roy's clever ideas in chapter 5 about less-expensive design and construction methods.)

We reached the decision to borrow money in a logical, reasoned manner. It was raining heavily, and the temporary tarpaper roof we had put on most of a decade ago was gamely keeping out as much as 60 percent of the rain. The kids were running in and out through the interior stud walls, pursued by Bonnie, whose enthusiasm for living in a pit was waning. Rob was taking his ease in the living room when twelve pounds of wet spitting feline fury fell through the ceiling into his lap, leaving behind an impromptu skylight, flesh wounds, and spousal determination for a rapid change of circumstance.

We decided to borrow some money and finish.

10. There's more than one way to skin a cat.

The cat who precipitated the decision made a lovely muff and alerted us to the possibility of alternative financing. We did the usual round of banks and credit unions but were unable to obtain money because we weren't "real" contractors. By being frank and noisy about the challenge facing us, we found that long-time acquaintances were willing to lend us money privately on a business-like basis. We secured the loan with our property and our word, borrowed a modest amount, and ended up with a home and dear friends to invite to it. It seems that there are folks out there who would rather lend money to friends than to a bank. We paid an interest rate that equaled what they would have made in term deposits, but which was, of course, less than the bank prime lending rate. No one suffered and we profited immensely. And in conclusion . . .

Our house became a metaphor for our lives. To build a house one must make a plan, then reduce it to its essential steps, make a list of materials in the order that they are needed, then find a way to obtain them. Assembling the components is a one-step-at-a-time process. You needn't become overwhelmed, because at any point there is only one thing to do. This philosophy provided us with a successful method for building a home, but it also brought order and progress to all parts of our lives. We began making plans about where we wanted to be five years hence in our careers, finances, material goals, and educational goals. We make those plans still, and credit them with giving our lives the direction that has put us where we are. And we're happy with where we are. Building your home may be the most stressful thing you ever do with your partner. (You're not foolish enough to think you can do this alone, are you?) Plan to develop communications skills that will help you to separate issues from personalities, and deal with disagreements in ways that don't threaten the dignity or worth of either's contribution. Finally, remember this always: insulation goes on the outside, vapour barrier goes on the inside. Forget this and your dignity and worth will not win the argument, because your pipes will freeze.

Rob Roy's Thoughts

Watt? No Strategies and Circumstances?

I met Rob and Bonnie at a delightful little motel near Chichen Itza on Mexico's Yucatan Peninsula. While not everyone you meet at Chichen Itza is mortgage-free—although most of the indigenous Mayans are—I like to think that Rob & Bonnie and Rob & Jaki wouldn't have come together if we weren't that way ourselves. The Watts were taking a year's sabbatical from their jobs, much easier to do without worrying about regular payments. Their delightful "case study" is more philosophical in nature, tempered with humor, a little pathos, good old-fashioned wisdom, and some sound advice based on experience. Strategies? Well, they're in the article, but there's a higher value to the Watts' story that would be trivialized by listing them out here.

≈

Land in Common:
The Cooperative Approach

by Jim Schley, Vermont

If the world were just, it would suffice to build a house.

—ARTHUR SCHOPENHAUER

In the spring of 1996, ten friends celebrated an unusual anniversary: we made our final payment on a ten-year bank loan for purchase of an old hill farm in Vermont.

The bank that agreed to offer this loan had considered us an experiment—not necessarily high-risk, but somewhat unpredictable. We were determined to own 160 acres in common, without subdividing the land, and to build our homes along shared driveways, which did not yet exist; the land also lacked a power line. For reasons not obvious to any of us, the bankers decided to take a chance. And while that bank changed ownership four or five times in the following decade, the members of the Blue Moon Cooperative Community steadily kept paying off the loan, month by month, until the day arrived when we owned the land unencumbered by the bank. One might ask which partner in the loan deal was the higher risk.

Any venture in collective ownership will have countless aspects that are unique, and our story is still unfolding. Let me summarize the key ingredients to our community's strategy for buying land and building homes, without mortgages.

We presently have five households living on the Blue Moon land, and several affiliated households in nearby towns. The cooperative has ten adult members, with eight children. Our equity as co-op members increases at an equal rate with each monthly payment we make. While those who were founding members have been paying longer, and thereby have higher equity than those who joined later, legally we own the land equally, and lease our home sites from the co-op (which is ourselves, and not a separate entity as in a land trust); these leases are for ninety-nine years, renewable by our inheritors, conditional upon their acceptance for membership in the co-op.

We employ one of our members as a bookkeeper, and we pay members for plowing and sanding our driveways and for supervising management of the tax-favored "working forest" land, which includes most of our acreage. In addition to the land and our driveways, we own in common a tractor, a plow truck, a workshop, a sugarhouse (for boiling down maple sap), a pond, and many tools that would be owned in multiples in a "normal" neighborhood.

I don't want to give the impression, from our present vantage point of almost fifteen years on, that our odyssey was less gradual, painstaking, and improvisational than it's been. In the beginning, the group met weekly for more than two years before we found land that we liked and could afford. During this time we worked exceedingly hard to learn the consensus decision-making process, getting to know one another as more than acquaintances. This was like a cross between forming a company and forming a clan. Prospective members joined and departed, some finding the number of meetings required not to their liking or the fundamentally easy-going nature of the group not "directed" enough in a spiritual or ideological sense.

At our frequent meetings we made lists of the ingredients we were seeking in our community, as we responded to advertisements listing land for sale. In the mid-1980s in our part of Vermont, land prices were rising, upwards of $2,000 per acre—there was a building boom, and it appeared that most of the old pastures and fields within commuting distance of the region's bigger towns would be rapidly "developed." At one point our original gang of six actively put out the word that we were receptive to widening the circle, and then six more people joined the discussion group. All of us were employed, with incomes varying according to profession (included among our number over the years have been several carpenters, several teachers, a midwife, an engineer, a software programmer, a food co-op co-manager, two editors, and a forester). At the time of our land purchase, none of us had much in the way of savings, but in candid discussions we found that some of us had access to personal loans from friends and relatives (ranging from $5,000 to $15,000). This networking gave us a pool of resources significantly greater than that available to any one household.

But throughout, we've shared much more than economic arrangements. Because there were so many of us, we didn't each have to deal with the realtor, the banker, the lawyer, the insurance company, the town's planning board, the road contractor, the telephone company, and so forth. We divvied up tasks according to interests or tolerance—conscripting people onto the dreaded By-Laws committee, when necessary. And although we built separate houses, all of us gained from cooperatively buying supplies, salvaging old buildings, and learning about solar electric systems.

In order to investigate different models for community ownership, we spent time visiting with veterans of various kinds of group-living experiments: communes, collectives, multi-family residences. The voice of experience proffered certain persistent lessons, including "Don't underestimate the importance of privacy as well as community," and "Be wary of purchase schemes where a few members of the group in fact buy the land on behalf of the rest," which will unavoidably result in a situation where some are real owners while others have merely symbolic equity, and are therefore "tenants" of the true owners.

Without for a moment discounting the importance of conviviality and goodwill in sustaining us through years of hard work, this group has also been the beneficiary of those clear and resilient principles that we devised for the governance of our partnership. Before plunging into the task of co-owning an actual piece of ground, we worked on devising a formalized, legal relationship within which our members can relate as neighbors, including provisions for managing financial transactions among the inevitable comings and goings that any such group will encounter over years together.

Early on, we abandoned our previous intention to constitute ourselves as a land trust, and instead, at the suggestion of a very inventive lawyer and accountant who works with food cooperatives throughout our region, began to explore the applicability of Vermont's "Cooperative Marketing Act." As the co-op's official articles of incorporation declare, our aim is to "conserve and responsibly manage the land . . . according to use values rather than market values and in a manner which maintains and improves the quality of its air and water resources, the productivity of its soil and the integration of its landscape." Moreover, our goal as a community is also to "nurture and sustain the human resources of the Cooperative through development of a . . . community among its members which recognizes both the autonomy of members and . . . responsibilities to the larger local and regional communities."

Our cooperative lawyer helped us create a social, financial, legal, and ecological structure, a consensus-based member council, which is composed of all of us, yet which is a structure that also stands alone. It is a vessel designed to be strong enough to withstand the departure of founding members, who would be compensated for their equity and receive a fair price for their home upon leaving the co-op.

We named our undertaking the Blue Moon Cooperative Community because early on, success seemed so improbable. We figured that "once in a blue moon" a gambit like this comes to fruition. And here's how the model has worked in practice over the past thirteen-plus years . . .

In 1986 we successfully negotiated a purchase agreement with the family that was selling a piece of essentially abandoned farm land. Because the existing access road was in terrible condition and because there were no power lines, the cost averaged $400–500 per acre, substantially less than the going rate in local towns. We paid $135,000 for the 280 acres we purchased, and immediately sold 120 acres to a relative of one of the co-op members for $50,000, with rights of first refusal for repurchasing that piece later (which we have chosen not to exercise). This meant that we needed $85,000 for our 160 acres.

Roof framing at Jim Schley and Rebecca Bailey's house in Vermont.

The basic fee for membership in the co-op was a one-time payment of $1,000, and we did not want to obligate members to pay a one-tenth share of the land purchase price. Instead, we raised a down payment of $30,000 by arranging loans at specified interest rates from people in our surrounding community as well as two loans from co-op members, likewise at specified interest rates—transactions that we treated as "outside" loans in order to avoid the implication that some of us owned a bigger share of the land. In other words, the co-op borrowed money from some of the members as though they were separate people, repaying them with monthly checks that cross paths with their own monthly payments into the co-op. Therefore each member's equity rises at the same rate, although certain people in truth invested more cash into the original purchase. Our cooperative lawyer's device of financial fiction has worked very well. At no point has any member expressed the feeling that, as co-owners, some of us are more equal than others.

Next we arranged a ten-year loan for the balance of our purchase price with the entirely conventional bank mentioned above, which treated our account as a "corporate" loan, made to the cooperative itself. While we all needed to file financial disclosure statements to satisfy the bank's confidence in this loan, and while legally we were all responsible for the loan, none of us as an individual contracted with the bank for the purchase of this land. Likewise with our purchase agreement, our liability insurance, our tax bill to the town for the non-residential property, and so on: each of these arrangements has been made collectively, with the co-op listed as the contractual party.

We pay an annually adjusted fee for membership, presently $160 per month. The membership fee combines funds for operating expenses (payment on loans, land taxes, driveway and road maintenance, repair of community vehicles, costs of managing our wooded lands, and administrative expenses) and funds that accumulate as an equity account for each member. This latter portion of our monthly fees is refundable in the event that a member decides to leave the group. If in a given year we collect more money for operating expenses than we actually require, the extra is refunded, as in other kinds of co-ops.

As for the five houses in which members are now living on the land, each of these ended up being financed by cash, from savings, or from personal (non-institutional) loans. Because our home sites have never

Cousins eating lunch: Steven Schley Jozef and Lillian Bailey Schley.

been severed or subdivided from the larger parcel of land, and because we lack the obligatory infrastructure such as electric power, none of us was eligible for a conventional bank mortgage for home construction.

Building costs were kept down by several strategies. Most of the labor was done by the homeowners themselves, with hired friends and volunteer work parties, while living off-site in affordable rentals. Each of the houses is modestly sized and straightforward in style and form. Each house has a solar electric array; one also has a solar hot-water system, and another will soon have a wind turbine. For wintertime heat we use woodstoves, since we have plentiful supplies of firewood close at hand; all of the houses were carefully sited for solar exposure and well-insulated to minimize the need for fossil-fuel heating. While our state taxes are paid collectively by the co-op, the local town assesses property taxes upon each household separately, which accommodates differing levels of size and finish.

When in 1996 we paid off the ten-year loan for purchase of the land, we built a stage in our pasture and invited more than a hundred relatives, neighbors, and friends to celebrate our break with the bank.

We are presently making steady progress on two smaller loans from individuals and two loans from the Cooperative Fund of New England, a lender that makes loans specifically to promote cooperative community projects (loans for which we were eligible only by virtue of being organized as a co-op). While four of the early members have departed—and been repaid for their equity—most of the original group are still living at the community. Doubtless there will be changes, foreseen and unforeseen, in the coming years, but we continue to be a good-natured and fun-loving neighborhood, very absorbed in the seasonal cycles on our gorgeous land, and in the growing-up of our children, who are the strongest daily reminders of the ties between these homes. Together we tap maple trees, pick and press apples, cut and transport firewood, gather for a meal at least once a month, and play music. These days we are fantasizing about several community building projects, including a sauna, a guest house, an outdoor bread oven, a workshop, and a garage for working on any number of old trucks.

While we were extraordinarily lucky to have found a willing and able collection of adults as large as this for a co-op land purchase, it seems that many would-be homesteaders could make their lives easier and their settlement process smoother by sharing the challenges with at least one other household—dividing the chores of dealing with realtors, lenders, town officials, and contractors among more people; sharing equipment and information, as well as driveways; and ending up less isolated and also less distributed over the landscape, reducing the psychological as well as the ecological stresses.

Rob Roy's Thoughts

Jim's story clearly shows the advantages of cooperative land purchase among like-minded people, as well as the benefits of mutual aid in the actual construction process. In the early years on The Hill, owner-builders derived many of the same benefits: lower per-acre land cost, and the sharing of skills, labor, and tools. Psychologically, there is the advantage of having a built-in support group, a benefit beyond price. Speaking as an outsider, it strikes me that one of the prime factors that makes Blue Moon so successful is the careful attention paid at the beginning to creating a clear, unambiguous agreement, every bit as important among friends (maybe more so) as among strangers.

Two homes at Blue Moon Cooperative share a driveway and telephone line, and initially shared a well. The Bailey/Schley house is on the right.

Strategies and Circumstances

1. Gained economic benefits from cooperative land purchase.
2. Community support for building our individual house.
3. Sharing of tools, skills, and knowledge.
4. Lived cooperatively with "housemates" to save on housing costs during construction.
5. Used lumber sawed on-site from our own logs.
6. Used plenty of recycled and bargain-priced materials.
7. Kept off the electricity grid.
8. Compact design, easier and cheaper to build and maintain.
9. Wood heat with propane back-up. Plenty of firewood all around.
10. Did most of the work ourselves, except site work, foundation, chimney, and plumbing.
11. Assisted the professionals, helping to keep the costs down while learning valuable skills.
12. Loads of help from family and friends.

OVERLEAF: *The chart on the following two pages summarizes the strategies used by the mortgage-free people featured in this chapter.*

Comparative Strategies Chart

Issue	Light	Holdt/Mapelli	Osby
The Land. **How did you obtain the land for the home? Cost?**	Belongs to parents. Worth $10,000.	Two acres of land was a gift from Sara's mother in 1993. Valued at $47,000.	Purchased land. Owner-financed. Located in newspaper want ad. 1.86 acres at $5,000 per acre.
The Grubstake How much did you have? Where did it come from?	Saved up $11,000 in 18 months. Laid by $4,500 in materials & tools. Borrowed $8,000 from Judith's parents to finish.	$15,000 to begin with from savings. Later, we borrowed $3,000 from Sara's mom to finish project. Worked it off.	About $5,000 in savings. We made lifestyle choices to save money.
The Temporary Shelter. Where did you live while building?	Lived with parents next door during construction.	On site in army tent for 8 months. Then 4 more months in an unused cabin.	Rented home with option to buy. Only $4/10$ of a mile from site. Now we rent it out, balancing payme
Low-Cost Home What strategies kept costs down?	Compact shape. Rubble trench foundation. Straw bale building. Salvaged materials. Did work ourselves with help from friends. Plastering party.	Cordwood masonry. Recycled lumber and other materials Milled wood from property. Bartered labor & materials. Got help from family and friends. Framing party.	Used locally milled framing timbers. Shopped for bargains Compact shape. Did most everything myself.
Code Issues. Any problems?	Once we got our plans stamped by a licensed engineer, we had no problem with getting a permit.	No problems. We were able to work with the building department.	I was able to build on an owner-builder permit.
Cost of home	$24,000 so far. Will spend $6,000 more to finish.	$20,000	$25,000
Size of home	1,836 SF gross; 1,360 SF usable	1,200 SF	1,500 SF
Year moved in	1997	1995	1990
Location	New York State	Washington State	North Carolina
Time of construction	6½ months	18 months	8 years

Comparative Strategies Chart

Butz	*Watt*	*Bailey/Schley*
Bought land "on contract" from owner. 15 acres, about $11,500.	Bought land on contract. $1,500 down; rest over 5 years. 16 acres cost $18,000.	Bought 160 acres with 5 other households. Each adult paid $1,000 co-op membership fee plus monthly payments for approximately 15 years.
$200! Borrowed the rest on a signature loan.	$3,750 savings to start. Later, we borrowed $15,000 from friends to finish the project.	$10,000 in savings; stockpile of salvaged materials and lumber cut & milled on-site; $10,000 in gifts from family; $7,000 loan from a co-op lender; cash from part-time jobs.
Rented a house in town 8 miles away. Had shelter on-site (tent, shed) to stay in on weekends.	Lived in a tent trailer while we built basement, another TS for 9 years!	Shared group house in nearby town, reasonable rent. Moved into our home w/o electricity or running water for first 5 months.
Post-and-beam is easy and quick. Kept it small, just 440 SF.	Basic box design. Rob's dad drew the plans. Friends helped on heavy labor; we did the rest ourselves.	Used mostly lumber milled on-site, salvaged or bargain materials wherever possible. Did all own work except site, foundation, chimney, and plumbing (we assisted professionals). Compact, off-the-grid design, no frills. Lots of volunteer help.
Standard building, so no problem with codes.	Standard construction, so no problems.	Local codes for owner-builders are laissez-faire, except state septic regs. No problem with the proper septic design and permit.
$5,000	About $26,250	$38,000
440 SF	1,000 SF on each of two finished levels	1,700 SF
1997	1980	1992
Wisconsin	British Columbia	Vermont
5 months	9 years	21 months for basic comforts, ongoing finish work

Onword

Chapter 7 shows that it is possible for all sorts of people living all over North America to own their own homes, mortgage-free. Folks from all walks of life are represented: artists, teachers, even my erstwhile editor at Chelsea Green. Lots of hard work and a willingness to put up with a certain degree of hardship are common to the six case studies related. Grubstakes varied from $200 up to $15,000. Some built while keeping their job(s) and others left their outside employment during the construction process. Two of our couples benefited from not having to buy the land, and this is not uncommon. Others benefited from some type of collective land purchase. Some toughed it out on the land while others rented or lived with relatives nearby. Almost all of the couples made good use of recycled materials and employed building methods and strategies that kept costs down.

Nowhere in this book do I mean to imply that there are any "free lunches" with regard to shelter cost. The people in these studies have not been unusually lucky; they have made their own luck and worked hard to make the best use of it.

Individually and collectively, the case studies of chapter 6 and 7 exemplify the concepts and principles offered in the first five chapters. My constant intent has been to provide you with principles for creating your own home, Mortgage-Free! I think of these principles as tools. We might provide two individuals with equal piles of building materials and tools. One may build a snug home; the other may see his lumber rot and his tools rust. Who can say? Everybody's different.

In summary, there are basic principles—or tools—that I would like you to take away when you have finished reading this book.

First, you can and should be mortgage-free. Your inalienable rights to "life, liberty, and the pursuit of happiness" are not easy to actualize while you're under the yoke of the death pledge.

Second, you can't build without the land. Chapter 2 outlines how to find and buy land. Some of the strategies, while unorthodox, might just work for you, as they did for Jaki and me, and for the heroes of chapter 7.

Third, you can't build without resources and some of these resources will, of necessity, be money. In chapter 3, I call these resources a grubstake. For many Americans, saving money is a task of Herculean proportion. After all, it's more fun to spend than to save, right? It doesn't have to be. Happiness is not really a function of material consumption, according to the great thinkers. Some of the most miserable people I know have been fat cats, and some of the happiest have been bare-footed Mayan children in the forests of Belize.

Fourth, the Temporary Shelter strategy detailed in chapter 4 is probably one of the most useful concepts employed by mortgage-free people in rural areas. Immediately, they stop paying shelter costs, they gain valuable building experience, they learn about the land, and they gain a useful building for the future, perhaps even a wing of their mortgage-free home.

Fifth, keep building costs down. This can be accomplished by building small and simply, using indigenous and recycled materials, and adapting various other planning and building strategies explained in chapter 5, too numerous to detail here.

When I set out to do something, I like to see how others have done it before me. I may not agree with everything they did, but I learn something in any case. My good friend and cordwood compatriot Jack Henstridge tells me, "None of us are totally useless, Rob. We can always serve as horrible examples!" I take a little pride that in all of my books, including this one, I have tried to share my errors with my readers, as well as my successes. People have told me that they've really appreciated that, with comments like, "You know, I was going to do that same (stupid) thing, but when I read of your experience, it saved me the trouble." Glad to help. In chapters 6 and 7, the Mortgage-Free Gang and I share mostly sound and successful strategies, but keep a watchful eye out for the clangers, too.

The above commentary recaps the book, thus far, but the book does not end here. The five appendices that follow are valuable resources to help you along the mortgage-free road. They are put in the back of the book not because they are less important, but because the information in them is more readily accessible in appendix form. Appendix 1 is a strategy chart to help you plan a course of action based upon your financial circumstances. I believe that appendix 2, at press time, is the most up-to-date list of building schools in print. These schools are an invaluable resource, particularly if you are considering an alternative building technique. Appendix 3 is an annotated list of books, videos, and magazines that expand upon the various topics discussed in the main body of the book. Appendix 4 explains some of the technical terms of land purchase. This is important information when you get to the point of needing it, but dry as a bone, which is why I tucked it away in the back of the book.

Appendix 5 is called "Amortization Tables." You might find the commentary before the tables to be interesting, and the tables themselves could be useful if you need to formulate a financial plan for land purchase.

Mortgage-Free! is not a magic wand. Despite all of the wonderful and scintillating wisdom in these pages, it is unlikely that you will achieve all that you want from your shelter as fast as you would like to have it. Patience may be the single most important requirement to achieve economic freedom and true security; not the thirty-year "patience" imposed upon us by lending institutions to achieve a false security, but the simple, daily kind of patience coupled with a strong desire to achieve one's goals. Not all who attempt to win this freedom by building their own homes will succeed. I hope that this book has helped you to decide whether you are the kind of person who will start with the odds in your favor. If your heart's not really in it, the odds are overwhelmingly against you. Do not begin the project. I will not want to receive your correspondence. But if you feel that you can in no way afford to delegate the responsibility of your own shelter to others, then examine your assets, formulate a plan of strategies, and stay with the plan, adjusting it as necessary to changing circumstances. The exact path is not so important, but know the general direction of your goal. If the train you are presently riding is going the wrong way, get off at the next station.

Lending institutions have all sorts of schemes to encourage homebuyers to go into even greater debt: lower down payments (higher mortgage!) and easing qualifications for mortgagees, just to name two. As I put this book to bed, in December of 1997, mortgage rates are relatively low, and it may be tempting to sign the death pledge. Do not be persuaded. Mortgages are brought to you by the makers of the plastic credit card, that other great enslavement device of the money masters. Mortgages and credit cards are at least as serious a problem as drugs in this country, and probably more addicting. We *sign up* for our addiction.

Henry Thoreau gave us a better idea 150 years ago. In the final chapter of *Walden,* he says:

> I have learned this, at least, by my experiment: that if one advances confidently in the direction of his dreams, and endeavors to live the life which he has imagined, he will meet with a success unexpected in common hours . . . If you have built castles in the air, your work need not be lost; that is where they should be. Now put the foundations under them.

Good night, Henry. And good night, dear reader. May your sun rise clear.

APPENDIX 1

Mortgage Freedom Strategy Chart

HOW TO USE THIS CHART

Intersect your income with your total savings (cash, bank accounts, and readily convertible assets) to determine the key number for the appropriate Strategies List. Example: If your income is $24,000 a year and you have already saved $8,000, read Strategy List 11. Also, have a peek at the lists directly adjacent to the one you're supposed to be looking at. This somewhat serendipitous chart is loosely based on incomes and property values in northern New York in 1997. Other parts of the country may be more or less expensive to live or build in (probably more.)

As time goes on and inflation takes its toll, salaries and savings of equivalent empiric value to the 1997 figures should be used. This chart and the accompanying strategies should be considered only as a rough guide. Your final plan of action must be based on a realistic appraisal of your own abilities, self-confidence, and personal circumstances.

INCOME → SAVINGS ↓	LESS THAN $2,000	$2,001– $15,000	$15,000– $35,000	OVER $35,000
LESS THAN $100	1	2	3	4
$100– $5,000	5	6	7	8
$5,000– $20,000	9	10	11	12
OVER $20,000	13	14	15	16

1

A. Carry on your merry way, as long as you do not expect others to support you. Only then are you truly free.
B. Join a religious commune or monastery.
C. Marry a rich spouse.
D. Get a job and move to List 2, 3, or 4, depending on your new income.
E. Find someone building a house. Exchange labor for experience, and room and board. Keep eyes and ears open to opportunities.
F. Build an ultra-low-cost house on squatted land. This is what birds and beavers do, as did Henry David Thoreau, so you're in good company. Read the first chapter of *Walden*.

Comment: Tomorrow is the first day of the rest of your life.

2

A. Try to find a job that pays more, or take an additional part-time job.
B. Do a "material fast" (if you aren't doing so already just to survive).
C. Read Strategies List 3.

3

A. Begin to assemble your grubstake.
B. Look for land to get an idea of what you want and what price you can expect to pay for it.
C. When possible, put a down payment on land. Know where future payments are coming from.
D. Lack of savings might be due to an undeveloped sense of economy, a common American deficiency. Read chapter 2 again and the books on economy listed in appendix 3.
E. Read, research, try to get some building experience.

4

A. Change economic philosophy. If you are unable to save money on your present income, you:

    a. Are paying too much for rent or mortgage. Change shelter situation.
    b. Have too many kids or one or two spoiled ones. I don't think I can help you.
    c. Have no sense of economy at all. Money runs through your

APPENDIX 1: STRATEGY CHART

fingers like dry sand. Your purchases depreciate rapidly in value, like snowmobiles, big cars, and banana splits.
B. Read chapter 2 again and the books on economy listed in appendix 3.
C. Go on a material fast for six months.
D. Alternative: Make no change at all. Maybe you are already leading the life that suits you best.

5

A. Find a job. Relocate, if necessary.
B. Begin adding to grubstake, using material fast.
C. While waiting for your economic situation to improve, start researching the building option . . . at the library!

6

A. Try to improve income situation, then:
B. Move to Strategies List 7.

7

A. Find land and secure it with a down payment.
B. Research the type of building you have in mind.
C. Look for opportunities to gain building experience.
D. Keep your job.
E. Build the Temporary Shelter and move in to eliminate shelter costs, increase grubstake accumulation and gain building experience.

8

A. Find land within commuting distance to your job and make a down payment. Be alert to owner-financing opportunities.
B. Keep your job, but build the Temporary Shelter in order to accelerate grubstake accumulation.
C. If you've followed (A) and (B), you have good potential for laying up a substantial grubstake in short order, even though you may have land payments to make. Take advantage of bargains on building materials and tools when opportunities arise.

9

A. Find and buy land. If not bought outright, you'll need a job to save for next year's payment. You'd better find a job anyway, as your grubstake won't last long unless you're presently living without shelter cost.

B. If you're adventurous as well as tenacious, make the move to the land. Many of my neighbors on Murtagh Hill started with less.

C. Use the Temporary Shelter strategy, possibly with a view to adding on to it.

D. While living in the TS, gather materials for the house.

E. Unless a regular income situation is entered into soon, you'll need to grow food and cultivate firewood for heat.

F. A part-time job, at least, would make things a lot easier.

10

A. Buy land.

B. Build a Temporary Shelter, perhaps as a core unit for an add-on house.

C. Keep replenishing the grubstake as it is spent for materials and/or land payments.

D. Add value to indigenous materials on the property. Cut logs for rafters, joists, log-ends, or to take to the sawmill for lumber. Gather and sort stones for a masonry stove or thermal mass.

E. Watch for bargains on both used and new materials.

11

A. Find and buy land. If the land is close to your work, build and occupy a Temporary Shelter to accelerate saving your grubstake.

B. Read and research about building. Attend a building school specializing in the desired building method.

C. Keep your job. Build part-time. Re-read the Butz, Osby, and Watt case studies in chapter 7 for inspiration.

D. Consider the add-on house strategy.

Comment: Giving up your job to build full-time is risky with this sort of grubstake. Living expenses can eat up the savings rapidly.

12

A. Buy land, or at least make a down payment.

B. If land is close to work, build a Temporary Shelter to accelerate saving your grubstake.

C. If you've followed (A) and (B), you have good potential for laying up a substantial grubstake in short order, but convert dollar savings to building materials or tools whenever the right opportunities come along.

Comment: I suspect that many of you see yourselves in this list of strategies. The income is a very valuable asset and should not be given up lightly (or at all, if you're one of the minority who are truly happy at your work).

13

A. What are you waiting for? $20,000+ is more than enough. With no job, you can relocate to where land is cheap and building inspectors are far and few between.
B. Buy land, build a Temporary Shelter, build the permanent house. If the land is bought on a land contract or owner-financed mortgage, know where future land payments are coming from.
C. Unless you are opting out altogether—I've no objections—have a clear idea about where your future living is going to come from.

14

A. Move to an area of low land values. You should be able to replace or improve on your present job almost anywhere.
B. Buy land.
C. Caretake a nearby home or cabin (or find another low-cost shelter situation) while you build a Temporary Shelter.
D. Move into the TS.
E. Build your house on a pay-as-you-go basis.

Comment: Low income, large grubstake. Interesting. I'm guessing that you must have scored a windfall while working at a minimum wage job.

15

A. Find and buy land.
B. Read about and research housing options. Attend a building school, if lacking in practical building experience.
C. If unhappy with your job, leave it and build your house, starting with a Temporary Shelter to save on grubstake depletion. The TS can be added to, or a new house built on a pay-as-you-go basis.
D. If relocating, keep alert to employment opportunities right from the start. Twenty, even thirty grand can disappear faster than you think.

16

A. Buy your land.
B. Read and research. Attend a building school if lacking in experience or knowledge.
C. Answer this question honestly: Are you happy at your work? If *yes*, stay with it. Build in your spare time. The Temporary Shelter strategy is optional. Don't use it if you're comfortable where you are, your land is nearby, and you are still able to save a decent amount of money each year. If *no*, make the move or find another job. You only get one life. You are in better economic shape than 90 percent of the owner-builders I've known. Your chances for success are very high, as you have already shown a sense of economy.
D. If you make an outrageous salary as a baseball player, movie star, or congressman—and I presume someone sent you this book as a joke gift—you can hire me to build your house, at a slightly less outrageous salary.

APPENDIX 2

Building Schools in North America

People enter into the building process with various levels of preparation behind them. Jaki and I have visited cordwood homes around the country, some built by people who just "winged" it, with no research outside of reading a magazine article. We've observed a large qualitative difference between those of the wingers and those built by people who study books on cordwood. Another leap in quality is apparent with people who use an instructional video to supplement their reading. Videos demonstrate how to do something in a way that a book can't, and show a finished quality of work. Finally—again, speaking in general terms—the best homes are the ones built by students who learn the techniques firsthand at cordwood masonry housebuilding classes. I have to assume that this generalization holds true for log building, straw bale construction, timber framing, even conventional stick-frame construction. If possible, then, try to attend housebuilding classes in the specific disciplines that you plan to use in your home.

Lists of building schools must be constantly updated, and I'm sure that some of the ones listed here will be impossible to reach by the time this book sees print. (Watch out for telephone area code changes, too, a frequent bugaboo nowadays.) Nevertheless, I believe this is the most comprehensive list available as of late 1997. It is intended as a reference source only; inclusion does not constitute endorsement. Contact the schools of interest to you and ask them to send you their course catalog. These will range from modest workshop brochures to comprehensive catalogs.

As travel is always a concern, information is organized by state, followed by the lone Canadian entry. If you know of a building school not listed, please send information about it to Earthwood, at our address below, or to Sandra Leibowitz, who maintains the *Eco-Building Schools Directory*, which she continually updates. See appendix 3, category 9. Write Sandra at 3220 N Street NW #218, Washington, DC 20007. Canadian sources are particularly sought after. Some of the information below was adapted from Sandra's directory, and is included here with her kind permission.

Fax numbers have the same area code and exchange as phone numbers, unless noted.

Arizona

Arcosanti, HC 74, Box 4136, Mayer, AZ 86333. Tel: 520-632-7135. Fax: 6229. Email: arcosanti@aol.com. Website: http://www.arcosanti.org/. Quarterly newsletter: *Arcommunique*.

Out On Bale, 1037 E. Linden Street, Tucson, AZ 85719. Tel: 520-624-1673. A clearing house for straw bale construction information, Out On Bale offers a periodic series of hands-on workshops as well as a research publication on straw bale building techniques. Their excellent quarterly journal is called *The Last Straw*.

California

Building Education Center, 812 Page Street, Berkeley, CA 94710. Tel: 510-525-7610. Fax: 0855. The Center's focus is on conventional construction, with classes ranging from one-day workshops to one and two-week "intensives" on Home Design, Owner Contracting, Building, and Remodeling. Courses are geared to California codes and conditions; for example: "Earthquake Retrofitting." A quarterly eight-page tabloid keeps you posted.

Cal-Earth Institute, 10177 Baldy Lane, Hesperia, CA 92345. Tel: 760-244-0614. Fax: 2201. Email: calearth@aol.com. Website: http://www.calearth.org. Cal-Earth's approach includes: "creating built environments in tune with nature through the four universal elements: Earth, Water, Fire and Air."

Real Goods Institute for Solar Living, 555 Leslie Street, Ukiah, CA 95482. Tel: 707-468-9292. Fax: 9394. Email: isl@realgoods.com. Website: http://www.realgoods.com. 1997 workshops included: Home Retrofitting for Energy Efficiency, Solar Electric, Residential Small Hydro Systems, Sustainable Building and Eco Design, Straw Bale Construction, Rammed Earth Construction, and others.

REW (Rammed Earth Works) Associates, 1350 Elm Street, Napa, CA 95257. Tel: 707-224-2532. Fax: 258-1878. Email: ewinst@aol.com. On-demand workshops in rammed earth construction.

Sacramento Owner Builder Center, 4777 Sunrise, Fair Oaks, CA 95628. Tel: 916-961-2453. Email: obc@psyber.com. Offers house design and housebuilding courses which are designed for novices, but are sophisticated enough for the semi-professional.

Colorado

SOLAR ENERGY INTERNATIONAL, Box 715, Carbondale, CO 81623. Tel: 970-963-8855. Fax: 8866. Email: sei@solarenergy.org. Website: http://solstice.crest.org/renewables/sei. SEI's Renewable Energy Education Program teaches the practical use of solar, wind, and water power. Workshops impart the knowledge and skills to design, install, and maintain renewable energy systems and to build state-of-the-art solar homes that are efficient, practical and earth-friendly.

RED ROCKS COMMUNITY COLLEGE, 13300 West Sixth Avenue, Lakewood, CO 80401-5398. Tel: 303-988-6160. Red Rocks is a regular community college within the Colorado State system. John R. Sperling is the Chairman of the Construction Trades Faculty. He can be reached at the shop (303-914-6209) or office (303-914-6362). Email: rr_John@rrcc.cccoes.edu. Website: http://www.rrcc.cccoes.edu. The trades faculty offers a variety of credit courses including carpentry, electrical, plumbing, solar construction technology, and many others.

Georgia

SOUTHFACE ENERGY INSTITUTE'S HOMEBUILDING SCHOOL, 241 Pine Street, Atlanta, GA 30308. Tel: 404-872-3549. Fax: 5009. Email: HBS@southface. org. Website: http://www.southface.org. Conducts both comprehensive nine-day homebuilding courses and more condensed weekend courses. Also conducts courses in passive solar design, and photovoltaic design and installation. Southface publishes a quarterly journal of building, *The Southface Journal of Energy and Building Technology*.

Maine

FOX MAPLE SCHOOL OF TRADITIONAL BUILDING, P.O. Box 249, Corn Hill Road, Brownfield, ME 04010. Tel: 207-935-3720. Fax: 4575. Email: foxmaple@nxi.com. Conducts workshops in timber frame construction, and infilling techniques such as wattle and daub, light straw and clay, and woodchips and clay. There are "traveling" timber frame workshops at various sites around the country. Fox Maple publishes *Joiners' Quarterly: The Journal of Timber Framing and Traditional Joinery*.

SHELTER INSTITUTE, 38 Center Street, Bath, ME 04530. Tel: 207-442-7938. Fax: 7935. Email: shelterint@aol.com. Website: http://www: mainecoast.com/shelterinstitute. Newsletter: *Shelter Notes*. Established in 1975, the Shelter Institute offers complete design and house-building classes, as well as timber-frame construction. Their book list has approximately 250 titles. Shelter Institute also provides timber-frame kits.

Massachusetts

HEARTWOOD OWNER-BUILDER SCHOOL, Johnson Hill Road, Washington, MA 01235. Tel: 413-623-6677. Fax: 0277. Offers a variety of workshops and comphehensive courses, including timber framing, contracting, basic and finish carpentry, cabinetmaking, and energy-efficient house-building.

Minnesota

COMMUNITY ECO-DESIGN NETWORK, P.O. Box 6241, Minneapolis, MN 55406. Voicemail: 612-306-2326. Email: erichart@mtn.org. Website: http://www.umn.edu/nlhome/m037/kurtdand/cen. Quarterly newsletter: *Eco-Design Times*. Workshops in straw-bale construction, and solar greenhouse design and construction.

GREAT LAKES SCHOOL OF LOG BUILDING, Snowshoe Trail, Sand Lake, Isabella, MN 55607. Tel: 218-365-2126 or 612-822-5955. Email: logcabin@ northernnet.com. Website: http://www.northernnet.com/logcabin. Established in 1975, Great Lakes School offers eleven-day courses in traditional log building, and, occasionally, five-day courses in foundation stonework.

NATURAL SPACES DOMES, 37955 Bridge Road, North Branch, MN 55056. Tel: 800-733-7107 or 612-674-4292. Fax: 612-674-5005. Email: info@ naturalspacesdomes.com. Website: www.naturalspacesdomes.com. Conducts owner-builder workshops to teach people how to erect their—Natural Space's—own dome frameworks, so the firm is really more of a manufacturer than a building school, but definitely worth checking out if you're into domes.

New Mexico

NATURAL HOUSE BUILDING CENTER, 2300 W. Alameda, #A5, Santa Fe, NM 87501. The Center conducts approximately ten one-week workshops per year in timber framing, straw-clay construction, earth plastering, and earth floors. As we go to press, the Center is looking for land in the Southwest upon which to relocate, so the best way to contact them is by email or through their website. Email: laporte@econest.com. Website: http://www.econest.com.

SOUTHWEST SOLARADOBE SCHOOL, P.O. Box 153, Bosque, NM 87006. Tel: 505-861-1255. Fax: 1304. Teaches a regular series of earth-building classes, focusing on adobe and rammed-earth techniques at various locations across the Southwest, and even in Costa Rica. Publishes *Adobe Builder* magazine.

New York

EARTHWOOD BUILDING SCHOOL, 366 Murtagh Hill Road, West Chazy, NY 12992. Tel: 518-493-7744. Website: http://www.interlog.com/~ewood. Earthwood conducts two- to five-day hands-on classes in cordwood masonry construction and workshops in earth-sheltered housing at our 6-acre rural campus. Regional workshops are conducted throughout North America.

Oregon

COB COTTAGE COMPANY, P.O. Box 123, Cottage Grove, OR 97424. Tel: 541-942-2005 weekdays. Fax and evenings: 3021. Semi-annual newsletter: *The Cob Web*. Teaches one- and two-week courses in natural building with unprocessed materials, such as cob and others. Conducts workshops all over the world.

GROUNDWORKS, P.O. Box 381, Murphy, OR 97533. Tel: 541-471-3470. Email: sparking@teleport.com. Website: http://www.teleport.com/~sparking/cob/door.html. "Groundworks is dedicated to teaching people, especially women, to sculpt their own low-cost, low-tech earth homes." Also offers co-ed workshops.

OUR BACKYARD FARM EDUCATIONAL RESOURCE CENTER, 1430 Willamette #267, Eugene, OR 97401. Tel: 541-933-2166. Email: jlauryan@efn.org. "Dedicated to sharing the skills of omni-considerate living, nourishing mind, body and spirit; building community through sustainability, simple living, and self-reliancy skills, beginning with the basics of housing, food and health." Accents cob-earth building and straw bale construction.

Pennsylvania

EAST COAST ALTERNATIVE BUILDING CENTER, 2801-A Taxville Road, York, PA 17404. Tel: 717-792-0551. Email: ecabc@juno.com; or larryjoesanders @juno.com. Conducts hands-on workshops in straw bale, cob, earth and plaster, and related fields. ABC expects to move to a new location soon, so their address and phone number may change. If unsuccessful by phone or mail, use the email addresses or try directory assistance for Larry Sanders in York, PA, and environs.

Tennessee

ECO-VILLAGE TRAINING CENTER, The Farm, P.O. Box 90, Summertown, TN 38383. Tel: 615-964-4324. Fax: 4474. Email: ecovillage@thefarm.org. Conducts workshops in cob and straw bale construction, and permaculture. Learn about intentional communities at the same time.

Texas

OWNER-BUILDER CENTER @ HOUSTON COMMUNITY COLLEGE, 4141 Costa Rica, Houston, TX 77092. Tel: 713-956-1178. Fax: 7413. Newsletter: *Home Improvement Journal.* "The Owner-Builder Center promotes energy-efficiency in residential construction in a hot, humid climate. We also teach quality construction practices applicable to Houston's climate, soil conditions, and vernacular materials."

Vermont

EARTH SWEET HOME INSTITUTE, RR 2, Box 955, Putney, VT 05346. Tel: 802-254-1135. Email: earthswt@sover.net. Website: http://www.enviro link.org/orgs/earthsweet. Courses in straw bale construction and photovoltaic electricity.

YESTERMORROW DESIGN/BUILD SCHOOL, RR 1, Box 97-5, Warren, VT 05674. Tel: 802-496-5545. Fax: 5540. Email: ymschool@aol.com. Website: http://www.yestermorrow.org. Yearly journal: *Trilithon.* Yestermorrow teaches a variety of courses and workshops for both laypersons and professionals, including one- and two-week design/build courses, and two-day workshops in such fields as straw bale construction, ecological house design, stone masonry, and solar design.

Washington

GREENFIRE INSTITUTE, PO Box 1040, Winthrop,WA 98862. Tel: 506-996-3593. Email: greenfire@ipc.org. GreenFire conducts workshops in straw bale construction and other sustainable building techniques in the Pacific Northwest.

Wisconsin

MIDWEST RENEWABLE ENERGY ASSOCIATION EDUCATIONAL INSTITUTE, Box 249, Amherst, WI 54406. Tel: 715-824-5166. Fax: 5399. The Institute conducts a variety of hands-on workshops in alternative energy and energy-efficient construction. Their Midwest Renewable Energy Fair, held each year on the summer solstice weekend in June, is not to be missed if you're interested in sustainable energy and building options.

Canada

PAT WOLFE LOG BUILDING SCHOOL, RR 3, Ashton, Ontario K0A 1B0 Tel: 613-253-0631. With over 20 years of log-building experence, Pat Wolfe offers hands-on courses and sells videos on log home construction.

≋

Annotated Bibliography

HOW TO USE THIS BIBLIOGRAPHY

Authors and publishers love to have you run out and buy their books, but the conserver economist will tell you to start at the library, borrowing a few each week. Many of the books listed here are out of print anyway, and the library—or a good used book store—will be the only place to find them. Remember that many libraries will be able to get books for you on inter-library loan. The added benefit of going to the library is that you'll find a myriad of other interesting books on the same shelves where you find the ones listed below. If your library uses the Dewey Decimal system, go to sections 643 (home renovation), the 690s (buildings), and the 720s (architecture) for a great start on your research. After reading the books, buy only those that you know you'll be referring to again and again. If you find yourself spending much over $100 for building books, you are probably not making the best use of the library or your money. OOPS at the end of an entry means, "Out of print. Sorry." Try a library or used book store.

The Categories

The sources are arranged into eleven categories, as follows.

1. Economic philosophy
2. Inspiration
3. Land
4. Building, overview
5. Self-contracting
6. Alternative and sustainable building
7. Renovation
8. Renewable energy
9. Miscellaneous
10. Magazines and journals
11. Building book suppliers

Some books, like John Connell's *Homing Instinct*, for example, would fit quite happily into two or more categories, so I have placed it where I believe it is most appropriate.

1. ECONOMIC PHILOSOPHY

The first two books in this list, by the immortals Thoreau and Hesse, have done more to instill in me a sense of empiric economics than all the rest of my reading combined.

Walden, Henry David Thoreau (1990, Running Press). The first chapter, "Economy," is all that needs to be read as far as low-cost living and building is concerned. It runs about 70 pages. Don't be surprised if you find yourself reading with equal pleasure the remaining 180-odd pages, mostly naturalistic observations, generously marinated in the unique Thoreauvian wit and philosophy. ISBN: 0-89471-879-7.

Siddhartha, Hermann Hesse (1982, Bantam). *Siddhartha*, a book of economics? Absurd. Yet it worked as such, and much more, too, during my grubstaking days. Rereading it after a lapse of many years, I find that it still weaves its magic. *Siddhartha* is a story of essential living, which is another way of saying empiric economics.

Your Money or Your Life, Joe Dominguez and Vicki Robin (1992, Penguin). This book has sold over 500,000 copies, and with good reason. If you follow the nine-step program described within its pages, it is a virtual certainty that your economic situation will improve. If you are in debt, you'll get out of debt. If you want to save money for your grubstake, or any other purpose, you will do so if you follow the steps. The book's purpose is to show you how to achieve "Financial Independence," defined as the point where your annual investment income equals or exceeds your annual expenditure. At this point, you are free from unwanted work. A mortgage-free home fits in perfectly with the plan. Some people who have started in debt have achieved FI in just a few years. Magic? No. Just good common sense by leaders in the field of low-impact living. Methodically written, but in an easy style. 350 valuable pages. Highly recommended. ISBN: 0-670-84331-8.

How to Survive Without a Salary: Learning How to Live the Conserver Lifestyle, Charles Long (1996, Warwick). Along with *Your Money or Your Life*, this is one of the two best guides for learning the economic techniques that facilitate the rapid procurement of the grubstake. Once you're free of mortgaged servitude, you may want to use Long's tested fiscal philosophies to free yourself from wage enslavement. For excerpts, see the sidebar in chapter 2. ISBN: 1-895629-68-3.

Possum Living, Dolly Freed (1978, Universe Books). One of the first of the "modern" books on the conserver lifestyle. I hope you can find it in a library. The subtitle is almost a review: "How to Live Well Without a Job and with Almost No Money." This book will help you save the grubstake. OOPS.

The Simple Living Guide, Janet Luhrs (1997, Broadway Books). Wonderful compendium of stories and resources, written by the publisher of *Simple Living Journal,* 2319 North 45th Street, Box 149, Seattle, WA 98103.

The Tightwad Gazette Book: Promoting Thrift as a Viable Alternative Lifestyle, Amy Dacyczyn (1993, Villard-Random House). This is a compendium of valuable money-saving tips from America's best-known tightwad. For years, Amy edited *The Tightwad Gazette,* a monthly newsletter on frugal living. This book is a collection of their simple but effective strategies. And, lest words like "frugal" and "tightwad" don't sound like your cup of tea, rest assured that the Dacyczyns and their growing family live a very high-quality life in their large New England farmhouse. ISBN: 0-679-74403-7. The sequel, more money-saving tips, is *The Tightwad Gazette II,* same author and publisher. ISBN: 0-679-75078-9.

2. INSPIRATION

The Prodigious Builders, Bernard Rudofsky (1977, Irvington). Vernacular architecture, integrating site with structure, and making use of indigenous materials. Good recipe. ISBN: 0-8290-0986-8.

Handmade Houses: A Guide to the Woodbutcher's Art, Arthur Boericke and Barry Shapiro (1973, A & W Publishers). ISBN: 0-89104-001-3.

The Craftsman Builder, Arthur Boericke and Barry Shapiro (1977, Simon & Schuster). ISBN: 0-671-25192-9.

Handmade Homes: The Natural Way to Build Houses, Arthur Boericke and Barry Shapiro (1981, Delacorte Press). ISBN: 0-440-03340-3.

These three books by Boericke and Shapiro have a common character and design. Each is composed of approximately 100 quality color plates showing details of houses molded by "vernacular architects" (a fancy name for people who roll up their sleeves and build themselves a home, usually with recycled or indigenous materials and often without plans any more complicated than what can be drawn on a hunk of birch bark). Each plate illustrates that shelter can be as free—in every sense—as the builder wants it to be. These books unlocked my imagination, and they could do the same for you. All are OOPS, unfortunately.

Shelter, edited by Lloyd Kahn (1973, Shelter Publications, P.O. Box 279, Bolinas, CA). Jaki and I found this book freed our preconceived notions about housing back in 1974. It is now back in print after several years out-of-print. The examples of vernacular architecture from all over the world make these basic points time and again: The appropriate building material is all around you; the appropriate house style is dictated by the climate and landform. Good basic stick-framing information for small temporary shelters will be found here, but also hard-to-find info on sod and adobe construction, domes, bamboo, thatch, and other vernacular building methods. ISBN: 0-679-76948-X.

Getting a Roof Over Your Head: Affordable Housing Alternatives (1983, Garden Way/Storey). This compilation of seventeen detailed case studies shows that there are all kinds of ways to approach the problem of affordable housing. I'll bet that most of the examples detailed are mortgage-free, too. One family moved a house at great savings. Another "raised a work crew" of eight children, all of whom helped in one way or another to build their labor-intensive stone house. Another article deals with renovating railroad stations, schoolhouses, even churches as homes. There are a couple of beautiful houses made from silos. Lots of good ideas here. I hope you can find a copy. ISBN: 0-88266-317-8. OOPS.

3. LAND

Finding and Buying Your Place in the Country, 4th edition, Les and Carol Scher (1996, Dearborn Financial Publishing, Inc., Chicago). This is the only book you need on buying land. It covers everything: looking for land, evaluating the land, financing, legal, the works. Les Scher is an attorney who specializes in country property. At the beginning of chapter 34 ("Do You Need a Lawyer?") he says, "If you follow the course I outline in this book, you should have no problems handling your land deal with minimal assistance from an attorney." He also tells you when a lawyer should be retained, and what the lawyer can do for you. All in all, this large 400+ page book is one you may want to purchase if you don't already have your land, as you will want to refer to it frequently. And it will be handy again if you ever want to sell your property. ISBN: 0-7931-1785-2.

How to Buy Land Cheap, 5th edition, Edward Preston (1996, Loompanics Unlimited). Are there still "deals" out there on land? Yes, but you have to work at it. Preston describes all kinds of out-of-the-ordinary means of buying land: tax sales, foreclosure sales, auctions, Bureau of Land Management (BLM) properties, Federal Deposit Insurance Corporation (FDIC) properties, federal and state lands, distressed sales, etc. Never have the words *caveat emptor* ("let the buyer beware") had so much currency as when bottom fishing for land. ISBN: 1-55950-145-6.

How to Buy Land, L. John Wachtel (1982, Sterling). Worth looking for in the library for the author's thorough approach to land evaluation. See sidebar in chapter 3. ISBN: 0-8069-7602-0. OOPS.

Grafting Fruit Trees, Country Wisdom Bulletin #A35 (Storey). A piece of land with "scrub" apples may be more valuable than you (or the seller) might think. Grafting is something like magic, except that it's real. This 32-page booklet tells you how. Other titles in the Country Wisdom series include all sorts of specialized gardening booklets: *Eggs and Chickens*, *Raising Ducks and Geese*, *Build a Smokehouse*, *Buying an Old House*, and *Buying Country Land*, over 100 titles in all. Storey also publishes lots of good books on gardening, cooking, beer and wine making, and building. See category 11.

4. BUILDING, OVERVIEW

Before You Build: A Preconstruction Guide, Robert Roskind (1997, Ten Speed). At last, Roskind's classic checklist is back in print, with everything you need to know before building your house: buying the land; choosing the site; access; permits; codes and inspections; financing; estimating; "inner resources"; and a lot more. Also available from the Building Education Center (see appendix 2). ISBN: 0-8069-7602-0.

The Best Home For Less, Steve Carlson (1992, Avon). As a local tax assessment officer, the author learned first-hand the conditions and considerations that kept valuations down. With his wife, he began planning a new home. "It was then that we made the serendipitous discovery that has evolved into the premise of this book. The steps we took to hold down taxes also helped us to hold down the costs of construction (and therefore the mortgage), energy costs, repairs, and virtually all other expenses." The book describes a myriad of clever and unusual design and building strategies, and in an entertaining manner. Also tells you how to fight your tax valuation, which can reduce the life-cycle cost of shelter for years and years. ISBN: 0-380-76540-3. OOPS.

Guide to Affordable Houses, Alex Wade (1984, Rodale). This classic work by a truly hands-on architect covers all the considerations of designing and building, shares design solutions from other countries, and even offers useful tips on finding low-cost property. This book is particularly strong on panelized construction, but deals with a variety of other techniques including rammed earth, kit houses, and even structural polystyrene foam houses. Chapter 1, "Financing Options," is a breath of fresh air with lots of practical tips to help save you money. Wade has authored several books in the field, all of them offering a fresh outlook on the subject of sensible, affordable, and energy-efficient housing. ISBN: 0-87857-511-1. OOPS.

A Design and Construction Handbook for Energy-Efficient Houses, Alex Wade (1980, Rodale). An earlier Wade, worth looking for. ISBN: 0-87857-274-0. OOPS.

Foundations and Concrete Work, edited by Kevin Ireton (1997, Taunton). Ki Light turned me on to an earlier incarnation of this excellent book. Thirty-two articles from *Fine Homebuilding* magazine cover foundations, block, and concrete masonry in depth, including uncommon information that is hard to find elsewhere, such as rubble trench foundations (see Light case study in chapter 7), surface-bonded block construction, radiant floor heating, pouring a slab, insulated foundations, steep site foundations, and about twenty-five related topics. The usual clear *Fine Homebuilding* graphics accompany the text. ISBN: 1-56158-182-8.

Homing Instinct, John Connell (1993, Warner). Written in very readable style by the founder of Yestermorrow Building School, this oversized, 400+ page compendium deals with both the designing and building of one's own home. Connell's illustrations are clear and his building ideas are state-of-the-art with respect to the new energy reality. Connell has great respect for the natural resources and the ecology of this fragile planet, and, without proselytizing, his gentle-down building philosophy comes across clearly. Highly recommended. ISBN: 0-446-51607-4.

Do It Yourself Housebuilding: The Complete Handbook, George Nash (1995, Sterling). Up-to-date, profusely illustrated, and entertaining, this huge, 700+ page volume covers ground work, framing (wall, floor, and roof), mechanicals (plumbing, electric, heating, ventilation, air conditioning), and finish work. If I were to recommend just one book as a reference for building a conventional home, this would be it. Well worth twenty-five bucks. ISBN: 0-8069-0424-0.

Architectural Graphic Standards, 9th edition, Charles G. Ramsay, George Ramsey, Harold R. Sleeper (1997, John Wiley & Sons). This huge book, which costs about $250, is filled with all sorts of useful information on building, including hard-to-find span tables for floor joists and rafters. Every library has a copy, if not the 9th Edition, then certainly an earlier manifestation. ISBN: 0-471-51556-6.

Building Construction Illustrated, 2nd edition, Francis D. K. Ching with Cassandra Adams (1991, Van Nostrand Reinhold). I think of this book as the poor man's *Architectural Graphic Standards*. Frank Ching's drawings are clear and concise, and show you the right dimensions for practically every aspect of design and construction, from room design to stairway construction. Lots of valuable tables, though not as many as *A.G.S.* ISBN: 0-442-23498-8.

The Real Goods Independent Builder: Designing & Building a House Your Own Way, Sam Clark (1996, Chelsea Green). Like John Connell's work above, Clark's contribution is another big book of fresh designing and building ideas. Clark focuses on traditional stick-framing techniques, because he believes strongly that this time-tested method is an economy of both dollars and materials. Sam, a professional builder himself, has worked closely with owner-builders for thirty years. ISBN: 0-930031-85-7.

The Visual Handbook of Building and Remodeling, Charlie Wing (1990, Rodale). Over one thousand illustrations show virtually every type of material for every building job. The text tells where each material is appropriate. I used this book a lot in my days as a housing rehabilitation specialist, and still refer to it for info that's hard to find elsewhere. Charlie Wing was founder of Shelter Institute, America's first owner-builder school (see appendix 2). If you happen to come across any of Charlie's other building books while browsing the library shelf, stop and have a look. He is one of the nation's most respected building writers. ISBN: 0-87857-901-X

5. SELF-CONTRACTING

You might as well derive the economic benefits of being the contractor on your own home, even if there are only parts of the project that you want to contract out. Anyone can do it, but it takes some work and study. The books listed here will tell you how.

Be Your Own House Contractor: How to Save 25% Without Lifting a Hammer, Carl Heldmann (1995, Storey). Good. Covers the ground, but a little thin. ISBN: 0-88266-266-X.

How to Be Your Own House Contractor: Remodeling, Additions, Alterations and Building a New Home, 3rd edition, Paul H. Rauch (1994, Brick House). Better. More information than Heldmann's book. ISBN: 0-931790-74-3.

The Complete Guide to Contracting Your Own Home, 3rd edition, Dave McGurty and Kent Lester (1997, Betterway Books). Best. The title is right. This is the most complete book on the subject I've seen, and even gets into related construction aspects of the project as well as all the paper strategies. "This book can save you from 25% to 42% on the home you build over a comparable home purchased through a real estate agent. Here are the major ways: Real Estate Commission, up to 7%; Builder Mark-up, up to 20%; Savings on Material Purchase, up to 4%; Cost Saving Construction, up to 2%; Doing Work Yourself, up to 9%. Total: up to 42%." ISBN: 1-55870-229-6.

Be Your Own Contractor, and Save Thousands, James Shepherd (1996, Dearborn Trade, Chicago). I haven't seen this one, but Builders Booksource (Category 11) speaks well of it, so keep an eye out: "The process of building a modern house is amazingly complex and yet fairly straight-forward when well organized. This book helps you see that process clearly. Not a 'how to build it' book, but an excellent overview with . . . helpful tips that even a pro could use." ISBN: 0-7931-1731-3.

How to be Your Own Architect, 2nd edition, Murray C. Goddard and Mike and Ruth Wolverton (1985, TAB Books, Blue Ridge Summit, Pennsylvania). How to design. Using drafting tools. Construction details. Planning electric and plumbing. Drawing plans for a small house. Making materials lists and estimates. This book covers the basics to live up to its title, but it isn't the only book of its kind on the subject. Look in the 728 (Dewey Decimal) section of the library. ISBN: 0-8306-1790-6.

The Complete Guide to Designing Your Own Home, Scott T. Ballard (1995, Betterway Books). Written by a practicing architect, this book tells you what you can reasonably do yourself and advises where professional help should be employed (and how to save money on it). Good on planning and designing. Good overview of the building process. ISBN: 1-55870-334-9.

6. ALTERNATIVE AND SUSTAINABLE BUILDING

The Passive Solar House: Using Solar Design to Heat and Cool Your Home, James Kachadorian (1997, Chelsea Green). Here are basic solar building principles to help you with the planning and design of a home that heats and cools itself with free energy. The author accents his patented solar slab design, now in the public domain, but his basic principles adapt well to a variety of designs. The first line of the book tells us: "All houses are solar." The question is, how can we make the best use of the solar energy that hits all houses? Kachadorian tells us how, and his excellent appendices make it possible to plan a solar home for all climates and latitudes. Any kind of house that you can design and build should incorporate passive solar techniques. ISBN: 0-930031-97-0.

Passive Solar Energy, Bruce Anderson and Malcolm Wells (1981, Brick House). Still one of the best overviews of how to use free heat from that big yellow thing up in the sky. ISBN: 0-931790-09-3. OOPS.

The Complete Book of Underground Houses: How to Build a Low-Cost Home, Rob Roy (1994, Sterling). Step-by-step details for the construction of a Log End Cave–type of earth-sheltered home, as shown in chapter 6. Surface-bonded block walls and plank-and-beam roofing are emphasized.

Waterproofing, drainage, and insulation are covered in detail. Five cold-climate designs and three warm-climate examples are featured as case studies. ISBN: 0-8069-0728-2.

How to Build an Underground House, Malcolm Wells (1994, Malcolm Wells Publishing, 673 Satucket Road, Brewster, MA 02631). Mac's dedication: "If you live in one of those naked, shameful, energy-wasting, vulnerable, rain-repelling things called an above-ground house—if you live, in other words, in just about any building in the United States—this book is for you." Oh, well, even though Mac left me out of his dedication, he did agree to draw some funny pictures for *Mortgage-Free!* Mac's "How to Build" book, just one of many he has written, is filled with design ideas not found elsewhere. By way of his inimitable text and drawings, he takes the reader through the construction of a modest 1,200-square-foot underground home. Write Mac for his books and plans list. ISBN: 0-9621878-3-6.

The $50 and Up Underground House Book, Mike Oehler (1992, Mole Publishing Co., Rt. 4, Box 618, Bonners Ferry, ID 83805). Truly the bottom line in low-cost earth-sheltering. Mike and I take different approaches to some of the structural and design philosophy details, but I commend his book for its imaginative approach to the problem of shelter. The $50 model ($22 went toward a stove and stovepipe) should be considered as a truly temporary shelter, but there is a value in that, as we have seen. Mike is still living in his $500 model after nearly 20 years. ISBN: 0-442-27311-8.

Earth Sheltered Housing Design: Second Edition, The Underground Space Center (1985, Van Nostrand Reinhold). Considered for years as the bible by those in the field, this very thorough study is now very hard to find. Not a how-to book, but very strong on design considerations for underground houses. ISBN: 0-442-28746-1. Look for two companion volumes, also published by VNR, *Earth Sheltered Residential Design Manual* (1982, ISBN: 0-442-28679-1) and *Earth Sheltered Homes: Plans and Designs* (1981, ISBN: 0-442-28676-7). All three books are OOPS.

The Underground House Book, Stu Campbell (1980, Garden Way/Storey). Good clear overview. Thorough, easy to read and understand, excellent illustrations. Backed by the technical expertise of architect Don Metz. ISBN: 0-88266-166-3. OOPS.

Alternative Housebuilding, Mike McClintock (1989, Sterling). Compares and describes several different alternative building styles: log houses, cordwood masonry, timber frame, pole houses, stone, adobe, rammed earth, and underground housing. About all that's missing is cob, tire houses and straw bale construction, techniques that have become better known in the 1990s. This large book provides an excellent overview of construction alternatives. ISBN: 0-8069-6995-4.

The Natural House Book, David Pearson (1989, Simon & Schuster). So many housing components today are manufactured from unhealthy materials: plastics, chemicals, even poisons. Natural materials, for the most part, are healthy materials. If you care about this—and you should—try to find a copy of this book, the best on the subject. It's also a visual delight and, as such, inspirational. ISBN: 0-671-66635-5.

Earth to Spirit: In Search of Natural Architecture, David Pearson (1994, Chronicle Books). A mind-freeing and exquisitely beautiful book showing vernacular architecture all over the world. A worthy companion to Pearson's *The Natural House Book*. ISBN: 0-8118-0731-2.

Complete Book of Cordwood Masonry Housebuilding: The Earthwood Method, Rob Roy (1992, Sterling). Part One describes the three styles of cordwood masonry construction: within a post-and-beam frame, within built-up corners (stackwall), and as a load-bearing curved wall. Part Two details step-by-step construction of the Earthwood house. ISBN: 0-8069-8590-9.

CoCoCo/94 Collected Papers, edited by Rob Roy (1994, Earthwood Books, 366 Murtagh Hill Road, West Chazy, NY 12992). This is a complete transcription of the papers prepared for the Continental Cordwood Conference of 1994, a gathering of virtually all of North America's leading cordwood masonry builders and innovators. Twenty-five papers (over 170 pages) cover new construction details, code issues, case studies, and historical perspective. No ISBN number.

Basic Cordwood Masonry Techniques, Rob and Jaki Roy (1995, Earthwood and Chevalier/Thurling Productions, West Chazy, NY). This 88-minute video is like a cordwood workshop in a can, and covers barking the wood, estimating materials, mixing the mortar, building the cordwood walls, pointing the mortar, laying up window frames, stackwall corner construction, and a lot more. ISBN: 0-930031-91-1.

The Sauna, Rob Roy (1997, Chelsea Green). Scandinavian immigrants arriving in the upper Midwest in the 19th century would build a sauna for their temporary shelter and live in it while building their home. This book tells about saunas, and accents cordwood masonry as a low-cost means of building your own. A cordwood sauna makes for an excellent TS, good hands-on practice, and a very useful outbuilding if you're planning on a cordwood home. ISBN: 0-930031-87-3.

The Backyard Stonebuilder, Charles Long (1985, Warwick). I liked his *Living Without a Salary* so much that I carried Long's book on stone masonry home from the library. Written with the same humor and common sense, Long takes the reader through several small stone masonry projects, with lots of good basic information applicable to foundation or house building. ISBN: 0-920197-19-1. Look for his earlier book, *The Stonemason's Primer*, which is OOPS.

Building with Stone, Charles McRaven (1989, Storey). Excellent treatment of stone masonry by a master builder. Good photographs, drawings, and advice. ISBN: 0-88266-550-2.

The Art of the Stonemason, Ian Cramb (1992, Betterway Books). Basic and advanced mason's techniques are shared by a fifth-generation master mason from Scotland. Arches, stairs, bridges, towers, and restoration are all covered. Great glossary of hard-to-find terms and plenty of old-timey wisdom. ISBN: 1-55870-225-3.

The Straw Bale House, Steen, Steen, Bainbridge & Eisenberg (1995, Chelsea Green). It's no secret that straw bale houses are among the most energy-efficient that can be built, with the highest R-value for walls of any of the natural (or sustainable) building methods. But straw bale construction has another compelling argument in its favor. The authors quote Matts Myhrman of Out On Bale (see appendix 2): "If all the straw in the United States after the harvest of major grains was baled instead of burned, five million 2,000-square-foot houses could be built every year." *The Straw Bale House*, a big beautiful 300+ page labor of love, is the most complete book on the subject to date. Check with Out On Bale for other straw bale books, videos, and their excellent newsletter, *The Last Straw*. ISBN: 0-930031-71-7.

The Rammed Earth House, David Easton (1996, Chelsea Green). At a workshop once, after a 15-minute tirade about the use of indigenous materials by my co-instructor, a student from (then) British Honduras, piped up: "Down where I come from, we ain't got no indigenous materials. We just use what's lying around." We allowed that would be okay. Maybe all that's lying around is earth. Dave Easton's book about this ancient building technique is by no means the first, but it is arguably the best. Like many other sustainable building methods, rammed-earth construction is labor intensive and materials cheap. A companion video is available from Chelsea Green. ISBN: 0-930031-79-2.

The Cob Builder's Handbook: You Can Hand-Sculpt Your Own Home, Becky Bee (1997, Groundworks, distributed by Chelsea Green). If you've got clay on site, you can build a cob house. Cob houses (and pubs) several hundred years old have survived the damp climate of southern England. Thermally, the buildings perform very well, and they are a lot of fun to build. Becky's clear text and illustrations cover the topic very thoroughly. ISBN: 0-9659082-0-8.

Pole Building Projects, Monte Burch (1993, Storey). A pole building can make an excellent temporary shelter, or even a low-cost permanent home.

While Burch covers the basic construction technique very well, most of the projects in this book are for small sheds, barns, or outbuildings, although there are plans for two small vacation homes. ISBN: 0-88266-859-5. Plans for a variety of pole-building houses can be purchased from J. H. Baxter Company, 1700 South El Camino Real, San Mateo, CA 94402. Tel: 415-349-0201.

The Timber Frame Home, 2nd edition, Tedd Benson (1997, Taunton). The original edition inspired Don Osby to build his beautiful timber frame home. This new edition has expert advice backed by clear and detailed drawings, and lots of wonderful color pictures. It's as complete a book as will be found on timber framing. ISBN: 1-56158-129-1.

Timber Frame Houses, various authors. (1996, Taunton). This is a collection of 33 comprehensive articles on timber framing from *Fine Homebuilding* magazine. Wonderful ideas and lots of color illustrations supplement the other books on timber framing. ISBN: 1-56158-150-X.

Build a Classic Timber-Frame House, Jack A. Sobon (1994, Storey). Working from plans, the author shows how to build a classic hall-and-parlor timber-framed house, with emphasis on economy, tradition, and independence. Hundreds of clear and detailed photos and drawings. ISBN: 0-88266-841-2.

The Independent Home: Living Well with Power from the Sun, Wind and Water, Michael Potts (1993, Chelsea Green). Tells how to create a self-reliant home that is comfortable, natural, and sustainable. Lots of ideas here that are hard to find elsewhere. ISBN: 0-930031-65-2.

7. RENOVATION

Renovation: A Complete Guide, 2nd edition, Michael W. Litchfield (1997, Sterling). An excellent resource for anyone with a house that needs work. At 566 pages, the book is extremely detailed . . . and well organized. ISBN: 0-8069-9775-3.

Home Renovation, Francis D. K. Ching and Dale E. Miller (1983, Van Nostrand Reinhold). "The opportunity to renovate can be the persuasive factor in deciding to purchase an older home. The home may be attractive for its charm and style, its spatial feeling, or its historical significance. You may like its established landscaping or its neighborhood. Its potential value may be well worth the effort required to renovate it." Home renovation is the way I got my start in mortgage-free living, 25 years ago in Scotland. This large book covers most of the situations you will encounter in renovating an older American house. Nobody draws more clearly than Frank Ching. See also his *Building Construction Illustrated* in category 4 above. And the equally detailed text covers the subject exhaustively. ISBN: 0-89815-036-1.

The Old-House Doctor, Christopher Evers (1986, Overlook). Written by a professional with a genuine love of old houses, Evers takes the approach of a doctor diagnosing and treating a sick patient. Thorough, and clearly illustrated with over 300 line drawings by Harriet Hason. Over 100 references in the bibliography, covering renovation and restoration up to 1986. And this is one building discipline that hasn't changed much in the past ten years. ISBN: 0-87951-090-0.

See also category 10, Magazines and Journals

8. RENEWABLE ENERGY

The Solar Electric House, Steven J. Strong (1993, Sustainability Press; distributed by Chelsea Green). This is the definitive work on solar electric systems for home use, covering all aspects of PVs from economics to the nuts and bolts of systems and equipment. ISBN: 0-9637383-2-1.

The Solar Electric Independent Home Book, revised edition, Fowler Solar Electric (1995, New England Solar Electric, Inc., 226 Huntington Road, Worthington, MA 01098). Many suppliers of photovoltaic components consider this the best all-around book for wiring your own PV system. I agree. ISBN: 1-879523-01-9.

Real Goods Solar Living Source Book: The Complete Guide to Renewable Energy Technologies & Sustainable Living, 9th edition, John Schaeffer and the Real Goods Staff (1996, Real Goods; distributed by Chelsea Green). This big resource book is both a primer in all sorts of renewable energy and a catalog of the components available to make them work in your home. Updated every year or two, so look for the 10th edition by 1998. Always shop around before buying components. Check *Home Power Magazine* (category 10) for current suppliers. ISBN: 0-930031-82-2.

The Solar Powered Home, Rob Roy (1996, Earthwood Building School / Chevalier-Thurling Productions). This 84-minute video examines the basic principles, components, set-up, and systems planning for an off-the-grid solar powered home. Sensible energy usage is covered. ISBN: 0-930031-92-X.

Wind Power for Home and Business, Paul Gipe (1993, Chelsea Green). At 400+ well-researched pages, this is still the most complete discussion of wind energy I've seen, although it needs to be supplemented with current information from *Home Power Magazine* (see category 10) and from today's manufacturers and suppliers, because the wind machine manufacturers are still in a state of flux as of 1997. Companies come and go, and their products are constantly changing. ISBN: 0-930031-90-3.

9. MISCELLANEOUS

Four-Season Harvest, Eliot Coleman (1992, Chelsea Green). Coleman lives in Maine, and eats his fresh, organically grown vegetables all the year round. He doesn't use magic, just sound gardening principles he has developed over the past thirty years. Written in plain, easy-to-follow language, the book takes you through composting, planning and preparing the garden, planting and cultivating, cold frames and tunnel greenhouses, and finally, root cellars and indoor harvesting. Highly recommended. ISBN: 0-930031-57-1.

The Contrary Farmer, Gene Logsdon (1994, Chelsea Green). Here, in 230 pages, is the quintessential philosophy primer for modern pastoral life. If you seek a homesteading way of life to complement your mortgage-free home, or even have in mind a small farm income, Logsdon's book will delight and instruct you. And he's a true conserver, what I call an *empiric economist.* ISBN: 0-930031-74-1.

May All Be Fed: Diet for a New World, John Robbins (1992, William Morrow). Our son, Rohan, was the biggest influence on our decision to become vegetarian at the end of 1996. This book was his ammunition, and a real eye-opener. Robbins makes a convincing case for vegetarianism on several fronts: health, economics, planetary survival, and more. Plenty of good recipes by Jia Patton and others help to make the transition easier. ISBN: 0-688-11625-6.

Pantry of the Four-Season Harvest: Old-World Ways to Preserve Fresh Fruits & Vegetables, by the Gardeners and Farmers of *Terre Vivante,* with an Introduction by Eliot Coleman (forthcoming, Chelsea Green). Food is most commonly preserved today by canning or freezing, techniques that are energy-intensive, and that reduce nutrients and flavor. This book revives traditional techniques for storing produce, such as root cellaring, preserving in oil, vinegar, salt, sugar, or alcohol, drying and dehydrating, and lactic fermentation, which not only enhance the foods' flavor, digestibility, and nutritiousness, but also require far less fuel in the processing. ISBN: 1-890132-10-1.

Wells and Septic Systems, 2nd edition, Max and Charlotte Alth (1992, TAB Books). One of the first considerations of your home building project should be the water and waste disposal systems. This book will prepare you to make intelligent decisions. Check out all applicable local health codes before going ahead with your systems. ISBN: 0-8306-2136-9.

The Humanure Handbook: A Guide to Composting Human Manure, J. C. Jenkins (1994, Jenkins Publishing, distributed by Chelsea Green). Most North American municipal health departments require that you have a septic system, a water-wasteful, expensive way of getting human waste out of sight. Jenkins has a better way. His humanure sawdust toilet is clean, cheap, and produces good organic compost for the garden. I personally know people who have been using his system for years and have had no problems. This book combines fun with plenty of useful hardcore information. 198 pages. ISBN: 0-9644258-4-X.

Build Your Own Kit House, Jonathan Erickson (1988, TAB Books). How to analyze, select, and buy a kit package; how to be your own contractor; site preparation; footings and foundations; utilities; finishing the job. ISBN: 0-8306-2873-8.

Eco-Building Schools: A Directory of Alternative Educational Resources in Environmentally Sensitive Design and Building in the United States, Sandra Leibowitz. Periodically updated. Available for $8 postpaid from the author at 3220 N Street NW #218, Washington, DC 20007 or from Earthwood (see category 11). Lots of information on over 30 building schools, including program content, educational setting and structure, and organizational framework. Inquiries, suggestions, additions, deletions, and changes should be addressed to Sandra Leibowitz. No ISBN number.

Communities Directory: A Guide to Cooperative Living (1995 edition, revised for 1996, Fellowship for Intentional Community, Route 1, Box 155, Rutledge, MO 63563). Kirkpatrick Sale calls this "the most comprehensive and accurate reference book ever published on community living." The two main parts of this huge 440-page work are "Feature Articles," a compendium of 31 comprehensive articles on all aspects of community living and organization, and "The Listings," information on 540 communities in North America and 70 more overseas. A two-page "Guidelines for Contacting and Visiting Communities" is invaluable if you want to get out there and learn about intentional communities first-hand. ISBN: 0-9602714-4-9. See also *Communities Magazine*, category 10 and Community Bookshelf, category 11.

Feng Shui: A Layman's Guide, Evelyn Lip (1987, 1996, Heian International, Inc., 1815 W. 205th Street, Suite 301, Torrance, CA 90501). There are lots of books out just now on feng shui, the ancient Chinese art of putting everything in its right place. This one is a short introduction and worth a look. In the Orient, many housebuilders consult a professional geomancer before designing or siting their home. Most of the principles are just plain common sense, but it's amazing how often they are ignored. ISBN: 0-89346-286-1.

Interior Design with Feng Shui, Sarah Rossbach (1991, Viking Penguin). The author shows how to arrange furniture, rooms, and the location of buildings to enhance your career, family life, health, and prosperity. The book combines good interior design sense with the ancient art of feng shui. ISBN: 0-14-019352-9.

Gales Directory of Publications and Broadcast Media (1996, Gale Research, 835 Penebscot Building, Detroit, MI 48226). Get local newspaper addresses for anywhere in the country. ISBN: 0-8103-5660-0.

Plans

There are dozens of books and magazines full of capsuled house plans. Look at a good magazine stand or bookstore. The form is fairly consistent; typically the book will show an idealized 3-D drawing of the home, and floor plans for each story. The square footage is given and there is a description of the home, written as if someone were trying to sell it—and, in fact, selling the plans themselves is the true commercial purpose of the books. Five sets of plans plus the materials list will typically cost between $300 and $550, depending on the size of the home. What you get for your money is a complete set of plans suitable for submission to paper people and to build from, either by yourself or by sub-contractors. There will be a typical wall section, exterior elevations, a foundation plan, roof plan, stairway and fireplace plans if needed, typical cross-section, and a kitchen cabinet plan (at a larger scale than the floor plans). You are also buying the license to build the home. Typical "Terms of Sale" read as follows: "All home plans sold through this publication are copyright protected. Reproduction is prohibited. A limited license is given to use the set of plans to build one, and only one, dwelling unit." All the companies selling plans, quite rightly, make it clear what you can*not* do: duplicate home plans, copy any part of a home plan to create another (called "creating a derivitive work"), or building the home without a license. In short, you must buy the plans to build the house. Nevertheless, I see these books as great for ideas, even though most owner-builders prefer to design their homes from scratch as well as build them.

One company (out of many) with at least twenty-one separate books of house plans is Home Planners, Inc., 3275 West Ina Road, Suite 110, Tucson, AZ 85741. Call them toll-free at 800-322-6797. The books vary in scope. Some of the more interesting titles are: *200 Budget-Smart House Plans*, *Starter Homes*, and *Empty-Nester Homes* (200 plans for retirees and childless couples).

Another big plans company which sells both books and quarterly periodicals filled with plans is L. F. Garlinghouse Co., Inc., 282 Main Street Ext., Middletown, CT 06457. For research, I bought *New Country Home Plans*, a quarterly which sells for $2.95 a copy. It had about 120 designs illustrated, roughly one on a page. Most of the houses were rather large, although there were a few compact designs. This is just one of several plan-filled periodicals from Garlinghouse. Again, prices vary according to number of sets of plans required and the plan number, but the range is $235 to about $600, including materials list.

Be aware that if your local jurisdiction requires an architect's stamp, this will run you a minimum of an extra $300, even though the plan is drawn by an architect in the first place. In New York, for example, all plans submitted for houses of 1,500 square feet or more must carry an architect's or engineer's stamp. Ki and Judith Light (see chapter 7) had their home-drawn plans stamped by an engineer for $100, and gained valuable information about their plan in the bargain.

10. MAGAZINES AND JOURNALS

Fine Homebuilding, The Taunton Press, P.O. Box 5506, Newtown, CT 06470. Each issue is packed with concise, well-illustrated, and generally well-written articles on a variety of construction techniques. Always inspiring and entertaining, a recent issue told you how to make a sawhorse, how to install electrical boxes and receptacles, about "Building a Straw-Bale House," and how to avoid common mistakes in concrete and masonry, building a porch, and repairing plaster. The Taunton Press also has an excellent books and videos list on all types of—mostly—conventional construction techniques. Call 800-888-8286 for the current catalog or to subscribe to *Fine Homebuilding*.

The Journal of Light Construction, RR 2, Box 146, Richmond, VT 05477. Tel: 800-375-5981 for subscription. Geared to the small contractor, *JLC* still has lots of articles and product information useful to the owner-builder. A recent typical issue had articles on soil compaction, building stairways, skylight flashing, and more. The same 800 number above will connect you to the JLC Bookstore.

Home Power Magazine, P.O. Box 520, Ashland, OR 97520. Tel: 800-707-6585 for subscriptions. Want to keep up with the fast-moving developments in homemade power? *Home Power* is the one-stop source. The magazine even runs on homemade power, so they know whereof they speak. Each issue is full of practical information backed by clear illustrations. All of the major players in components advertise in *Home Power*, so each issue acts like an up-to-date source list.

Mother Earth News. For subscriptions, write the magazine at P.O. Box 56302, Boulder, CO 80322-6302 or call 303-678-0439. *Mother* was America's best how-to country living magazine during the 1970s, but let its readers down badly during the me-now 1980s and even went through a section 11 reorganization which left its "lifetime" subscribers in the lurch. But the magazine has bounced back in the 1990s, again publishing useful, practical articles about building, energy, gardening, and country life in general. I've even resubscribed.

Back Home, P.O. Box 70, Hendersonville, NC 28793. Tel: 704-696-3838. Started, staffed, and co-operatively owned by seven of the original staff members of *Mother Earth News* (including Don Osby who wrote his own case study in chapter 7), *Back Home* has stayed true to the original format of presenting enough useful information in an article for the reader to act upon. Every issue has at least one building article, usually incorporating natural materials in some way or another, and there are always a variety of articles on gardening and other homesteading projects and activities. *Back Home* is down home, and is run by the people who walk the walk as well as talk the talk. Now a bi-monthly.

Backwoods Home Magazine, P.O. Box 40, Montague, CA 96064. Tel: 916-459-3500. *Backwoods Home* is often confused with *BackHome*, because of the similar titles. Very political, but there are frequent articles on low-cost building methods, farm and garden, and, of course, guns and gun politics. This magazine will appeal to self-reliant and survivalist types, particularly those who find themselves somewhat right of center.

Countryside & Small Stock Journal, W11564 Hwy 64, Withee, WI 54498. Calls itself "America's Homestead Journal." Lots of info on small stock raising, but also a lot about the homesteading lifestyle in general. A recent issue had five articles on "Finding a Homestead." Always at least one piece on building, often using indigenous materials.

This Old House. Editorial offices: Time Publishing Ventures, Inc., 20 West 43rd Street, New York, NY 10036. Subscriptions: P.O. Box 830783, Birmingham, AL 35282-8772 or call 800-898-7237. I bought this slick glossy magazine at the newsstand on a whim, not expecting much from it. I found myself caught up in articles on glass blocks, wooden shingles, adobe, fixing wet basements, and "The Menace of Mold and Mildew." If you like the PBS series, you'll love this companion magazine.

Old House Journal. Editorial offices: 2 Main Street, Gloucester, MA 01930. Subscriptions: P.O. Box 50214, Boulder, CO 80323-0214 or call 800-234-3797. This one is directed more toward authentic restoration than *This Old House*. Lots of the restoration suppliers advertise here. If restoration is what's on your mind, back issues are available (call 508-281-8803) or look for *The Old-House Journal: Guide to Restoration*, a large one-volume reference available from their Old-House Bookshop at the Gloucester address. Or call 800-931-2931.

Joiners' Quarterly: The Journal of Timber Framing & Traditional Joinery, P.O. Box 249, Corn Hill Road, Brownfield, ME 04010. The subtitle says it all. Hardcore following. Thirty-five percent of all new subscribers order a complete set of back issues for reference. A recent issue had an article about manufactured straw-core wall and ceiling panels. The journal is connected with the Fox Maple School (see appendix 2).

The Caretaker Gazette, 1845 NW Deane Street, Pullman, WA 99163. Phone/fax: 509-332-0806. E-mail: garydunn@pullman.com. Website: http://www.angelfire.com/wa/caretaker. Want to check out an area before you settle there? Become a caretaker for wealthy landowners with second homes, companies, nature retreats, ecological preserves, or national and state parks. *The Gazette* provides contacts. At press time, a six-issue subscription was $24.

Communities: Journal for Cooperative Living (Fellowship for Intentional Community, Route 1, Box 155, Rutledge, MO 63563). Subscriptions are $18 for 4 issues from *Communities*, 138 Twin Oaks Road, Louisa, VA 23093. Each issue of this fine quarterly journal accents a different aspect of living in intentional communities: making a living, sustainable building and design in community, ecovillages, growing older in community, etc. Updates on communities are included and the REACH column is a kind of national bulletin board for people looking for community and vice-versa. Back issues are available.

11. BUILDING BOOK SUPPLIERS

The first five listings are publishing companies with good lists of building books. The final four listings are catalog companies that sell building books and others pertinent to the topics raised in *Mortgage-Free!* In all cases, send for their current lists.

Publishers

Chelsea Green Publishing Company, P.O. Box 428, White River Junction, VT 05001. "Books for sustainable living." For a catalog, call 800-639-4099. Chelsea Green, in partnership with Real Goods Trading Corporation, publishes the excellent on-going series called Real Goods Solar Living Books.

Sterling Publishing Company, Inc., 387 Park Avenue South, New York, NY 10016. Call 800-367-9692 and ask for their Sterling Craftsman Book Catalog. Besides building books, Sterling is very strong on wood-working and crafts.

Storey Communications, Inc., Schoolhouse Road, Pownal, VT 05261. "How-to books for country living." Strong on gardening, building, cooking, crafts, animals, and beer-making. Call 800-827-8673.

The Taunton Press, Inc., 63 South Main Street, Box 5506, Newtown, CT 06470-506. Specializes in building books, with the same attention to detail and fine graphics found in Taunton's Fine Homebuilding magazine. For a catalog, call 800-888-8286, operator 354.

Betterway Books, 1507 Dana Avenue, Cincinnati, OH 45207. Tel: 800-289-0963. Lots of useful building, designing, and self-contracting titles.

Booksellers

Edward R. Hamilton, Falls Village, CT 06031-5000. This large mail-order catalog has thousands of discounted titles in every category imaginable, including fiction. The building books are found in the "Do It Yourself" section. There are some real bargains here. You'll even find some of the titles in this bibliography at greatly reduced prices. Write for a catalog.

Builders Booksource, 1817 Fourth Street, Berkeley, CA 94710. Specializes in building books. Call 800-843-2028 Monday through Friday. Has over 5,000 titles in stock. This is the best source for books on building codes.

Earthwood, 366 Murtagh Hill Road, West Chazy, NY 12992. Call 518-493-7744 for current book list. Carries about 40 titles, mostly about alternative building methods, including quite a few of the ones listed in this appendix.

Community Bookshelf, East Wind Community, Tecumseh, MO 65760. Phone: 417-679-4682. This is the one-stop source for books, videos, and tapes on intentional community, but the list also includes sections on Ecology, Food, Indigenous People, and more.

APPENDIX 4

Before Closing

Before closing on land, with or without a house on it, here are some important considerations which are not covered elsewhere in this book.

Make sure that there are no back taxes due on the land. Check with the town or county tax collector's office. The seller should pay any outstanding taxes. They must be paid before closing for you to get clear title to the land.

Make sure you know if others have rights (reservations) on the property. Such rights or reservations can include water, timber, grazing, and/ or mineral rights. Know the situation and decide whether or not it is acceptable to you.

If you are buying the land on contract or through a mortgage, make sure that you have the right to prepay the principal. Les Scher suggests that your loan agreement contain a clause that "the principal and interest are payable in installments of X dollars or more." Remember, prepaying on a mortgage is one of the best investments you can make.

ABSTRACT OF TITLE AND TITLE INSURANCE

Make sure that the title is searched back at least as long as the statute of limitations in your state, which can vary by quite a bit. The written record of this title search is called an *abstract of title*. No abstract of title is complete until it is recertified with your name on it. If you are retaining an attorney for the land transaction, this is one of the areas where he or she can be most valuable. Decide whether or not you want title insurance, the most important purpose of which (in my view) is to guarantee good title and legal access and right-of-way. Les Scher argues strongly in favor of it in his very thorough chapter called "The Title Search, Abstract of Title and Title Insurance Policy." Although title insurance costs vary, Scher says that a $50,000 policy will typically cost about $400. This is a one-time premium.

As a counterpoint, a surveyor friend of mine warns that "title insurance covers you for everything except what might actually happen." I have never taken out a title insurance policy on any of the many properties that I have bought, but I have always been clear about the chain of title prior to purchase, and the properties have always been covered by

Warranty Deeds. This may say nothing more than that I've been lucky, and, in fairness, I am not a big advocate of insurance in general. Insurance companies don't return nearly as much of their take to clients as do state lotteries. And I don't buy lottery tickets either.

Lending institutions will insist upon title insurance. Paper people tend to scratch each other's backs. But the object of this book is to stay away from lending institutions.

TERMS OF PURCHASE

If you haven't managed to be the beneficiary of gifted land, the best method of securing land is to buy it outright. This is nice for those who can afford it, but, more commonly, the bargain will involve a mortgage, deed of trust, or a land contract. By the mortgage or deed of trust methods of buying land, the buyer receives a deed to the property, which he or she records. A mortgage, by now, should be fairly self-explanatory. With a deed of trust, a trustee will hold the deed until the land is paid for.

By the land contract method (also known variously as installment sale contract, land sale contract, land contract of sale, or conditional sales contract), no deed is delivered to the buyer until all payments are made. This is risky business if not done just right. Les Scher, who specializes in land dealings, says, "I recommend that you never buy on contract unless you have no alternative. If you have no other choice, at least be sure you have some essential protections written into the land contract." Scher lists these protections in chapter 21 of *Finding and Buying Your Place in the Country*. Of paramount importance to the buyer—you—is that the contract be recorded in the county clerk's office so that the seller will not be able to encumber the property in any way, or even sell it again to one or more additional parties.

I am less fearful of buying or selling land "on contract" then Les Scher, but I am not a lawyer, and I don't even play one on TV. But if the proper protections are included, and they have been explained to you to your satisfaction and understanding by counsel looking after your interests, then go ahead. Buying country land on contract is fairly common where I live and I know of many successful land purchases made this way, and am not personally aware of any horror stories, although I know they're out there. The bottom line is that if you, the buyer, fail to meet the terms of the contract, you will lose the land. Usually, this means keeping up the payments, but there may be other conditions that could trigger foreclosure. And never buy land from someone who is still paying for it themselves on contract or by way of mortgage. If they lose the land, so do you.

A mortgage is a legal agreement of financing. The owners of the land may "finance the deal" themselves and hold the mortgage, or a lending institution may hold the mortgage. My experience is that financing by the owner is very often less costly in terms of interest than a bank mortgage. Many sellers are willing to "give terms" because they benefit on their income tax by not taking all the money at once. Holding the mortgage themselves is better for them, and may be better for you.

With lots of middlemen—what I call Paper People—removed from the transaction, it is usually possible to settle upon a lower interest rate than the bank is offering. Both buyer and seller can benefit. You get a lower mortgage rate, but the sellers can get a higher return on their money than if they put it in a certificate of deposit.

If push comes to shove, you, the buyer, will have better protection with a deed and a mortgage than with a land contract. If the sellers are willing to sell under contract, see if they will go the full deed and mortgage route. (Egad, I said something good about a mortgage!) Jaki and I had a five-year mortgage on our first piece of property on The Hill. Sometimes they are a necessary evil.

KINDS OF DEEDS

For the most part, deeds fall under two different categories. One, the Full Covenant and Warranty Deed (also called, simply, a Warranty Deed) gives the buyer the assurances that the seller in fact owns the land he or she is selling. The seller warrants it so. A Quitclaim Deed, on the other hand, transfers only the rights that the seller has in the land, which might be none at all. It is quite legal to offer for sale a Quitclaim Deed on the Brooklyn Bridge. Les Scher strongly admonishes land buyers to reject Quitclaim Deeds out of hand, although there are instances where such a deed may have some value. In a couple of property situations here on The Hill, my surveyor friend found certain "clouds" on the title of some parcels. One lady lost her property to the county for back taxes, for example, but the surveyor felt that there was some question about the legality of the foreclosure. Even though these events had transpired many years previously, his advice was to purchase a Quitclaim Deed from the now elderly lady to clear the title. It didn't cost much, and the lady finally and unexpectedly got something for her property.

If you buy land at a tax sale, you will eventually be given a Tax Deed, which usually has a little more substance than a Quitclaim Deed, but not nearly as much as a Warranty Deed.

Amortization Tables

HOW TO USE THE TABLES

Monthly mortgage payments are listed for interest rates of 6% to 14% and for loan amounts of $1,000 to $100,000. Other loan amounts are easily figured by adding two or more monthly payments together. For example, to find the monthly payment for a $45,000 loan at 6% for 20 years, use the first (6%) chart below and find the 20-year column. Add the monthly payment for $5,000 ($35.83) to the monthly payment for $40,000 ($286.58), resulting in a monthly payment of $322.41.

Similarly, for mortgage rates of 7%, 9%, 11%, and 13%, a very close approximation can be interpolated quite easily. For example, to find the monthly payment for repaying a $100,000 loan at 7% for 20 years, jot down the figure for $100,000 at 6% for 20 years, which is $716.44, and the figure for $100,000 at 8% for 20 years, which is $836.45. Average the two numbers: 716.44 + 836.45 = 1,552.89 / 2 = 776.445 (you can round up to the nearest cent). The real answer, from charts, is $775.30, just $1.145 off. Don't worry, lenders have extensive charts and computerized programs to help you out.

THE *BOTTOM* BOTTOM LINE

I hope you'll never need these figures, but while they are close at hand, please have a look at something very interesting. Please turn to the 10% chart and check out the impact that the term of the loan (number of years) has on the monthly payment. Take a $50,000 loan at 30 years, 25 years, and 20 years. The monthly payments are, respectively: $438.79, $454.36, and $482.52, not all that much different, really, to save 5 or even 10 years of indentured servitude. And when the payment amount is multiplied by the number of payments (respectively 360, 300, or 240), the results are equally interesting. If paid back in 30 years, the total amount paid is $157,964.40. If paid back in 25 years, it's $136,308. And, in 20 years, it's $115,804.80. Just an extra $43.73 a month (a meal out for two) can save you ten years and $42,159.60! Remember that the loan was only for $50,000 in the first place. This is why making the largest payments you can afford and prepaying principal are the best strategies you can employ if some sort of a loan is absolutely necessary.

Monthly Mortgage Payment

INTEREST RATE: 6%

Amount Borrowed	Term of Mortgage (Years)					
	5	10	15	20	25	30
$1,000	19.34	11.11	8.44	7.17	6.45	6.00
5,000	96.67	55.52	42.20	35.83	32.22	29.98
10,000	193.33	111.03	84.39	71.65	64.44	59.96
20,000	386.66	222.05	168.78	143.29	128.87	119.92
30,000	579.89	333.07	253.16	214.93	193.30	179.87
40,000	773.32	444.09	337.55	286.58	257.73	239.83
50,000	966.65	555.11	421.93	358.22	322.16	299.78
100,000	1,933.29	1,110.21	843.86	716.44	644.31	599.56

INTEREST RATE: 8%

Amount Borrowed	Term of Mortgage (Years)					
	5	10	15	20	25	30
$1,000	20.28	12.14	9.56	8.37	7.72	7.34
5,000	101.39	60.67	47.79	41.83	38.60	36.69
10,000	202.77	121.33	95.57	83.65	77.19	73.38
20,000	405.53	242.66	191.14	167.29	154.37	146.76
30,000	608.30	363.99	286.70	250.94	231.55	220.13
40,000	811.06	485.32	382.27	334.58	308.73	293.51
50,000	1,013.82	606.64	477.83	418.23	385.91	366.89
100,000	2,027.64	1,213.28	955.66	836.45	771.82	733.77

INTEREST RATE: 10%

Amount Borrowed	Term of Mortgage (Years)					
	5	10	15	20	25	30
$1,000	21.25	13.22	10.75	9.66	9.09	8.78
5,000	106.24	66.08	53.74	48.26	45.44	43.88
10,000	212.48	132.16	107.47	96.51	90.88	87.76
20,000	424.95	264.31	214.93	193.01	181.75	175.52
30,000	637.42	396.46	322.39	289.51	272.62	263.28
40,000	849.89	528.61	429.85	386.01	363.49	351.03
50,000	1,062.36	660.76	537.31	482.52	454.36	438.79
100,000	2,124.71	1,321.51	1,074.61	965.03	908.71	877.58

Monthly Mortgage Payment

INTEREST RATE: 12%

Amount Borrowed	Term of Mortgage (Years)					
	5	10	15	20	25	30
1,000	22.25	14.35	12.01	11.02	10.54	10.29
5,000	111.23	71.74	60.01	55.06	52.67	51.44
10,000	222.45	143.48	120.02	110.11	105.33	102.87
20,000	444.89	286.95	240.04	220.22	210.65	205.73
30,000	667.34	430.42	360.06	330.33	315.97	308.59
40,000	889.78	573.89	480.07	440.44	421.29	411.45
50,000	1,112.23	717.36	600.09	550.55	526.62	514.31
100,000	2,224.45	1,434.71	1,200.17	1,101.09	1,053.23	1,028.62

INTEREST RATE: 14%

Amount Borrowed	Term of Mortgage (Years)					
	5	10	15	20	25	30
1,000	23.27	15.53	13.32	12.44	12.04	11.85
5,000	116.35	77.64	66.59	62.18	60.19	59.25
10,000	232.69	155.27	133.18	124.36	120.38	118.49
20,000	465.37	310.54	266.35	248.71	240.76	236.98
30,000	698.05	465.80	399.53	373.06	361.13	355.47
40,000	930.74	621.07	532.70	497.41	481.51	473.95
50,000	1,163.42	776.34	665.88	621.77	601.89	592.44
100,000	2,326.83	1,552.67	1,331.75	1,243.53	1,203.77	1,184.88

Index

R

rafters, 169, 178, 225
rainwater collection, 243
raised-bed gardens, 102–103, 217, 230
real estate agents, 8, 75–76
recreation, 17, 48, 189, 245–46
rectilinear house design, 167
recycled building materials, 39, 125, 126–27, 179, 205–206, 225–26, 234
Redfield, James, 51, 84
refrigerators, 136
relocation. *See* moving/relocation
"remote site" systems, 97–98
renewable energy. *See* alternative energy sources
renovations, 197–98, 216, 330–31
rent/renting, vii, 4, 10, 24, 45
repair. *See* houses/housing
resale value, 88, 159, 160
"right of survivorship," 112
Robbins, John, 43, 105
Robbins, Roland Wells, 129
roofs and roofing, 126–27, 157, 169, 178, 186, 231
root cellars, 141, 170, 172
round house design, 166–70
rubble trench foundations, 87, 171, 258–59
Rudofsky, Bernard, 93
runs, defined, 138
rural areas. *See* land choice; mortgage freedom
Rural Development (agency), 80
Rylander, John and Edith, 282–83

S

safety. *See* health and safety
salary. *See* income
salvage. *See* recycled building materials
sandbag construction, 95
saunas, 137, 138, 141, 150, 245–46
savings, 6, 10, 31, 32. *See also* grub-stakes
Scher, Les and Carol, 75, 76, 112, 114
Schley, Jim, 110, 194, 222, 294–301, 303

Schor, Juliet, 18
Seguin, Susan Warford, 129
self-contracting. *See* owner building
self-discipline. *See* savings
self-employment. *See* work
seller's costs, 8–9
septic systems, 39, 90–91, 135, 140, 234
shallow (dug) wells, 89
sheds, as temporary shelter, 122, 124–30
shelter. *See* houses/housing
Shockey, Cliff, 24
silos, 125
site integration, house design and, 110, 156–57, 191, 193, 226–27, 232, 234
skylights, 187
slabs, 183–84, 205. *See also* floating slab foundations
slabwood, 127–28
sleeping arrangements, 134, 226
Smit, Isaac, 167, 170–71
smoking, 46
"soakaways," 140
sod houses, 94–95
solar design, 15, 86, 183–85, 186–87. *See also* photovoltaic (PV) panels
solar gain, 99, 226, 236
southern exposures, 11, 186–87, 193, 226, 236
spending habits. *See* consumerism/consumption; savings
squares, compared to circles, 167, 170–71
squatting, 12, 81–83
stairs, 190–91
stewardship. *See* land stewardship
storage areas, 136, 170. *See also* food, production/storage
stoves, 135, 185. *See also* masonry stoves
straw bale construction, 88, 255–63
Structural Skin™, 247
stump houses, 130–33
styrofoam. *See* Dow Styrofoam™
surface bonding, 233
sweat equity, 160

CHELSEA GREEN

Sustainable living has many facets. Chelsea Green's celebration of the sustainable arts has led us to publish trend-setting books about organic gardening, solar electricity and renewable energy, innovative building techniques, regenerative forestry, local and bioregional democracy, and whole foods. The company's published works, while intensely practical, are also entertaining and inspirational, demonstrating that an ecological approach to life is consistent with producing beautiful, eloquent, and useful books, videos, and audio cassettes.

For more information about Chelsea Green, or to request a free catalog, call toll-free (800) 639–4099, or write to us at P.O. Box 428, White River Junction, Vermont 05001.

Chelsea Green's titles include:

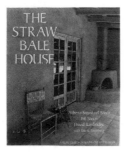  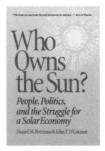

The Straw Bale House
The Independent Home:
  Living Well with Power
  from the Sun, Wind, and
  Water
Independent Builder:
  Designing & Building a
  House Your Own Way
The Rammed Earth House
The Passive Solar House
The Sauna
Wind Power for Home &
  Business
The Solar Living Sourcebook
A Shelter Sketchbook
Mortgage-Free!
Hammer. Nail. Wood.

The Flower Farmer
Passport to Gardening:
  A Sourcebook for the
  21st-Century Gardener
The New Organic Grower
Four-Season Harvest
Solar Gardening
The Contrary Farmer
The Contrary Farmer's
  Invitation to Gardening
Forest Gardening
Whole Foods Companion

Who Owns the Sun
Gaviotas: A Village to
  Reinvent the World
Global Spin: The
  Corporate Assault on
  Environmentalism
Hemp Horizons
A Patch of Eden
A Place in the Sun
Renewables are Ready
Beyond the Limits
Loving and Leaving the
  Good Life
The Man who Planted
  Trees
The Northern Forest